POISONED
APPLE

POISONED APPLE

▼

THE BELL-CURVE CRISIS AND HOW OUR SCHOOLS CREATE MEDIOCRITY AND FAILURE

BETTY WALLACE AND WILLIAM GRAVES

St. Martin's Press   New York

Design by Basha Zapatka

Library of Congress Cataloging-in-Publication Data
Wallace, Betty
    Poisoned apple : the bell-curve crisis and how our schools create mediocrity and failure / Betty Wallace
and William Graves.
        p.   cm.
"A Thomas Dunne book."
    ISBN 0-312-11876-7 (hardcover)
    1. Ability grouping in education—United States.   I. Graves,
William.   II. Title.
LB3061.W25 1995
371.2'5'0973—dc20   94-46240
                                                          CIP

First Edition: March 1995
10 9 8 7 6 5 4 3 2 1

For my son, Matthew Wallace, and in memory of my father,
Thad Hez Cloer.
—B.C.W.

For my wife, Karin, and our children,
Emma, Mark, and Max.
—W.G.

Here is Edward Bear
coming downstairs now,
bump, bump
on the back of his head
behind Christopher Robin.
It is, as far as he knows,
the only way of coming
downstairs,
but sometimes he feels
that there is another way
if only he could stop bumping
for a moment and think of it.
—A. A. MILNE,
Winnie the Pooh

CONTENTS

▼

F O R E W O R D

▼

I knocked on Betty Wallace's door at the North Carolina Department of Public Instruction in Raleigh in 1986 to learn about textbooks, but I learned much more. I was education writer for *The News & Observer* in Raleigh and was trying to figure out why public school textbooks had become so bland and shallow. Wallace, who oversaw the state's textbook adoption process, described some of the forces working against challenging, readable textbooks. Among them were public education's preference for age-based grouping and uniform instruction. Texts had to be written to grade level, which is to say the average level for children of a given age. This gave them a dull, artificial quality.

Betty saw dull books as just one symptom of the deeper problem in public education. High student dropout rates, ability grouping, mediocre achievement, and student failure all flowed from a mass education system's preoccupation with age-based average achievement and with students who deviated from the average, a fundamental flaw she called the Bell-Curve Syndrome.

In my visits to schools across North Carolina and the nation, I too was concluding that public education's flaws were embedded deep in its foundation. Clearly, requiring students to earn more course credits or to spend more days per year in the classroom would not solve the serious ills of public schools. More money was not making much of a difference either. Betty and I agreed that public education would never improve as it needed to without correcting fundamental structural problems. After many discussions, we set out in 1990 to describe those problems in a book.

At the same time, Betty moved to Henderson, North Carolina, one of the nation's worst, to become superintendent of the Vance

County School System, and I moved to Portland, Oregon, to cover education for *The Oregonian*. As we worked, Betty began carrying out the revolutionary reform she had designed over the past decade. So in 1992, on the advice of our editors, we reorganized this book to focus more heavily on solutions and to show how Betty was applying them in her ground-breaking work in Vance County. Much of what we report on Vance County is based on her view of what occurred. I also, however, visited Vance County schools twice and interviewed local community leaders, administrators, teachers, students, and parents for their perspectives on what Betty did there.

Since Betty Wallace embarked on her adventure, scores of other educators across the country also have begun breaking out of the mold of traditional education. Much of this school change, however, is unfolding in haphazard and piecemeal ways. This book provides a rationale for sustaining these changes and a plan to give them more coherence.

We draw heavily on examples from Oregon and North Carolina simply because that is where we live and work. Similar examples could be found in every state in the nation.

Oregon and North Carolina, though, do in some ways represent the extremes of the nation's public education system. North Carolina has an old, heavily centralized state school system, while Oregon is young, with a relatively small central bureaucracy and strong local control. North Carolina serves twice as many students as Oregon in half as many school districts. North Carolina in recent years has posted the lowest Scholastic Assessment Test (SAT) scores in the nation; Oregon students have the highest scores among states that widely use the college entrance exam. Both states rank among the nation's leaders in their aggressive attempts to overhaul their schools.

—William Graves

ACKNOWLEDGMENTS

▼

We are indebted to scores of educators, parents and children across the country who shared their insights and invited us into their schools and classrooms. Among them: teacher Fran Lee and Principal Ann Gerson at Creston Elementary School in Portland; education writers Harriet Tyson and Margaret Evans Gayle; David E. Barbee, education technology expert in Washington, D.C.; Linda Dudley, former principal of Paint Branch Elementary School in College Park, Maryland; principal Nancy Hays and teacher Judy Darby at Boeckman Creek Primary School near Portland, Oregon; principal B. J. Wise at Silver Ridge Elementary in Silverdale, Washington; principal Paul Erickson and teacher Lynda Darling at Vocational Village High School in Portland; teacher Valerie Anderson at Oregon Outreach in Portland; principal Colin Karr-Morse at Marshall High School in Portland; test experts Richard Stiggins and the late Walter Hathaway, both of Portland;

Also, in Vance County, our thanks to: principal Ginger Miller, teachers Wanda Dawson and Robert Pirie, and the faculty at Zeb Vance Elementary; principal Oddis Smith and the Pinkston Street faculty; and other Vance County educators, Bernard Allen, Larry Beckham, Mamie Gunter, Laura Joyner, Betsy Wright, Gloria Lunsford-Boone, Dorothy Peace, Trudy Tidwell, Grace and Vic Vickery; the Kiwanis Club of Henderson, Mike Faulkner and the Kittrell Grocery Store gang, and residents of the Beacon Light housing project.

Thanks also to numerous educators and friends in Macon County, North Carolina, who contributed to Betty Wallace's education and career, including: Lucy Bradley, Marie P. Stuart, Jo Ann Ammons, Lonnie Crawford, Mildred Martin, Harry Moses, Gary

Roland, Sue Sams, Alice Slagle, Bob Sloan, John Crawford III, George Wallace, and the Macon County Public Schools.

Others who have contributed as mentors and advisers to our understanding of history, politics, power, and learning include: state legislator Liston Ramsey, Vance County historian George Templeton Blackburn II, editors Robert W. Chandler of *The Bulletin* in Bend, Oregon, and Claude Sitton of *The News and Observer* in Raleigh, North Carolina; reporters Tammy Stanford, Sarah Wente, and Tim Simmons; educators Gerri Blackwood, Bob Bridges, Guerney Chambers, Nancy Davis, Kay Daughtry, Linton Deck, John Dornan, Bob Edwards, Dudley Flood, John Jordan, George Kahdy, Betty Oxendine Mangum, Jerome Melton, Karen McNeil-Miller, Reginald Mintey, John Murphy, Betsy Nelson, Don Nielsen, Glenn Orr, Bill Peek, Jay and Cotton Robinson, Joe Walters and Martha Woody; and professors Carvin Brown, David Mullen, and Harry Williams of the University of Georgia in Athens.

We also must include here our gratitude for support from members of our families: Ollie Cloer, Paul and John Cloer, Shirley Rocha, Joyce Viale, Lola Raab, Earl Graves, Jill Adair, Jack and Douglas Graves, Mark and Dolores Steichen, and Karin Graves.

Special thanks to Bill Geroux, reporter for the *Richmond Times-Dispatch*, for his thoughtful insights and suggestions after reviewing portions of the manuscript. We also are deeply grateful for the hard work of our literary agent, Anne Edelstein, and for guidance and support from our editors at St. Martin's Press: David Sobel, Bill Thomas, Thomas Dunne, and his assistant, Neal Bascomb.

Finally, we thank *The News & Observer, The Oregonian,* the Education Writers Association, and the German Marshall Fund for the resources, support, and opportunities they gave Bill Graves to visit schools across the United States, Holland, and Germany.

Poisoned
Apple

PROLOGUE

▼

Betty Wallace climbed to the ridge one last time to watch the sun rise above the Great Smoky Mountains and splash over Skeenah Farm. She followed the well-worn cow path up past the black pines through a stand of dogwoods up to the hardwoods above. She passed the black walnut trees and circled the ginseng seedbed she and her father had planted two seasons ago.

Wallace reached the top, curled up in the crook of a big oak, and watched the day break. The air was heavy and moist. Leaves dripped with condensation. Soon the cattle would wind their way through the woods up to the good grass in Ollie McConnell's meadow. Long shafts of light stroked the trees and sparkled through the dripping leaves, producing a shimmering wonderland. She looked across to Fish Hawk Mountain. In the winter the mist froze in a rime along the ridgeline, but on this July morning in 1991, it was lifting in the heat to reveal her parents' farm. She saw her father walking in the distance to the barn as he had thousands of times before. The small man with flowing white hair had farmed the black earth here in the Blue Ridges of the southern Appalachians for nearly nine decades. Down below she could see the sun play on the tin roof and the rough-sawn hemlock siding of her own century-old cabin, perched solidly on huge field boulders.

Wallace breathed it all in, the damp smell, the crackle of drying leaves, the winding trails, and the memories this country evoked: the pulp wooders, the hounds, the fox and coon hunters, and the girls, as her father called their black Angus heifers. This is where she grew up, where time seemed to stop, where the natural spring of her family's old homestead had never gone dry. Here in the heart of Skeenah, the Cherokee word for spirit world, she drew strength for her next adventure into the world beyond the ridgeline. She'd had many adventures in her forty-seven years, ranging as far away as Russia, China, and Nome, Alaska.

Never, however, had she faced more of a challenge than the one that stretched before her to the East in North Carolina's rolling, rural Piedmont. She was about to become the first female superintendent of Vance County School District. It was among three districts out of 134 that the state was threatening to take over because of low student achievement. Wallace thought of little else but her new job during her short stay in the mountains; now it was time to go to it.

She took a final long breath, pushed back her full, gray-streaked black hair, and headed back down to the house, occasionally breaking into a run as she used to do as a child. Unlike her slight but tough father, she grew up strong and stout, and struck a more solid figure as she descended the hillside. Her gray Buick, packed with suitcases, and her dismayed mother waited below. There was no reason to rush off, her mother reminded her.

"There's plenty for you t'do here," she said. "It's a good life."

Wallace smiled, hugged her mother, and went out to the barn to tell her father good-bye. He adjusted his Husqvarna chainsaw cap. He knew what she was taking on and offered some practical advice.

"Just lay right in there no matter how tough it gets," he said. "Remember, when you're dealing with son-of-a-bitches, you just haf'ta figure out some way to out-son-of-a-bitch 'em."

Wallace climbed into her old car and headed out of the high country. She drove down through the Blue Ridge Mountains, past the Nikwasi Indian mound, through Watauga Gap, over Cowee Mountain, through the ancient Indian trading crossroads of Dillsboro on the banks of the Tuckaseigee River, over the Balsams and Black Mountain and through Swannanoa Valley and Pisgah Forest. She came down out of the foothills onto Interstate 40, heading east over a 300-mile stretch along the northern Piedmont that would take her through McDowell County, Winston-Salem, Greensboro and Durham, then northeast on Interstate 85 to Henderson, the county seat of Vance County. As the countryside flattened, Wallace swayed to the country melodies of Garth Brooks and Reba McIntyre on her radio and let her thoughts drift to the job. She smiled as she remembered a recent article in Raleigh's The *News & Observer*, the major newspaper for the eastern half of the state, about Vance County school board's search for a new superintendent. The board chairman, Eugene Gupton, wasn't worrying about the legal details of fair hiring practices. He told the newspaper, "I think a majority of this community believes we should have a superintendent who believes in God and goes to church regularly." But the board never probed Wallace's religious views, because she offered something that no other candidate could: a plan. The board was made up of one white and three black women, two white men, and one Lumbee Indian man. These leaders wanted someone to deliver their school district from a ten-year academic decline and from the humiliation of a takeover by the North Carolina legislature and state Board of Education.

During her two interviews with the board, Wallace had outlined her plan for leading Vance County students to a more promising future. She would reorganize the school system. Like most districts in the United States, Vance County judged and sorted students based on how their academic performance compared to the average and to others the same age. Schools did not expect children who fell below average to be able to learn as much as those above average. Those in the bottom half, sometimes called the forgotten half, were tracked into basic, remedial, and special education classes that failed to prepare them for adult life. Because of their below-average status, they lost confidence in their ability to learn, and, in time, many also lost heart, quitting school before they finished.

Wallace proposed organizing schools so they would expect all children, not just some, to reach the high achievement levels necessary to compete in the modern world. Instead of grouping children by age, she would group children by educational needs. Schools would set learning goals that defined just what students should know and be able to do at various stages of their education. Students would be judged on their progress toward the goals rather than on how they compared to others the same age. They would advance at their own pace rather than at the collective march of the traditional school. The system would focus on goals rather than comparisons, on individuals rather than groups. Instead of requiring students to fit the system, the system would adjust to fit the needs of each student. For starters, Wallace proposed eliminating grades and grade levels.

It was a radical plan. A growing number of schools, districts, even states across the nation were reorganizing to focus on learning goals, a movement often called outcomes-based education. Few, however, also were eliminating grade levels and grades. But if Wallace's plan was bolder than most, the Vance County school board also was more desperate than most. Neither she nor the board fully understood the turmoil this venture would bring.

Wallace had no illusions, however, about the status of Vance County and its schools. The district was overwhelmed by poverty, violence, and low student achievement. If she could show students performing at high levels under these conditions, she would prove that all students could succeed in schools just about anywhere.

Vance County forms a long rectangle that hugs the Virginia border near the midpoint of North Carolina's long east–west span. It lays only about forty-two miles north of the prosperous Research Triangle Park, a high-technology industrial center fueled with brain power from North Carolina State University in Raleigh, the University of North Carolina in Chapel Hill, and Duke University in Durham. But Vance County and its 38,000 residents might as well be a thousand miles away.

The years have been hard on the once-thriving land of plantations, small farms, and cotton mills. Abandoned cars, rusty farm machinery, and dilapidated trailer homes now pile up next to decaying two-story homes that once had had elegant names. The red clay soil that produced healthy crops of tobacco and cotton for generations now leaches water from tables polluted with pesticides and petroleum products. Few people now live off the land, and the average income per family was less than $12,000 in 1990. The northern half of the county, up where the arms of the John H. Kerr Reservoir reach down from Virginia, is so rural it fairly swallows people. Some county officials suspect children are growing up in the rural border country without ever going to school. The county still wrestles with deep-rooted racial tensions. Its adult illiteracy, teenage pregnancy, and women and child poverty rates all are among the highest in the state. Out of one hundred counties, it has the state's seventh-highest rate of child abuse and twenty-fourth-highest rate of violent arrests.

Henderson, once the stately Southern county seat, calls itself the Gateway City because it is the first city Interstate 85 passes through after it drops across the Virginia border from Petersburg. Now, however, Henderson's nickname carries a darker meaning, for it has become a gateway for interstate drug trafficking that feeds local crime. Henderson had long been a mill town, dominated by Harriet and Henderson Yarns, still the county's largest employer with 1,700 workers. The mill, however, lost its formerly broad control over the townspeople after bitter strikes and unionization attempts in the 1950s. The well-known union organizer Norma Rae led battles just two counties away in Roanoke Rapids, while families in Henderson were torn and split by fire bombings, drive-by shootings, and gang assaults. The battles in Henderson became so violent in 1958 that the National Guard was summoned to restore order and camped in town for nearly five months. Some residents still can recall putting up fences around their homes and hearing bullets ricochet off the cotton mill water towers at night. But those fights are over. The county is now battling drugs, crime, and poverty. The fourth- and fifth-generation children of families that established Henderson are moving on to raise their families in Greensboro, Charlotte, and Atlanta. Vance County's cultural and economic fabric is becoming increasingly threadbare.

The public schools reflect the county's social and economic stress. In 1991 the school district enrolled about 7,000 students, 61 percent of them black and 39 percent white. Fifty-eight percent of them were poor enough to qualify for free and reduced-price meals. Their test scores were among the lowest in the state; their dropout rates among the highest. Vance high school seniors posted among the lowest Scholastic Assessment Test college entrance exam scores in the state, where average SAT scores in recent years have ranked forty-eighth to dead last in the nation. Vance County's ten elementary, two middle, and two high schools suffered a steady academic decline during a decade in which the state was spending hundreds of millions of dollars to upgrade its schools. Paralyzed at the top by corruption, racial division, and politics, the district had been replacing superintendents like coaches on a losing team. Betty Wallace was the sixth in twelve years.

All this weighed on her as she pulled off Interstate 85 into the Gateway City and drove under the portico of Henderson's Holiday Inn. Dead tired after the eight-hour drive, she stretched, sighed, and stepped into the motel to register. There on the front desk lay the *Henderson Daily Dispatch,* with a bold headline spread across the front page: BOARD WITHHOLDS NEW SUPERINTENDENT'S NAME. Wallace chuckled to herself. The board obviously did not feel bound by a state law that required it to disclose the name of a new hire. Well, tomorrow everyone would know. Soon, she vowed, she would know the people of Vance County, just as they would soon know her plan for their children.

For the next two months, Wallace suspended her personal life and immersed herself in the people of this weary county. She filled her days talking to her teachers and staff and her evenings talking to any community group that would listen. And she listened too. She could hear vestiges of the past in the residents' distinct accents, in the abbreviated dialect of black mothers shopping with their children in the Winn-Dixie supermarket or in the soft, aristocratic, Virginia-inspired accents of those who dropped their r's and rounded their ou's in words like "around." She tried, unsuccessfully, to resurrect her high school Spanish in conversations with the migrant workers she met while washing her clothes at the Dabney Drive Laundromat. Much of Vance County's history was dark and cruel, yet its people still had hope, still longed to redefine themselves. They were hungry for change, and in that craving, Wallace and Vance County's people found common ground. Word got around that Wallace was accessible, willing to speak and to listen, and invitations poured in.

On one hot, moist summer night, Wallace agreed to address a black congregation in a small cinder-block church in the middle of a tobacco field outside Henderson. She approached the concrete steps, pausing to shake wet and friendly hands all around. This Wednesday night prayer meeting crowd was larger than usual because the new superintendent was visiting. A neighboring church congregation had been invited.

"We've never had a school superintendent visit us before," said a handsome young man holding a newborn baby. "We're glad you're here."

A tiny woman clasped her heavily veined hands around Wallace's and asked, "What do you do?"

"I'm the superintendent of schools," Wallace replied.

"But what do you do?" the woman asked again, more insistently.

Wallace had trouble providing a clear answer. She must speak more plainly, she thought, as she entered the church. No jargon. No theory. People wanted to know how schools would help their children. She loosened her collar.

After announcements and prayers and a song, "Prone to Wander, Lord, I Feel It," Wallace was called to the pulpit. She had hoped just to answer questions, but the minister wanted her to give a speech. She looked out across the sea of hands rhythmically waving colorful paper fans, and her mind swirled. She opened her mouth, but the words did not spill out the way they usually did. In fact, there were no words at all. Her tongue felt dry. Time slowed, the fans moved in slow motion, and for a moment she despaired. She collected herself, licked a salty drop of sweat from her lip, and plunged in. Finally the words began to flow. She later recalled her presentation going about like this:

"I go out talking with groups of people every night," she began, "and everywhere I go in Vance County, I ask people what they want for their children. And they all say the same thing: 'I want my children to do better than I have done. I want them to grow up healthy. I want them to have the things they need. I want them to read and write well and to learn mathematics and to prepare themselves for a good job.'

"People say, 'I am worried that other people will take advantage of my children, that our money will buy less and less, and that we will all be even poorer than before. I am worried that my children will have to leave Vance County to make a living. I am worried that my children will not get their share of the American Dream.' "

Wallace did not feel she was speaking very smoothly, but people were listening. Fans passed slower before their thoughtful eyes. She wiped sweat from her own and proceeded.

"People say they want our schools to be better so that our children can learn the things they need to know. They want their children to do well in school and to feel that they can learn anything they want to learn.

"People want their children to be smart."

A quiet "Amen" startled Wallace, and she saw that it came from the little woman with big veins in her hands. When Wallace paused, the woman raised her red paper fan in the air and said, "She's telling it right." Some other voice joined in with "Amen. A-men."

"People want their children to get a fair shake in the world," Wallace continued. "And they want their children to be able to judge for themselves what is good. They want their children to know if they're getting the right price for their tobacco, if they're paying too much for tires, and which size Tide is the best buy at the grocery store."

"Amen."

"They want their children to have a bank account . . ."

"Amen."

". . . and to know how to save money and to write checks."

"That's right."

Wallace caught the rhythm and flow of this exchange and began pausing for responses. She spoke about the promise of knowledge. She described how learning can fill human lives with joy from birth to death, how it can deliver the poor to prosperity, how it can enrich the lives of an entire generation with a fullness of meaning that extends far beyond the benefits of a good job.

"People want their children to take care of themselves . . ."

"Tell it, sister."

". . . and to be healthy . . ."

"Yeeessss. Amen. That's right."

". . . and to feel good about themselves . . ."

"Uh-huh."

". . . and to learn new things . . ."

"Amen. Aaamen."

". . . and to feel the *joy* of learning. . . ."

"Tell it, sister, it's the truth!" came an old voice where a red fan waved high in the air.

Wallace finished, surveyed the blue and red and yellow fans swaying before her, and was overwhelmed by her affection for this warm audience. She felt a deeper bond to these people and her mission in Vance County. As a stream of sweat trickled down her spine, she added her own quiet "Amen."

She felt both hope and a humbling dread as she drove home in the afterglow of this encounter. Wallace was at once buoyed by the congregation's support and daunted by the journey she was asking it to make. The scope of the challenge before her quickly became apparent in talks with principals and teachers and in visits to schools with remedial labs, desks in neat rows, and sets of identical textbooks lining classroom shelves. Vance County schools had all the symptoms of a system deeply entrenched in traditional, group-oriented practices. Wallace had taken command of a district that fully embraced education's worst enemy—the bell curve.

CHAPTER 1

▼

THE BELL CURVE

Betty Wallace sensed something awry in the framework of public education soon after she began teaching high school English in Cobb County, Georgia. Like most beginning teachers, she was startled by the large number of students who lacked even a basic grasp of reading and writing. How had they managed to get so far still knowing so little? Her misgivings deepened as she watched public school alienate her own son, Matthew.

By the time Matthew entered school, Wallace had worked as a teacher and curriculum coordinator in Charlotte, North Carolina, and become an assistant superintendent in Macon County, up in the mountains where she grew up. Matthew was always bright and inquisitive, but school left him unfulfilled. He learned more from the mountains. His mother would come home and see his head bobbing above Skeenah Creek where he invested hours stalking salamanders, leeches, and dragonflies and monitoring the gestation of tadpole eggs. He followed his grandfather through the woods and learned the names and traditional medicinal uses of plants and the types of lumber useful for construction. His grandmother taught him how to pick wild branch lettuce, to preserve food, and to grow a dozen varieties of onion. "Life wouldn't be worth livin' without onions," she said as she showed him features of shallots, sweet Vidalias, and the strong wild onions indigenous to the mountain woodlands. Matthew asked neighbors to teach him how to salt down a deer hide and to mount a snake skin. He read voraciously in comic books, classic literature, and Volkswagen manuals written in German. More than once Wallace found calls to Germany on her phone bill as a result of Matthew's quest for records and parts for his 1954 VW. In the open classroom and laboratory of the Smoky Mountains, Matthew learned more about science, language, and the wonder of life than he ever did in school. His mother suspected Matthew was typical of many or even most American children. If so, what did that say about schools?

This question nagged at her as she studied from 1976 to 1980 for her doctorate in education under Professor David Mullen at the University of Georgia in Athens. Mullen had been charged with organizing Afghanistan's first formal education system, and he pulled Wallace into his research. Starting from scratch forced the educators to ask fresh questions about the purpose of public education. Wallace decided schools could and probably should have a variety of roles. Some, for example, might emphasize science while others could specialize in arts, humanities, business, or health care. But all schools shared two responsibilities: to perpetuate the culture they served and to give all children the knowledge and skills they needed to become effective adults.

When she applied that standard to the American public education system, Wallace had to conclude it failed on both counts. Needless to say, large numbers of students did not graduate with the skills they needed to be effective adults. Moreover, schools had become abstract, distant, and alien to other endeavors in the American culture. Where else, for example, were people grouped by age?

After earning her doctorate, Wallace went to work for the North Carolina Department of Public Instruction. Her first job was director of the department's Western Regional Education Center in Canton, where she worked four more years. Then in 1984 she moved to department headquarters in Raleigh to become deputy assistant state superintendent for curriculum and instruction. This gave her a bird's-eye perspective on the problems afflicting public education. From Raleigh she could clearly see how large, uniform, dehumanizing public schools across the state were demanding students conform to mediocre standards that left large numbers either bored or frustrated. Education had become preoccupied with average achievement and with those who deviated from it. In essence, Wallace concluded, schools were trying to force children into a bell-curve pattern of academic achievement. This was the weak beam causing the framework of education to twist and sag. This was the practice that was hurting children in classrooms across the country. A morning visit to Fran Lee's fourth-grade classroom at Creston Elementary School in Portland, Oregon, reveals its poison.[1]

Lee steps up to the chalkboard to give her students a lesson in grammar and punctuation. She points to an odd cluster of words: did you leave champ, your dog eat?

"Who can correct my sentence?" she asks.

Eager arms shoot up. Lee calls on some of the volunteers, they suggest changes, and soon the sentence makes more sense: Did you let Champ, your dog, eat?

Not all children, however, were raising their hands. For a few, such as Desirée, the top speller in this class, this exercise poses no challenge. For others, such as Jimmy, it is nearly incomprehensible. A vast academic canyon separates Jimmy and Desirée. It shows in their writing.

Desirée writes a full page about her school with passages like: "The food is OK. I like their chicken nuggets the best. You should try them." Jimmy writes two incomplete sentences about falling into a puddle. "Wan day I was waking done the stret satile it rand and I tript in a pudl I was so mad I frect." Desirée has gained command of language; Jimmy has not. Later, when they have twenty-five minutes for silent reading, Desirée whips through thirty-four pages of *Dear Mr. Henshaw* by Beverly Cleary. In the same period, Jimmy struggles to concentrate as he slogs through only portions of five pages of the more basic *The Cat Who Went to Heaven* by Elizabeth Coatsworth. When Lee goes over arithmetic homework, Jimmy is still searching through his book for the correct page number. He daydreams during the next lesson and, after getting his next assignment, fails to finish a single addition problem by the time some students nearly are done.

It makes no educational sense to put Jimmy and Desirée in the same class for the same lessons. But then Creston Elementary, like most American schools, does not group students on the basis of educational needs. Instead, students are put together because they share the same age and neighborhood. That's about all they have in common. Most modern American classrooms include children with a wide range of academic skills and economic, social, and ethnic backgrounds. Fran Lee's is probably less diverse than most. Even so, half of her twenty-six students are poor enough to qualify for federally subsidized free- or reduced-price lunches, one lives with a family that does not speak English, one is a Pacific Islander, one an American Indian, one Hispanic, and one black. During the year, three students moved into Lee's class while four others left. Test scores show her students' academic skills in math and reading range from first-grade to eighth-grade levels or averages. They are different children with different backgrounds and different educational needs.

Yet Lee is charged with teaching them as if they were all the same and all prepared to spend the same amount of time on the same lesson in each subject every day. She is expected to cover a curriculum developed by central office specialists who follow statewide guidelines and expected to teach all of her students out of the same textbooks, selected from a list approved by state and district selection committees. These materials are all designed for the achievement level educators deem average for fourth graders. Most of Fran Lee's students, however, aren't average. Only five of her students, for example, scored in the average range on reading tests. Most are at various levels above and below the broad average range defined by test scores.

Lee, who has spent three decades in the classroom, does as much as any person can to accommodate these differences. Administrators say she's one of Portland's best. She spends extra hours preparing more challenging assignments for her more advanced students, such as Desirée. "I expect more of those kids, and they know it," she says. She also looks for chances to pull Jimmy aside for extra help. Still, her first responsibility is to the group. Sometimes, to reach everybody, she says, she aims her group lessons "for the lowest common denominator." Her extra efforts to compensate for differences separating Jimmy and Desirée make school still a pleasant, or at least tolerable, place for both. But they are well aware of the academic gulf that divides them. On a day when Desirée is pulled out of class for special honors as student of the month, Jimmy is pulled out for special help in a federally funded remedial reading program called Chapter 1. The gulf will only widen as these two students progress through school.

Desirée will face a continuous battle against boredom, at least until she is allowed to move into the more challenging college-bound academic track in high school. Jimmy, on the other hand, will continue scrambling to catch up in remedial classes. But unless he does, which is unlikely, he will grow increasingly frustrated and discouraged with school, lose drive, fall farther behind, grow to believe he is not very smart, and possibly give up and drop out. He already fights a sense of defeat, though he has fared better with Lee than with his previous teachers, his mother said. His older brother, who also fell behind the pack in elementary school, is repeating eighth grade after two years of failure. Most students will experience some measure of Desirée's boredom and Jimmy's frustration as they encounter subjects that come easy and hard.

By the time they reach high school, large numbers of students have become disenchanted with school and learning. Unless they are bound for college, they are reluctant to read, write, or do homework. Teachers give assignments that not just some, but most, of their students fail to complete. Some students simply don't have the basic skills to handle the work. English teachers try to teach Shakespeare, as the curriculum demands, to students who still have trouble reading the newspaper. Math teachers try to teach algebra to students who have not yet learned their multiplication tables. Both teachers and students are frustrated.

Schools for Some

Until very recently, widespread school failure did not produce serious social consequences. Americans willing to use their hands, backs, and enterprise did not need much more than a basic education to earn a good living on farms and in factories and shops. But today even a high school diploma will not give most young people access to jobs that pay enough to support them in even a modest lifestyle, which may explain why 58 percent of unmarried adults between twenty and twenty-four years of age still live with their parents. Good jobs demand more education. Yet our schools graduate more than 1 million young people a year who are ill-equipped either to go to college or to work. The education demands of good-paying jobs will be even more rigorous when Jimmy and Desirée complete high school in 2001. Now more than ever before, American schools have a moral responsibility to give every student, not just some or even most, high academic skills. Yet few, if any, American schools are even coming close to meeting this responsibility at this time.

The old way, still the prevailing way, and for most children the only way, is no longer good enough because it allows only some children to succeed. At its heart, public education is a brutal system of winners and losers. Children's success hinges on how their academic performance compares to that of others of the same age. Their fate depends on where they rank relative to the average—in other words, their place in a normal distribution, or what statisticians call the bell-shaped curve. Much of what is practiced in American schools is based on this "deep, unspoken, unquestioned assumption," notes David T. Conley, a professor of education at the University of Oregon.

"It is difficult to overestimate the pervasiveness of this mode of thinking or the difficulty of challenging its acceptance by educators," he writes.[2]

U.S. public education embraced the bell curve early in the century. The curve had emerged earlier as a nineteenth-century discovery by Carl Friedrich Gauss of Germany. Gauss showed that natural occurrences, such as the weight of adult geese or the girth of fifty-year-old men, will tend toward an arithmetical average. Most mature male Embden geese, for example, weigh twenty-six pounds, which is the average, or norm. The occurrences of mature geese weighing more or less than average diminish as the margin separating them from the average widens. In other words, given one hundred Embden geese, you would typically find thirty-two that weigh a pound more or less than the twenty-six-pound average, but only four that weigh more than three pounds above or below average.

Gauss showed that when these weights are plotted on a graph with a vertical axis representing numbers of geese and a horizontal axis representing weight, they describe a bell-shaped curve. (See Figure 1.1.) The curve's peak represents the average, and the line then slopes away on each side as it moves away from average. This pattern, also called the Gaussian or normal curve, occurs often in the distribution of natural and chance events. It also is sometimes called an error curve, for deviations or errors in precise measurements, say with a ruler, will produce a bell-shaped distribution. Gauss probably plotted the curve after observing some natural characteristic, such as the height of eighteen-year-old men, and then wrote the mathematical formula that would describe the same curve.[3]

In reality, however, many natural characteristics do not produce bell curves but irregular, skewed curves. This is usually true, for example, of human accomplishment: for the age at which men marry, the patents held by inventors, the number of publications of research scientists, the amount of music written by composers, yearly earnings—*and* student achievement.[4] This is because human accomplishments are more a function of will and effort than of inherent, naturally occurring qualities such as intelligence.

Educators, however, assume achievement reflects intelligence more than will or effort. Most instructional practices stem from this assumption. Students are grouped by age for mass instruction on the assumption that their academic abilities will describe a bell

Figure 1
Normal Distribution in Weight of 100 Mature Male
Embden Geese

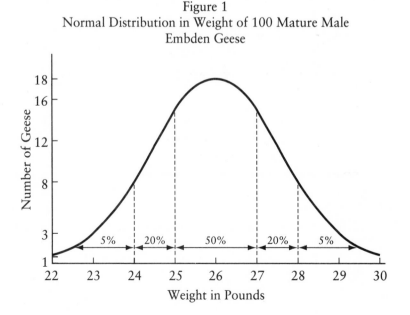

curve. Since most fall in the average range under the dome of the curve, most can profit from group instruction geared to that average. Or so the theory goes. In every corner of the education system, group instructional plans are aimed at the average. Teachers teach to the middle or grade level, synonyms for the average. Publishers produce textbooks written to grade level. Curriculum experts design courses for the average. So in reading, for example, educators have concluded that most second graders—that is, *average* second graders—begin class in the fall ready to read simple sentences. Fifteen percent will still be mastering letters, sounds, and beginning words, and another 15 percent will be independent and fluent readers, but most will be reading simple sentences. This would represent a range of achievement levels that could be charted as a bell curve. A second-grade teacher, then, logically teaches from second-grade reading textbooks that open with stories using simple sentences.

This approach misses the mark, though, for students who are still learning words or who are already independent readers. Schools try to compensate for these students with special classes. For those who lag behind, schools offer remedial classes designed to help them catch up to the pack. For those who are ahead, schools offer gifted classes that occupy them with learning projects while they wait for the pack to catch up. By the secondary level, however, schools give up trying to keep children in a single group. They begin sorting them into at least three tracks: the basic, the general, and the advanced. Implicit in this organization is the assumption that only the advanced are smart enough to take challenging courses they need to prepare for college. Consequently, only about 30 percent of America's graduates are prepared to go on to four-year colleges. Less is required of the other 70 percent, so most of them leave school prepared neither for work nor for college.

There are at least three flaws in this structure.

First, instruction and expectations are geared to students performing at average levels, which tend to be mediocre. These practices give rise to a system fine-tuned to mediocrity. In its landmark 1983 report *A Nation at Risk,* a presidential commission got front-page headlines for warning a rising tide of mediocrity threatened our schools. But how can we expect otherwise from a system that inherently strives for mediocrity?

Second, the system's fixation with the average has created an evaluation system that judges students more on how they compare to the average than on what they know. This system fosters an unhealthy social hierarchy that pits students against one another in repeated comparisons. It promotes the myth that every class and every school includes some students who are smart enough to make it and some who are not. Intelligence certainly varies among students, but even so, virtually all students are smart enough to reach high levels of academic achievement if they are willing to work hard. Schools should set high expectations for all students, not just 30 percent.

Finally, public education has institutionalized the bell curve as a prescriptive rather than a descriptive tool—as if the curve were a law of nature. With grades, tracking, and other instructional practices, schools force students into a bell-curve pattern of achievement whether that fits them or not.

In a country that is becoming increasingly diverse, such a pattern usually does not fit. Few students are average in all things. So group instruction geared to the average is going to miss the mark for nearly all students some of the time. Actually, it probably misses the mark for most students most of the time because their achievement range is so vast. Students typically don't come to a teacher in neat bell-curve packages. The achievement curves are just as likely to be skewed, because students of the same age today often have vastly different ranges of experience and, therefore, widely differing knowledge and skills. One-third of all three-year-olds and more than half of all four-year-olds attend preschool. Thus about half the children entering kindergarten have one or two more years of schooling than their peers, some of whom have rarely seen a book. Most American classrooms are now so diverse that they include some students who spent part of their lives living in other countries, speaking other languages. Portland, Oregon, public schools enroll students capable of speaking fifteen major languages and another thirty more obscure ones. According to the 1990 U.S. Census, 32 million Americans speak a language other than English in their homes. That represents a 38 percent increase over the previous decade. The census counted 907,563 children ages five to seventeen who do not speak English very well or at all. The U.S. Department of Education estimates that 2.2 million children in the nation's private and public schools have a limited command of English. Further, the economic gap separating children's parents has expanded over the last two decades. Between 1975 and 1990, the earnings gap between white-collar professionals and skilled tradespeople widened from 2 percent to 37 percent; the gap between professionals and clerical workers increased from 47 percent to 86 percent.[5] When children are so diverse, it makes no sense to give them all the same lesson based on a group average.

Consider, for example, a fictional second-grade classroom of Mr. Braintree. Like most modern American classes, Braintree's twenty-four students have a range of reading levels that reflects their cultural and economic diversity. Two students are immigrants and still learning English. Four more are still learning the alphabet and phonics. Seven can read some words and phrases. Two can read simple sentences. Five can easily read more complex sentences. Three more can independently plow through most newspaper stories, and one can comfortably digest adolescent literature as a fluent reader. If we were to chart the reading achievement levels of Braintree's second graders, it would not form a bell curve but rather a skewed, double-humped curve. (See Figure 1.2.) If Braintree was determined to teach the whole group one lesson geared to the average, he would have to settle on having them read beginning stories with simple sentences. But as the figure shows, this level, while average for the class, fits the needs of only two students. Braintree's lesson would be either too hard or too easy for his other twenty-two students. With this range of achievement, there is no way he can reach even a third of his students with a single lesson set to one level. Similarly, the actual achievement curve in reading for Fran Lee's class is skewed, with more students scoring above and below than within the average range. (See Figure 1.3.)

Other grouping and instructional methods will allow teachers to meet the needs of all rather than just some children. Instead of grouping children by age, for example, educators could group them by achievement levels. They could take all children still learning English and put them in one group. Put all children learning their letters, phonics, and first words in a second group; those learning to read phrases and simple sentences in a third; and so forth. These

Figure 2
Distribution of Reading Levels
in Mr. Braintree's Class

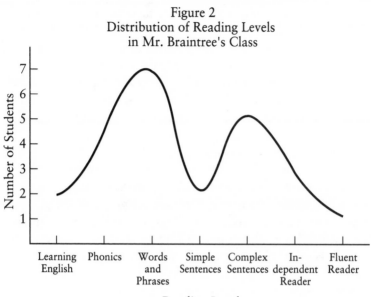

Reading Levels

Figure 3
Distribution of Reading Scores in
Fran Lee's Fourth-grade Class

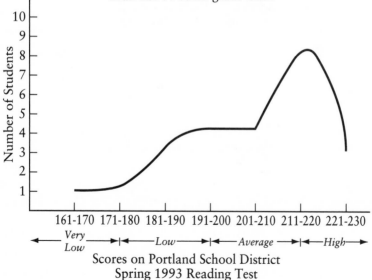

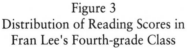

Scores on Portland School District
Spring 1993 Reading Test

groups, each based on a different achievement level, could be viewed as stairs ascending to the final goal—reading fluency. Each child then should be free to ascend this staircase at his or her own pace. (See Figure 1.4.) This structure might put three six-year-olds in three different groups: One with two years of preschool experience might be ready for beginning sentences, another exposed only to kindergarten might need more work on letters, and a third might be ready to read longer sentences.

The staircase structure is widely used and accepted in sports, performing arts, and other educational endeavors outside of public schools. Swim teachers, for example, group their classes by achievement levels rather than ages. They would not think of putting a six-year-old who had mastered the crawl stroke in a beginners' class with children still mustering courage to dunk their heads just so she could be with others her own age. Instead she would be placed in an intermediate-level class with other students ready to learn the frog kick and breast stroke.

When Emma Graves, the author's daughter, decided to take bal-

Figure 4
Staircase Grouping
(Children grouped by achievement levels rather
than age. Each step is a different group.)

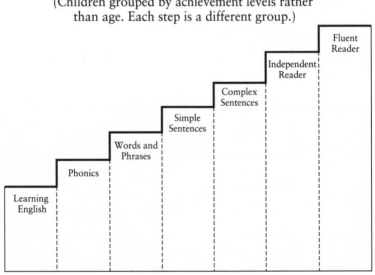

let lessons at age fourteen, the Oregon Ballet Theater put her in level one with other beginners, most of whom happened to be seven- and eight-year-olds. Ballet teachers would consider it absurd to group their children on the basis of age.

Public education could serve all students instead of just some by rejecting its rigid, age-based structure and shifting to a staircase structure such as that used by swim and ballet schools. At first glance, this might look a lot like the tracking or ability grouping that we see in remedial and gifted classes. But achievement grouping differs from ability grouping in three fundamental ways.

First, it holds high standards for all students, not just some. It assumes that progress up the achievement staircase is more a function of effort than intelligence. It assumes that all students are smart enough to reach the top. Some children might need to spend more time than others in the beginning swim class, but their teachers expect them all eventually to learn how to swim. No one is locked into lower levels.

Achievement grouping also is fluid. It does not force students to move from one level to the next in whole groups. A student can advance whenever he is ready, whether it takes him three or thirteen months.

Finally, students in achievement groups are not judged on the basis of how they compare to others of the same age. Instead they are evaluated on what they know and are able to do and compared against a standard of performance. When they meet the standard at one level, they move to the next. There are no losers. Everyone who tries advances.

Schools can break away from age-based grouping in other ways. Some schools, for example, group children of mixed ages and achievement levels, much as they were grouped in one-room schoolhouses earlier in the century. Teachers find ways to guide these students along various learning paths at the same time. They might use computers to individualize math, trade books to individualize reading, and tap the skills of advanced students to tutor those at lower levels. They also sometimes turn to the larger community outside the classroom for learning opportunities, much as teachers in one-room schools were forced to do. These methods allow teachers to group children of various ages and achievement levels and still meet individual needs. They work better, however, when combined with staircase achievement grouping and performance standards.

Public schools must shift to more fluid structures and individualized instruction if they are ever to succeed in preparing all, or even most, students to be effective adults in the modern world. The current system, with its compulsive bond to a bell-curve pattern of student achievement, is harmful to more than half of America's children. It will never work much better than it does now. The bell curve always has a dark side that penalizes students who fall in its gloomy shadows.

By rejecting bell-curve assumptions about student achievement and grouping children by their educational needs, however, schools can usher virtually all children to high levels of academic achievement. The uniform, age-based U.S. public education system does not fit the nation's increasingly diverse culture. Americans need a school system flexible enough to respond to individuals rather than one that demands individuals conform to its rigid, monolithic ways.

The bell curve serves as both a model and a fitting symbol of an archaic public education system. It describes a broad swath of mediocrity flanked by a sliver of excellence and a ribbon of failure. It is a pattern we've all grown up with, as familiar and seemingly benign as an old schoolhouse bell. But we can no longer afford to be lulled by this warm familiarity. This bell's invitation to learn rings hollow.

CHAPTER 2

▼

THE BELL-CURVE SYNDROME

Teaching practices based on the bell curve compromise learning in American schools the way low levels of lead subtly damage the brain. They have limited the education of generations of Americans, always hurting some children far more than others. The bell curve's poison seeps through schools largely unnoticed. But educators are too familiar with its frustrating symptoms: widespread low student achievement, dull textbooks, watered-down basic and remedial classes, pervasive mediocrity, high dropout rates, discipline problems, demoralized teachers, and large numbers of misplaced, angry, alienated children. These symptoms feed on one another, giving rise to a syndrome that is worse than the sum of its parts: the Bell-Curve Syndrome.

Educators rely on a bell-curve pattern of performance both to define average or grade-level student achievement and to identify students who deviate from the average. Both practices feed the syndrome in differing but overlapping ways. In the first, educators focus on norms or average student performance to prescribe instruction. What suits the average child becomes the standard instructional path and pace for all children of a given age group. Tests reveal the average. Textbook publishers and curriculum designers then base their materials on these averages. Teachers rely on textbooks and curricula to instruct children, who are then tested to yield a new average or norm. In this cycle, the education system continuously adjusts its instructional thermostat to average—or, one might argue, mediocrity. Each stage of the cycle produces dark consequences that become part of the Bell-Curve Syndrome.

Testing and the Quest for Average

Uniform national tests such as the California Achievement Test became widely used in schools during the 1980s in response to political demands for accountability. The release in 1983 of *A Nation at Risk* stirred political leaders to invest heavily in public education. The nation collectively increased its spending on schools by $98 billion between 1983–84 and 1991–92 to $213 billion, marking a 50 percent increase in spending in eight years after adjusting for inflation.[1] Political leaders wanted to see results and a way to measure them, so in response, educators commonly turned to a faulty barometer—norm-referenced tests.

Rather than using measures that tell parents what their children know and can do, administrators sought tests that showed how students compared to the average performance of others of the same age. Underlying this choice was the assumption that student achievement would naturally describe a bell curve and that education's first priority was to identify where each student belonged on that curve. The tests widely used by schools were aptly called norm-referenced tests. "Norm" refers to the peak of a normal curve, or the average, so one can think of these as average-referenced tests. They do their job. They tell educators what the average basic skill performance is for students across the nation at every grade level. Results for these tests usually are reported as percentiles. A student who scores at the sixtieth percentile, for example, has scored above average since he is above 59 percent of his peers and behind only 40 percent. A student scoring at the fiftieth percentile would be at about average. This tells a teacher or parent how a student compares to her peers but nothing about what she can read, write, or do in math.

Norm-referenced tests have other drawbacks. They make it possible for only some students to earn respectable scores, emphasize the performance of groups over individuals, and focus on low rather than high standards.

In a system that judges students on their relative performance, no one can look good without someone looking bad. It is literally impossible for all students to succeed. Whatever the average, there must be students below it, and they are relegated to some measure of failure status.

"We have a system in which 50 percent of the kids experience failure," said the late Walter Hathaway, former director of research and testing for the Portland School District in Oregon. "If we started out to design a system that would hold kids back from the beginning, we couldn't have come up with a system more effective than the system we have."

Even should a group of students achieve at high levels, some members will be forced to occupy the losers' slots in a norm-referenced system. If second graders by some quirk were on average capable of multiplying fractions, those who could only multiply whole numbers would be deemed failures. Conversely, educators and parents tend to become complacent about student performance as long as it is at or above average, though the average by world standards may be low. It would be of no consolation for a pilot to learn that his airplane is flying higher than average if it is still headed into the side of a mountain.

Since being above average is the prevailing American standard of excellence, every state education system in the nation has found a way to meet it. John Jacob Cannell, a doctor from West Virginia, revealed this seemingly impossible phenomenon in 1988. He showed that 90 percent of American school districts, and all fifty states, claimed to be scoring above the national average on standardized tests. If the national average is a true average, the number should be 50 percent and no more. In 1989 Cannell found forty-eight states still boasting their children score "above the national norm." Cannell called this the Lake Wobegon effect, referring to the fictional community where "all the children are above average" created by radio humorist Garrison Keillor.

Testing experts say the Lake Wobegon effect occurs because testing companies use the same national norms for five to seven and, in some cases, even ten years. The norms are established through an expensive process that involves a national representative sample of 250,000 to 500,000 children, said Michael Kean of Monterey, California, vice president of public and government affairs for CTB Macmillan/McGraw-Hill, which sells about 10 million tests a year to public and private schools. These norms would remain valid for years if all teachers used the test for the first time each year. But in practice, many teachers give their students the same test year after year until teachers become so familiar with it that they can prepare students for specific questions, Kean said. Students do better than they would without this expert coaching, and a majority end up scoring above average. The actual average rises above the official norm. Hence, the Lake Wobegon effect.

Cannell said some teachers also resorted to cheating to make the grade.[2] While Kean believes that Cannel overstated the scope of fraud, he acknowledged that some districts misuse norm-referenced tests to sort students or judge teachers when they should be only one of many evaluation tools. According to Kean, "You should use multiple measures for making any education decisions."

In any case, the Lake Wobegon effect underscores American education's preoccupation with the average.

Norm-referenced tests also encourage educators to focus on the progress of groups rather than individuals. It is the average score of the group, not individual results, that reflects on educators. As long as a class, school, district, or state posts average group scores at or above the norm, it appears successful. By this standard, schools can enroll many students who are failing—as nearly every school in the nation does—and still be deemed successful.

Finally, national norm-referenced tests tend to focus on rudimentary skills in reading, language, and mathematics, since those are easiest to measure on a massive scale with multiple-choice tests. A $1 million study released in late 1992 by the National Science Foundation concluded that 95 percent of the questions on the most frequently used national tests measure low-level skills such as memorization and arithmetic rather than higher-level reasoning and problem solving.[3] These standards simply aim too low. Because teachers feel compelled to focus on preparing children for these kinds of science tests, for example, they have little time to do science, said George Wood, an Ohio University education professor and author of *Schools That Work*.

"If you're teaching toward filling-in-the-blank and multiple-choice answers, he says, "that's what you'll get back from your students."[4]

National tests help educators fix their course on the peak of the bell curve much as a pilot might steer his ship toward a distant bluff. Tests guide instruction. Teachers naturally try to teach their students what they will be expected to know on the test, and when standards sink, so does the instructional level. Tests focused on rudimentary skills have encouraged teachers to engage in dull and unchallenging instruction that relies heavily on worksheets and practice drills. Critics such as Monty Neill, associate director of FairTest, the National Center for Fair & Open Testing in Cambridge, Massachusetts, say these "drill-and-kill" exercises foster "dumbed-down curricula."

"The powers-that-be of testing have helped ensure that too few students receive a high-quality education," Neill wrote in an essay for *The Washington Post*. "Classrooms often have turned into test-coaching centers that fail to upgrade educational quality."[5]

While all students should have strong fundamental academic skills, they must know far more to be effective adults in the modern world. But student achievement patterns over the last decade show that far too many of them do not.

Patterns of Performance

The heavy emphasis on basic skills in American schools has paid off with modest gains in student performance on low-level academic tasks. But there has been little improvement in higher skills such as analysis, synthesis, problem solving—what teachers often call critical thinking skills.

The clearest evidence of these trends lies in the results of tests conducted by the Educational Testing Services for the National Assessment of Educational Progress, a division of the U.S. Department of Education. The tests are given periodically to national samples of students at ages nine, thirteen, and seventeen to assess their proficiency in reading, mathematics, history, geography, science, and civics. The national assessment translates the scores into proficiency levels, which, unlike the comparative scores of norm-referenced tests, provide some explanation of what students know and can do. For example, between the 1977–78 and 1991–92 school years, student performance on rudimentary or basic math skills climbed, but performance on advanced operations showed little improvement.

"Our major improvements are at very low levels," said Iris Carl, past president of the National Council of Teachers of Mathematics, upon release of the 1992 report.[6]

The results showed that only 2 to 4 percent of students in the three age groups tested performed at superior levels. Nearly 40 percent failed to reach basic levels. Similarly, the proportion of seventeen-year-olds reading at basic levels climbed from 96 to 98 percent between 1970–71 and 1989–90. But the proportion reading at advanced levels during that period remained unchanged at an abysmal 7 percent.[7] Here are some other findings from these assessments:

- Students at ages nine and seventeen were reading slightly better in 1990 than they were in 1971, but thirteen-year-olds showed no improvement. Minority students made the biggest gains.

- Large numbers of students tested in 1988 had some command of basic history facts, but their interpretative skills were relatively weak. Among twelfth graders, 89 percent knew basic historical information, but only 5 percent demonstrated an ability to interpret it.

- Performance in science improved slightly between 1976–77 and 1989–90 for children tested at ages nine, thirteen, and seventeen. The proportion of thirteen- and seventeen-year-olds with a command of high-level science skills, such as the ability to analyze procedures and findings and to integrate specialized scientific information, has never been large and remained unchanged during this period.[8]

These results reflect public education's focus on minimum rather than high standards. Further, they tend to mask the widespread failure of huge numbers of individual American children because they are reported in terms of groups and averages. On science tests administered by the Educational Testing Service (ETS) between 1976–77 and 1989–90, the average scores of seventeen-year-olds climbed modestly. Even so, 494,000 high school seniors still could not apply basic scientific information, and 1.5 million—*more than half*—were unable to analyze scientific procedures and data.

ETS results in other subjects show similar failings. In 1990, 1.3 million U.S. high school seniors were unable to perform reasoning and problem solving involving fractions, decimals, percents, elementary geometry, and simple algebra. In 1989–90, about 41,600 of the nation's seventeen-year-olds were unable to read well enough to understand combined ideas and short uncomplicated passages.[9]

Meanwhile, there is other evidence that student performance in more advanced skills and knowledge is actually declining. Fewer students, for example, are earning high scores on the verbal portion of the Scholastic Assessment Test (SAT; until recently called the Scholastic Aptitude Test), a college entrance exam and one of the few consistent indicators of nationwide student achievement over decades. While the number of students taking the test has remained constant at about 1 million, the number scoring above 600 points out of a possible 800 has dropped from 116,630 in 1972 to 74, 836 in 1991.[10]

U.S. education standards are astonishingly low, even in suburban high schools, writes Thomas Toch, education writer for *U.S. News & World Report* and author of *In the Name of Excellence:*

> What might be called a "conspiracy of the least"—an unwritten, unspoken pledge between students and teachers to put as little energy as possible into their work—is endemic in inner city secondary schools. But the problem pervades many suburban schools as well. Classes start late. They end early. Teachers lead discussions off the assigned topic, filling time with irrelevant digressions. . . . Order, not education, seems to be the priority in many suburban classrooms.[11]

An increasing number of university faculty members say that even the nation's top high school graduates are arriving at college poorly prepared. "There is a general alarm among faculty members that students today just can't do the same kind of work that students could do 10 or 15 years ago," Richard Rosser, executive director of the National Association of Independent Colleges and Universities, told *The Boston Globe.* "They are not as rigorously trained, particularly in the communicative skills—the ability to write, the ability to speak."[12]

American students are not reaching the standards met by students elsewhere in the world, which will jeopardize their future and the U.S. capacity to sustain a competitive workforce in a world economy.

"Not only do they have great trouble going beyond basic rote skills to reasoning and problem solving, but their capacity for engaging in these more advanced mental activities has actually declined in recent years," write Ray Marshall and Marc Tucker in their book *Thinking for a Living.*[13]

US West, the telephone company, has seen the proportion of applicants failing its basic skills test for entry-level jobs climb from 23 percent in 1983 to nearly 80 percent in 1992. The failure rate has grown so high that the company is having problems finding enough qualified people to interview for vacancies. Yet the tests are easy, requiring only an achievement level deemed average for seventh or eighth graders, said Steve Nielsen, the company's former director of external development. "It has questions like 'Here's a list of words; alphabetize them,' " he said.[14]

Meanwhile, students in other industrialized nations are reaching high achievement standards. Twenty-five percent of Canadian students know as much chemistry as the top 1 percent of American students. Only 2 to 3 percent of American students can match the median score of Japanese students in math.[15]

U.S. thirteen-year-olds scored among the lowest in mathematics and in the bottom third on science achievement in a 1988 international test also given to students in Canada, Ireland, Korea, Spain, and England. In a math assessment of fifteen countries in 1991, U.S. thirteen-year-olds scored higher than students in only one country, Jordan. They scored at about the same levels as teens in Slovenia and Spain and significantly lower than teens in eleven other countries. In a series of science tests administered between 1983 and 1986, U.S. fourteen-year-olds scored lower than their peers in ten other countries, including Poland, Hungary, and Korea, better than their peers in the Philippines, and about the same as teens in five other countries.[16]

Average student achievement in the United States over the last two decades has hardly budged despite massive increases in spending aimed at improving student performance. Millions of high school juniors and seniors are performing at levels so low that they will be functionally crippled in an adult world that demands high academic skills. They are the victims of a system that uses norm-referenced tests to keep its thermostat set on average, usually a low standard. The disappointing pattern of learning in American schools—generally mediocre performance for the group and abysmally low achievement for millions of individuals—is probably the most serious symptom of the Bell-Curve Syndrome.

Teaching to the Middle

Curriculum and textbook designers draw on test results to develop instructional guides for teachers. They thereby reinforce an instructional system geared to average student performance. These one-size-fits-all grade-level curricula presume that if teachers expose all children to the same lessons for the same amount of time, the children will all acquire the same knowledge. This naturally misses the mark for many if not most students who aren't performing precisely at grade level.

Public school curricula also encourage teachers to focus on groups rather than on individuals and to worry more about what they teach or cover than what students learn. In many districts and states, the curriculum is painstakingly detailed in scope and sequence from kindergarten through grade 12. In North Carolina, for example, state curriculum designers in the state Department of Public Instruction developed a seventeen-volume set of curriculum guidelines. These guidelines tell each teacher of each subject at each grade level what must be taught throughout the year. Oregon, on the other hand, produces a statewide framework or broad guidelines that local districts can modify as they choose. Local districts then develop their own courses of study, though most stick close to state recommendations.

These highly defined curricula pressure teachers to march students through their lessons as if they were on a group tour in a museum. The curriculum writers decide which halls the students march down and which works they will spend their time viewing. Teachers cannot tolerate stragglers in the museum of knowledge, nor do they dare to allow the more curious and energetic to race ahead or stray down inviting corridors on their own. Such departures jeopardize the group's progress.

Diversity puts teachers in a bind. They know they can seldom reach every child with a single lesson. So they try to teach to the "middle," the average or grade level of their class (or, as in the case of Fran Lee at Creston Elementary, the lowest common denominator). Teachers give what individual attention they can for advanced students who already know the material and for students who are behind and having trouble grasping it. But doing so is never easy, and large numbers of students are either frustrated or bored, which can give rise to disenchantment and discipline problems.

In recent years, teachers at all levels have complained that the curriculum is too crowded, forcing them to cover too much content. They must choose between racing through the full curriculum and leaving some, or even most, of their students befuddled or slowing down and teaching less to more children. A history teacher, for example, may have to choose between helping students understand the causes of the Civil War and leaving them in the dark on the Cold War or glossing over the former to show them President John F. Kennedy at the Berlin Wall. Since they are under pressure to cover the curriculum, many, if not most, teachers will zip through the lessons, leaving students with a cursory understanding of American history.

Howard Gardner, professor at the Harvard Graduate School of Education, calls this "pressure for coverage" the greatest enemy of understanding in public schools. "If you feel that when Week One is over, you have to move on to the lessons in Week Two—whether or not the kids understand—you absolutely guarantee that understanding will not occur," he writes.[17]

The group-oriented design of school curricula also gives public school instruction an assembly-line quality. The system pushes students from class to class and grade to grade, giving them new pieces of knowledge and skills at each stop as if it were installing circuit boards into computers. In attempting to refine this assembly-line system, curriculum designers have divided knowledge and skills into increasingly smaller and more abstract parts. It is difficult for students to see the relationships among history, art, literature, and science when each is taught separately by separate teachers who rarely talk to one another. Within subjects, knowledge and skills are further refined. English curricula, for example, separate reading and writing and grammar. Students learn grammar by studying unrelated sentences or phrases, say to identify prepositions. In a report called *Becoming a Nation of Readers,* a distinguished commission of ten educators and researchers concluded:

> Research suggests that the finer points of writing, such as punctuation and subject-verb agreement, may be learned best while students are engaged in extended writing that has the purpose of communicating a message to an audience. Notice that no communicative purpose is served when children are asked to identify on a worksheet the parts of speech or the proper use of *shall* and *will.*[18]

In American schools, learning has become so abstract that students rarely see connections among the subjects they study or between their lessons and their lives. This is one reason they lose interest in school. They work abstract geometry problems on paper instead of going into the school gymnasium with tape measures to figure out the cost per square foot of replacing the floor. They read about the Civil War without ever visiting a battlefield. They read about the stars and planets without ever looking at the night sky. They see the world through the lackluster window of textbooks. Teachers commonly hear students complain: "Why do we have to learn this?" Because of the curriculum's assembly-line structure, teachers often respond: "Because you'll need it in the next grade." That answer suggests that the main purpose of learning is to prepare students to survive in the school system rather than in the real world. And that misguided purpose is why so many students eager to know the world are alienated by schools.

The grade-based curricula of American schools foster group-oriented, abstract instruction geared to the middle or average child. They pressure teachers to emphasize what they teach or cover over what students learn. As a consequence, some students don't learn what teachers teach; others already know it or see no meaning in it and become bored and alienated. Student motivation declines as teacher frustration climbs. Discipline problems ensue. These outcomes are in some ways indirect consequences of bell-curve assumptions about student learning. However, they all stem directly from education's preoccupation with instruction geared to the average. They therefore qualify as symptoms of the Bell-Curve Syndrome.

Bland Textbooks

If curricula supply the blueprints, textbooks provide the materials to build instructional programs in American schools. Publishers draw heavily both on the results of norm-referenced tests and on state curricula in an effort to produce books that match both. These efforts, however, have resulted in dull, shallow texts that focus on low-level skills and knowledge. Textbook critic Harriet Tyson says publishers have responded to the anxiety of teachers, who dominate district textbook selection committees, over their students' test performances.

"Instead of designing a book from the standpoint of its subject or its capacity to capture the children's imagination," Tyson writes, "editors are increasingly organizing elementary reading series around the content and timing of standardized tests."[19]

Because textbook companies must sell their books nationwide, they cannot write books tailored to match specific district or even state curricula (though computer technology is beginning to change that). Instead, they look for curricula topics common in most states. This has created a malady educators call "mentioning," the practice of cramming too many topics into one textbook. Prose plagued by mentioning darts from one subject to the next without providing context, depth, or transitions. History books summarize the Second Continental Congress or the Watergate scandal in two paragraphs.

Entire science books are glossaries masquerading as textbooks, Tyson says.

Textbooks usually have more influence on classroom instruction than the curricula they are based on. In fact, many educators see textbooks as a de facto national curriculum. Anyone who has taught in public school will understand why teachers rely heavily on texts. They are daily expected to deliver at least five, sometimes more, forty-five-minute lessons. Typically they have at most one period a day to prepare. It is as impossible for a teacher to prepare five interesting presentations a day as it would be for a pastor to prepare five daily sermons or for a politician to develop a new speech at every campaign stop. Japan limits the amount of time a teacher may spend in front of a classroom to no more than four hours a day. In China, teachers in Beijing teach no more than three hours a day. While schools in these countries share many of the structural problems plaguing American schools, they have advanced in at least this one area. Teachers in Japan and China have nearly half of their workday set aside for preparing good lessons.[20]

Without such a luxury, American teachers turn to textbooks, which come with questions at the end of each chapter and a variety of supplementary worksheets, activities, lesson plans, and ready-made tests. Teacher's editions include scripts of questions to ask students and of the answers to expect of them. In fact, textbook companies have discovered attractive supplementary materials have more influence on sales than the textbooks themselves.

Publishing companies use readability formulas to write textbooks to grade level. These formulas are based on what educators have determined to be the average number of syllables per word and words per sentence that best fit students at each grade level. Some formulas also draw on lists of words considered familiar to children at various ages. These formulas can be useful in describing books that best suit children at various stages of reading proficiency. Publishers, however, use them actually to guide the author's pen. Authors write sentences to fit the word count for a given grade level. Doing so represents another example of educators using norms in a prescriptive rather than descriptive way. They force written works to fit into a mold just as schools require students to fit a predetermined academic level.

Constrained by readability formulas, textbook writers produce a stiff and stale prose that usually lacks the vigor, variety, and color of more natural writing. Worse still, writes Tyson, in an effort to keep sentences short, as dictated by formulas, "the words and the phrases that help a novice reader infer the correct relationships between ideas and events are often stripped away." Elementary textbook writers omit large words because they violate reading formulas. So in Paul Leyssac's translation of Hans Christian Anderson's "The Emperor's New Clothes," the sentence: " 'Magnificent!' 'Excellent!' 'Prodigious!' went from mouth to mouth," is changed to: " 'How marvelous,' they echoed the emperor, "How beautiful." Similarly, textbook writers squeeze some juice out of Rudyard Kipling's "How the Camel Got His Hump," by changing "a great big lolliping humph" to "a great big humph."[21] Two great children's writers, Beatrix Potter and E.B. White, say children should not be denied fine and fancy words. White writes:

> Anyone who writes down to children is simply wasting his time. You have to write up, not down. . . . Some writers for children deliberately avoid using words they think a child doesn't know. This emasculates the prose and, I suspect, bores the reader. Children are game for anything. I throw them hard words, and they backhand them over the net. They love words that give them a hard time.[22]

The dull, Dick-and-Jane style of formula textbook prose persists through all levels of public schools. Here, for example, is a paragraph from a textbook written for fourth-grade social studies classes in North Carolina:

> Feeling that President Lincoln would ruin the South, the southern states decided to form their own country. They said Mr. Lincoln was no longer their president and that they would elect their own president. They would make their own laws. They would take care of them-

selves. President Lincoln, however, said this was against the law. Each side, the North and the South, formed armies. They would fight out their differences. From 1861 to 1865 they did fight. This was called the Civil War. It was the worst war in American history.[23]

No wonder you never find a child curled up next to a fire on a cold, rainy night reading a textbook. Nor, for that matter, will you find adults, even teachers, reading them unless they have to. Most professionals in other careers have deep affection for the tools of their trade. Carpenters like the feel of a good hammer and love killing time in a hardware store. A hairdresser prizes fine scissors, an artist his paints and brushes, a surgeon her scalpel. But you'll be hard pressed to find a teacher who likes spending free time browsing through textbooks in a curriculum library. Add dull textbooks to the Bell-Curve Syndrome.

Textbooks, tests, and curricula in public education are designed based on the premise that a large majority of students are performing at grade level or average, as would be described by a bell curve. Collectively, they chart one shallow, broad course for the mainstream. However, educators also use tests to identify students who don't fit into the mainstream and steer them down special paths, benefitting some and harming others.

Grading on a Curve

Every child's experience in public schools is profoundly influenced by how his or her skills and knowledge compare to those of others of the same age. Educators expect the academic performance of any group of children of the same age to show normal deviations and produce a bell-curve pattern. They also equate achievement levels with ability or intelligence. Only those on the high end of the curve, those deemed brightest, are expected to meet high academic standards. The system assumes that the rest are not smart enough. It sorts students into a bell-curve pattern of instruction—a mainstream curriculum with branches for those who deviate from the average.

The most blatant example of this prescriptive use of the bell curve occurs in grading. When teachers say they grade on a curve, they mean a bell curve. On a test, for example, teachers grading on a curve will rank the scores of their students and give As to the top 7 percent, Bs to the next 15 percent, Cs to the middle 56 percent, and Ds and Fs to the rest. The bell curve that results mirrors norm-referenced testing, in that students are judged against their own average. Just as with norm-referenced tests, there will be winners at the cost of losers; As and Bs are balanced by an opposing number of Ds and Fs—no matter how much or little the class as a whole learned. What American adult doesn't recall those school days when teachers would return tests and show the distribution of grades on the chalkboard? The high-achieving student would draw scornful glares from classmates for raising the curve. The primary aim of grades in this system is not to gauge learning but to sort students, says Richard J. Stiggins, director of the Assessment Training Institute in Portland, Oregon.

"We have people operating on the assumption that achievement of necessity must be distributed over a normal curve," he said. "As a teacher in a sorting system, I'm the best I can be when my grades are normally distributed. That is the definition of good outcomes in a sorting system."

Administrators expect to see teachers produce grades that reflect some semblance of a bell curve. Teachers who issue too many As are suspected of being too lax; those who issue too many Ds and Fs risk being labeled too demanding. A high school teacher in a Portland, Oregon, suburb was fired in 1993, in part for failing too many students. The principal compared the teacher's failure rate against the school average and said it reflected his inability to motivate students. In fact, the young teacher had an engaging teaching style and a passionate grasp of literature, and was widely considered exceptional by both his colleagues and students. But he also had high standards and was convinced that all of his students could meet them if they were willing to try.[24] In the same month he lost his job, Adele Jones of Georgetown, Delaware, was fired from her math teaching job at Sussex Central High School for giving out too many Ds and Fs. John McCarthy, the principal, said the low grades were hurting students' self-esteem. Some of those students rallied to Jones's defense, carrying signs with statements such as "I Failed

Ms. Jones' Class and It Was My Fault," or "Just Because a Student Is Failing Doesn't Mean the Teacher Is."[25]

Stiggins says that expecting teachers to show a bell-curve distribution of grades cannot be defended.[26] Even if the achievement of large numbers of students of the same age did produce a bell-curve pattern, this pattern would not show up in every classroom. Any statistician will confirm that a classroom of twenty-five or thirty students is too small to produce a predictable bell curve except by chance.

Educators know how harsh and humiliating this evaluation system can be for students on the low end of the bell curve. A steady stream of Ds and Fs usually is discouraging enough to drive a student out of school, which is one reason administrators fired Adele Jones. It is also why administrators have allowed the bell curve to shift or skew toward the high end over the last three decades. This makes Bs rather than Cs the average grade. Even American colleges and universities have tolerated this grade inflation. One-fifth of all entering college freshmen in 1990 had high school grade averages of A minus or above. Between 1958 and 1988, the average grade at Dartmouth rose from C to B.[27] Most English majors at Harvard University earn averages hovering between A and A minus, laments William Cole, an instructor of Romance languages and literature there. The "gentleman's C" for bland and perfunctory work has been replaced by the "gentleperson's B," and the A minus is gaining ground, he says.[28] These distortions of the curve obscure the meaning of grades still further. While student achievement has remained static over the last decade, grade averages climb. Their significance also varies from school to school, as a panel of educators reviewing federal remedial education programs reported:

> Today, in the absence of standards, grades on report cards overstate the performance of students in high-poverty schools, misleading students and parents and concealing the urgency for reform. On average, seventh-graders in high-poverty schools who received A's in math scored around the bottom third (35th percentile) on the math standardized test, far below the national average. By comparison, A students in low-poverty

schools scored at the 87th percentile. Indeed, an A student in a high-poverty school would be about a C student in a low-poverty school.[29]

Grades create a cruel dilemma for teachers. They know that Ds and Fs demean children, yet they have no other way to hold students to high standards. If they set their standards too high, the failure rate becomes intolerable. Because most teachers are reluctant to relegate students to failure, they are inclined to lower their standards. These symptoms, too, belong to the Bell-Curve Syndrome.

Sorting Children

School systems routinely sort students on a broad scale using norm-referenced national test scores plotted on a bell curve that spans the nation. Yet there is reason to question whether these distinctions are even valid. As noted in Chapter 1, human accomplishments, including student achievement, tend to produce irregular or skewed curves rather than bell-shaped ones. Norm-referenced and intelligence tests always produce bell-shaped curves because their designers create them to do so. They select and field-test each question, making sure it produces a bell-curve distribution of results. Test items that do not are discarded. The tests, thereby, ensure that student achievement will conform to a bell curve.

Students typically do not have to be in school long before these tests tell them how they stack up against their peers. Often they are sorted into ability groups for reading in primary grades. On its face, this practice resembles the achievement grouping used by swimming schools. The difference is that educators equate achievement levels with ability and assume that students in lower levels are less capable of learning. They therefore tend to expect less of students in lower groups. Sorting students by ability leads to a sorting of expectations that sticks with children throughout their school careers.

For children on the low end of the bell curve, ability groups often become academic quagmires that deny them high academic expectations throughout their school life. Educators call them slow, learning disabled, at risk, or underachievers, meaning under grade level or under average. Once they've been so branded, students truly are at risk because it is almost as difficult for them to tear away these labels as it is to remove tattoos. Because teachers expect less of them, they produce less. In time, they lag so far behind their peers that they are shuffled off to special classrooms, where they can get remedial help and their school district can pick up some federal dollars. But these remedial classes often become an educational wasteland, or what Joseph Berger of *The New York Times* called a "Kafkaesque cul-de-sac" from which there is no escape. Berger described how this system claimed the two sons of Margarita Otero Parker, who lives in New York City's Lower East Side. Both boys were labeled emotionally disturbed, though there was nothing wrong with them, Berger said. Julio Otero, now in his twenties, became so disenchanted with the dull and juvenile classes he was condemned to that he finally dropped out after grade 10. His brother, Christopher Parker, "a tall 14-year-old with lively green eyes and a talent for drawing cartoons, has been chafing in most of his classes since the third grade," Berger writes. The younger brother said he spent too much time visiting guidance counselors, going to work programs at a cycle shop, taking field trips to museums or pizza parlors, and being generally patronized with what he considered "baby work." Berger continues:

> All he craves is to sit in a real classroom, to hear a spirited lesson. Thousands of the genuinely handicapped belong in special classes. But too often, critics say, assignment there is not driven by a handicap, but by money and expedience.
>
> The Board of Education likes the classification because it can collect federal and state money to pay for small classes and teachers and counselors it otherwise cannot afford. (A disabled child's schooling costs $17,000 a year, almost three times as much as a mainstream child.) The school unions like it because, even in threadbare budgets, teachers must be hired for the handicapped.
>
> The special education juggernaut has channeled one of every eight New York children—123,000 in all (that's

a $2.09 billion cost)—into handicapped classes, more than double the 1979 figures. Yet 75 percent fall into two amorphous categories—learning disabled and emotionally disturbed.[30]

Note that the two special education categories in which the nationwide percentage of students have climbed rather than dropped over the last fifteen years are learning disabled and seriously emotionally disturbed. Between 1976–77 and 1988–89, the proportion of students classified as learning disabled climbed from 2 percent to 5 percent. That represents an increase from 796,000 to 1.9 million students. The emotionally disturbed classification grew by 376,000 children.[31]

John Taylor Gatto, New York State Teacher of the Year for 1991, became so disenchanted with an education system that "found its scientific presentation in the bell curve" that he quit teaching. He said he couldn't bear to hurt children any more. In a brief essay in *The Wall Street Journal,* he describes how it works:

David learns to read at age four; Rachel, at age nine: In normal development, when both are 13, you can't tell which learned first—the five-year spread means nothing at all. But in school, I will label Rachel "learning disabled" and slow David down a bit, too.

For a paycheck, I adjust David to depend on me to tell him when to go and stop. He won't outgrow that dependency. I identify Rachel as discount merchandise, "special education." After a few months, she'll be locked in place forever.

In 26 years of teaching rich kids and poor, I almost never met a "learning disabled" child; hardly ever met a "gifted and talented" one, either. Like all school categories, these are sacred myths, created by the human imagination. They derive from questionable values we never examine because they preserve the temple of schooling.

That's the secret behind short-answer tests, bells, uniform time blocks, age grading, standardization, and all the rest of school religion punishing our nation.[32]

Efforts to compare children against national averages begin as early as kindergarten with readiness tests used like entrance exams. The tests are given with the best of intentions. Teachers want to prevent children from beginning kindergarten before they are ready so they don't begin behind and encounter immediate failure. On its face, this seems reasonable enough. It is the same kind of thinking that led the nation's governors and President Bush in 1988 to agree on school readiness as one of their six education goals for the year 2000. The goal states simply that all children will begin school ready to learn. But consider what that really must mean. All children, after all, are ready to learn. They've been learning from the moment they were born, possibly even before, while still in the womb. By the time they are five, they've already learned the complex framework of a language. And how can a child begin school already behind? What educators are saying, and what Americans routinely accept, is that all children should be ready to learn the same lesson at the same level at the same time and at the same pace. Unreasonable goals lead to absurd practices such as requiring kindergartners to take entrance exams. While educators may institute the tests based on some notion of protecting children from school failure, they actually introduce failure to every child they turn away. Instead of requiring all kindergartners to be ready for what schools have prepared to teach them, teachers should be ready to teach each child whatever he or she is prepared to learn.

Through ability grouping or sorting in the early grades, public schools are rejecting kindergartners and locking more than a million children a year into remedial and special education classes that deny them the learning they need. Add these problems to the Bell-Curve Syndrome's growing list of symptoms.

Tracking

Ability groups formed in the primary grades evolve into academic tracks by the time students enter secondary schools. Three basic tracks—reflecting the low, middle, and high sections of a bell curve—survive in American middle and high schools as carryovers from the early part of century when public educators routinely sorted students for college and various levels of work. Students in the low track endure general science, basic English and math, and usually are allowed to take heavy loads of nonacademic courses, such as weight-lifting and auto repair. Students in the high track fill honors, advanced placement, foreign language, and upper-level science and math classes. Across the United States, only 20 percent of all graduates leave high school with three years of science and math and two years of a foreign language. The proportion is 16 percent for black students, and 12 percent for Hispanic, 22 percent for white, and 42 percent for Asian.[33] The rest take a wide path dominated by general courses with an academic rigor falling somewhere between the high and low levels. Students can move among these tiers, but few can stray far from the high track and expect to be ready for college.

Tracking lowers academic expectations and undermines the quality of education for most students, studies show. A 1990 middle school study for Johns Hopkins Center for Research on Elementary and Middle Schools showed ability grouping increased from fifth through eighth grade, eventually affecting 75 percent of all students in at least one subject. In an analysis of 20,000 students in grades 10 to 12, researcher Adam Gamoran of the University of Wisconsin found a wide achievement gap separating students in different tracks, wider even than the gap between students who remained in school and those who dropped out after grade 10.[34]

Still, tracking remains a pervasive practice in American schools. The RAND Corporation issued a study report called *Multiplying Inequalities* in July of 1990 that described widespread math and science ability grouping not only at the secondary level, but even in the elementary schools. The report is based on a 1986 National Science Foundation survey of 1,200 public and private schools and 6,000 of their teachers. The survey showed that 65 percent of elementary school math and science classes are classified as slow, medium, or fast track. Moreover, the Second International Math Study supported these findings by showing that U.S. schools do more extensive ability grouping than any other country studied.[35] Eighty percent of secondary schools track students in three or more levels.

"Considerable evidence suggests that tracking, especially in secondary schools, fails to increase learning generally and has the unfortunate consequence of widening the achievement gaps between students judged to be more or less able," the RAND report says.[36]

Tracking has been tolerated for generations in public schools because it served the assembly-line economy of the industrial age. But in the computerized workplace of the information age, graduates from the lower tracks face severe consequences.

Until Betty Wallace arrived in Vance County in July of 1991, for example, Northern Vance High School tracked its 1,000 students for a world that had disappeared with the rusting factories crumbling nearby in Henderson. Students lucky enough to land in the fast track took such courses as physics, calculus, chemistry, and world history. They then could go on to an institution such as North Carolina State University in Raleigh and study chemical engineering. When they graduated, they could find a high-paying job that would allow them to buy a home and support a family.

But what about a high school classmate who took three years of automobile repair classes and no more academics than required? This student will not be prepared for college or to work on cars. He may have learned how to clean carburetors, replace valves, and repair brakes. But he will be lost when he opens the hood of a modern car and looks at the mysterious black boxes and wire webs that connect the engine to computers. He cannot understand modern auto repair manuals, let alone operate the computer they are stored in. At best, he might land a job at a gas station, repairing flats, changing oil, and pumping gas for $6 an hour. This student will scramble to support himself and cannot hope to afford a home or to support a family. Students who move through the undemanding general track in high schools across the nation face similar dead ends. They have no hope of improving their lots without more education.

Until a generation ago, people could earn a good living without a good education. But today's students aren't competing in the past or just with American workers. They are competing with a worldwide labor force. This is what has changed.

Employers looking for unskilled labor can find it much cheaper elsewhere. Nike Shoe Company doesn't manufacture a single shoe in the United States. Instead it contracts with companies in other countries, such as Indonesia, where it pays workers 15 cents an hour to produce a pair of shoes it sells in the United States for $70.[37] A New York insurance company finds it cheaper to have its clerical work done in China. A manager can dictate a letter by satellite to a clerk in China, who then types the letter into a computer and ships it back—all about as fast as having it done by a secretary next door.[38]

For highly skilled jobs, American employers also look abroad. U.S. companies import about 1 million workers a year to fill high-skilled, high-paying jobs that they cannot fill with Americans, says Willard Daggett, director of the International Center for Leadership in Education. They turn to Japan, South Korea, Germany, and other countries, some of which are educating virtually all of their youth at levels that only our top students reach. In late 1992 the Economic Policy Institute produced a bleak picture of the American workforce in a report called "The State of Working America." The report showed a sharp drop over the past two decades in the number of manufacturing jobs that had provided high salaries for millions of unskilled or semiskilled workers throughout much of the post–World War II era. The jobs either have gone overseas to low-wage countries or have been automated out of existence. General Motors, for example, has not hired a single new production worker since 1986. Consequently, the report showed, the 1991 wages for high school graduates had dropped by 26.5 percent for males and 15.4 percent for females since 1979.[39] Society has little room for those who cannot manage complexity, says Linda Darling-Hammond, a professor of education and codirector of the National Center for Restructuring Education, Schools and Teaching at Teachers College, Columbia University. She writes:

> These changes signal a new mission for education—
> one that requires schools not merely to "deliver instructional services" but to ensure that all students learn at high levels. In turn, the teachers' job is no longer to "cover the curriculum" but to enable diverse learners to construct their own knowledge and to develop their talents in effective and powerful ways.[40]

unable to benefit) or deserve less (they are considered unwilling to benefit). But one could also argue that they need more—more able teachers, more instructional resources and supports.[44]

Education researchers have repeatedly documented the high correlation between children's performance in school and the level of education and income of their parents. Children of parents with low income and education achieve at lower levels in school than children from more affluent, better-educated families. A disproportionate number of minority students come from poor families and so, as a group, predictably score below average on achievement tests and get routed into low tracks.

The Coleman Report was one of the first large studies to document this correlation. Led by James S. Coleman, a sociologist then at Johns Hopkins University, and released in 1966, this massive survey studied 650,000 students, 60,000 teachers, and 4,000 schools. Coleman and his associates found that minority students started school knowing less than their white peers and fell farther and farther behind as they progressed through school. The report seemed to confirm that the influence of family background and values was so powerful that schools could make little difference in a child's learning. The quality of school didn't seem to matter.[45]

That was the wrong conclusion, but it continues to be widely accepted in public education. Schools expect less of poor students because they usually end up on the low end of the bell curve. Sorting of expectations begins in kindergarten when some students show up at school knowing more than others. Those who know more tend to come from middle-class and affluent families, and those who know less come from poorer, less stable families or from other countries. Yet the situation has little to do with intelligence and everything to do with experience. Compared to their more affluent peers, children from poor families typically are exposed to more television, fewer books, less travel, and fewer opportunities to engage in conversations with adults. They are denied a rich learning environment at home, so they learn less and arrive at school knowing less.

These differences are apparent in Marcia L. Carpenter's kinder-

Tracking steers the majority of American students ii mediocre academic regimens that prepare them neith nor for higher education. About 817,000, or 25 percent lic school students quit high school before graduating who do graduate, about one-third enroll in two-year c another 30 percent enroll in four-year colleges. About h in four-year colleges earn a degree within six years.[41]

The large number of dropouts and ill-prepared gradua the nation's high schools each year also can be counte(toms of the bell-curve syndrome.

Sorting by Class

Academic sorting in public schools has reflected and i class distinctions since it was started early in the century. ! cation historians believe the system was designed purpose serve class distinctions. In any case, a higher proportior and minority students end up in the low and general trac they are denied the chance to take upper-level math an(courses. A 1987 transcript study by the U.S. Department c tion showed that Hispanic and African-American stude fewer math, science, and foreign language courses than th(and Asian peers.[42] The RAND study found similar results:

> First, their access to high-track science and mathem ics classes diminishes as the minority enrollment at th school increases. Second, those who attend racia mixed schools are more likely than their white peers be placed in low-track classes. There is thus a "dout jeopardy" effect.[43]

While educators will argue that students are sorted approp based on differences in aptitude, RAND found that tracking capped them with lower expectations:

> Students judged to have low ability may get less be cause they are thought to need less (they are considere(

garten class at Club Boulevard School in Durham, North Carolina. Eight of her lowest students live with single parents, some born to teenagers. Most are poor. One restless boy, for example, is the son of an alcoholic mother who was dead and a father who was in prison. Other students in this class, however, come from stable families, spent years in preschool, and have been exposed to reading, numbers, computers, music lessons, and travel. Not surprisingly, they know more than the poor students. Thomas Adams, who happens to be black, comes from a stable middle-class home and can read books written for sixth graders.[46]

Thomas and the other more affluent students know more than their poorer peers because of their experience, not because they are any smarter. Given the chance and confidence, poor children are capable of learning just as much as their wealthier classmates. But most schools will compare the achievement levels of students from low-income families to group averages and conclude they are "at risk" of failing. Because they are below average, they will be sorted out for special classes and low tracks where less will be expected of them. They will then fall farther behind and the achievement gap will widen, just as the RAND study showed.

Whole schools and districts can suffer from this malady because they too are compared against averages. Oregon, for example, uses a socioeconomic index to rank schools based on the proportion of students drawn from poor families with low educations. These rankings accompany test scores. Predictably, schools with the poorest children tend to have the lowest test scores; those with the wealthiest children, the highest. The state encourages parents to compare their children's schools only to those with similar socioeconomic ranking. Again, the implication is that it is unfair to expect as much from a school serving low-income families as from one serving the middle class and rich. Because American schools and their textbooks, tests, and curricula are geared to average education needs, they are geared to the white, middle-class students who still dominate the culture. As American society grows more culturally and economically diverse, however, more and more students in school do not fit the mainstream. And to the degree they differ, they encounter the frustrations of an unsuitable group pace, labeling, tracking, and unfavorable comparisons. In many inner-city schools, the majority of students are from low-income families or other countries and founder in a system designed for their white, middle-class peers. Four Portland elementary schools have the highest proportion of poor and minority children in Oregon and the lowest reading and math test scores. Similarly, the half-million children in Chicago schools score far below state and national averages on standardized tests because two-thirds of those children come from poor families. Most Chicago students are black and Hispanic, but it is poverty, not race or culture, that has denied them exposure outside of school to language and knowledge. Even white middle-class students bog down in a system that ill-fits and frustrates the majority of its children. So it is not surprising that former U.S. Secretary of Education William Bennett called Chicago public schools the worst in America.[47] Nor should it be any surprise that Vance County schools, dominated by poor students, ranked among the three lowest-achieving districts in North Carolina.

American schools purport to sort students by ability for appropriate levels of instruction. In practice, they do so by class and race, relegating poor and minority children to low-level instruction that dooms their chances of learning enough to earn decent livings as adults. This injustice is yet another feature of the Bell-Curve Syndrome.

Ability vs. Effort

American educators equate the differences in achievement they see among students the same age with differences in intelligence. More often, though, achievement variations reflect differences in experience and effort. While some students are brighter than others, these differences are not as pronounced as educators have led us and themselves to believe. Even their so-called slow students are capable of writing well, thinking clearly, and understanding calculus, physics, and chemistry. All children are capable of learning as much as public schools demand of them, just as they all can learn to swim, ride bicycles, and drive cars. Educators, parents, and students place too much importance on innate intelligence or ability and too little on effort.

Tests used to measure this intelligence put a heavy emphasis on the primacy of narrow aspects of language, ignoring other vast regions of human intelligence. This fact was observed two decades ago by Philip Morrison, professor at the Massachusetts Institute of Technology:

> Too many creative—and less articulate—artists, craftsmen, healers, farmers, experimenters, and musicians stand in the way. I await not normal curves (no such bells ring for me!) but quite different evaluations that respect human interests and predilections, human specialties, human diversity, and human talent. IQ rings off key. If it is presently useful to schools, then that use is forced.[48]

Professor Howard Gardner, of Harvard, proposed a convincing theory of multiple intelligences in his book *Frames of Mind*. Humans, he says, have at least seven forms of intelligences. Three shaped by objects of the physical world are spatial, which figures heavily in art; logical-mathematical, dominant in science; and bodily-kinesthetic, manifest in dance. Two other forms—language and music—reflect features of auditory and oral systems rather than objects. Finally there are what Gardner calls the personal intelligences: knowledge of self and others.[49] All these intelligences exist in varying degrees and combinations in all humans, he says, with some playing heavier roles than others in the lives of most. All of these intelligences can be cultivated. In Japan, for example, large numbers of people have learned to play musical instruments extremely well under Suzuki instruction. Modern schools, though, emphasize some intelligences over others. Gardner writes:

> Among those observers partial to spatial, bodily or musical forms of knowing, as well as those who favor a focus on the interpersonal aspects of living, an inclination to indict contemporary schooling is understandable. The modern secular school has simply—though it need not have—neglected these aspects of intellectual competence.[50]

What's more, schools overemphasize the importance of differences among students in those forms of intelligence they do recognize, such as linguistic and logical-mathematical. The most tragic consequence of public education's misplaced emphasis on intelligence appears at about third or fourth grade, when some children start believing they are not very smart. They begin accepting the low expectations teachers have for them. Researcher Carol Dweck of Columbia University says these children have adopted an "entity" theory about their own ability to learn—a belief that they have been born with a certain amount of ability that determines how smart they are. Most children don't begin school thinking this way, Dweck says. Instead, they hold the "incremental view" that a person gets smarter by learning things and trying hard. Surprisingly, Dweck found that even bright students suffer when they adopt the "entity" theory because they tend to expect learning to come easily. When they encounter a difficult academic task, they quit rather than tackle it for fear that they might otherwise discover they are not as smart as they thought. What they do to feel smart and what they must do to learn new things are at odds. For this reason, many students who eventually came to see themselves as born smart start slipping academically and getting bad grades as they move into middle school.[51]

On December 10, 1992, a national commission called a news conference in Washington, D.C., to recommend overhauling the federal Chapter 1 program, which spent $6.1 billion in 1993 on remedial reading, writing, and math for about 5.5 million disadvantaged youngsters. The key problem with Chapter 1, the commission concluded, is that it expects too little of students and those low expectations become self-fulfilling. The commission recommended setting high rather than low standards for Chapter 1 students, who are disproportionately represented by poor and minority children. "There is ample evidence to show that under optimum teaching and learning conditions—those with high expectations and skilled instruction—children will learn at high levels," the commission concluded.[52]

This fact has been proven repeatedly in schools in Europe and Asia, and even in some schools and classrooms in the United States. Consider, for example, Leon Poelman of The Netherlands, who at age nineteen expertly adjusts the pneumatic system that controls the flaps on an airplane wing in a training center operated by Fokker Aircraft Services in the southern town of Hoogerheiden. Three years earlier Poelman graduated from a vocational school, Holland's bottom academic track. Yet even at the bottom, Poelman learned enough math and science to be trained as a mechanic for the U.S. Air Force F-16 and the Boeing 737. He knows English well enough to read maintenance manuals written in the language.[53] All students in The Netherlands, no matter what track they follow, learn a second language. By 1995 they all will be expected to learn two other languages. It is not uncommon for students there and elsewhere in Europe to learn three languages other than their own. Only a fraction of U.S. students, however, learn even a second language.

Asian cultures also expect high performance out of all of their students, largely because of a belief that academic achievement flows from hard work, not innate intelligence. In Japan and China, write researchers Harold W. Stevenson and James W. Stigler, high test scores reflect diligence, not superior intelligence. Similarly, they say, low scores are viewed not as a sign of stupidity but an indication that students must persist in working harder to learn their lessons. In the United States, by contrast, expectations for "low-ability" children are reduced.

"We suggest that the American emphasis on innate abilities is harmful and is undermining the pursuit of public education—indeed, of democracy itself," the authors write.[54]

Therese Knecht Dozier, 1985 National Teacher of the Year, intimately knows how the cultural values of ability and effort affect student learning. She has seen U.S. and Asian cultures and schools firsthand. She was born to a Vietnamese woman and a former colonel in Hitler's army, who had joined the French Foreign Legion to escape prosecution. A U.S. couple adopted and raised her. She has taught in Singapore and in Columbia, South Carolina, Miami and Gainesville, Florida, and was appointed special adviser to U.S. Secretary of Education Richard W. Riley in 1993. She described the depth and complexity of the cultural problems separating U.S. and Asian schools in a speech to the Education Writers Association on April 4, 1992.

My experiences living and teaching in the Republic of Singapore and my work with honors classes in the United States have convinced me that we face a fundamental problem in education today, an insidious barrier to achieving the academic excellence we all want for our children. We have fallen into the unconscious trap of categorizing people on the basis of their assumed innate abilities. We often take the attitude that some of us "have it" and some of us don't. I hear it all the time. Just the other day, my next door neighbor told me, "Let's face it, not everyone has the ability to do calculus. I certainly couldn't do it. We can't expect all students to take chemistry or to learn a foreign language." And yet in other countries, that's exactly what is expected. There is no ability grouping in Japan, for example. The slower student is expected to keep up with the faster. It is assumed that everyone is capable of success and achievement.

... My Asian students in Singapore were no smarter nor more talented than my American students. They ranged the whole gamut of abilities. Their I.Q.'s were no better than anyone else's.

But there was a difference. They worked harder. It's as simple as that. They worked harder. When my American students were having trouble in my class, they immediately took the attitude that the course was too difficult for them. They just didn't have the academic ability to do well and they needed to drop down to a lower level. By contrast, my Asian students never took that attitude. They would simply say, "I must try harder."

... The emphasis in this country on innate ability is very dangerous. It determines how we view children, and therefore, how we teach them. And it causes our young people to either write themselves off, or over-estimate the importance of being smart. We often begin to track students as early as the first grade and identify some as "gifted and talented" (those are the ones who "have it") and some as remedial (those are the ones who don't). We then set up our education system to ensure that the remedial students don't ever "get it" because they are never challenged and exposed to demanding curricula. And let's not kid ourselves, no matter what we call these groups—the bluebirds or the robins—our students know exactly who we think "have it" and who we think don't and they behave accordingly."

As a result of the Asian cultural conviction that with effort all children are capable of learning and understanding high levels of knowledge, virtually all do, though some must work harder than others. Observers say that Japanese high school graduates, for example, typically know as much in science, native language, and mathematics as most college graduates in the United States.[55]

A growing number of U.S. educators are properly beginning to see an ethical dilemma in expecting less of some children than of others based on where the students' test scores fall on the bell curve. One of them is Roger Elford, principal of Owosso High School in Michigan. In the 1991–92 school year, Elford agreed to let an English teacher mix general-track students with the college bound in a college-preparatory English class. Counselors selected fifteen students at random from the general track. As they purposely did not tell the teacher which students were from the general track and which were headed for college, she expected them all to do college-preparatory work. And they all did. Knowing that, Elford says, how can the school continue to justify tracking? How can it deny college-preparatory lessons to all of its general-track students? "We need to prepare kids to meet different expectations for a new world," he says.

No one knows this better than Jaime Escalante, the famous math teacher who prepared scores of poor Hispanic students at Garfield High School in East Los Angeles to take and pass college-level advanced placement calculus tests. In 1987 Garfield had 129 students take the AP calculus exams administered by the Educational Testing Service, more than all but three high schools in the nation. In most cases Garfield sent more students than each of the nation's most prestigious private schools, including Exeter, Punahoe, New Trier, Evanston, and Hunter College High. And Garfield produced more than a fourth of all the Mexican-American students in the nation who passed the exam. Escalante attributed his students' success to hard work or what he called *ganas,* the urge to achieve.

"The only thing you got to do over here, you got to work with *ganas,*" he told his students. "You don't have to have a high IQ, not like the ones that have one twenty, one forty IQ. Myself, I have a negative IQ. So the only thing I require of you is the *ganas.*"[56]

U.S. public education has been built like a poor argument on a series of flawed assumptions. At the base is the assumption that student achievement must describe a bell curve. From that faulty assumption stem others: that only some students are smart enough to reach high academic standards, that teachers can serve most students by teaching to the average, and that grade-level achievement is sufficient. These assumptions give rise to faulty instructional practices. Children are grouped by age and judged against the average; tests, curricula, and textbooks are tuned to mediocre, grade-level standards; and millions of children are sorted into remedial, special education, and low-track classes, generally by race and class, where they are never expected to learn as much as others. The consequences are severe. Millions of children become discouraged with school within their first years. Millions become convinced they are not smart enough to learn as much as their peers. Their self-worth plummets. Nearly a million students a year quit before finishing school. Only a fraction of those who do finish are prepared for college. The rest enter adulthood ill-prepared, with weak basic skills and a lifelong grudge against formal schooling. These are the faces of the Bell-Curve Syndrome, a disease that is weakening the economic and social health of the nation.

At its bell-shaped heart, the U.S. public education system is as un-American as collective farms. It rejects a good education for all in favor of a mediocre education for most and a deficient education for many. Too many people are ill-informed in an age when understanding government requires a sophisticated education. Schools are putting democracy at peril. Not only do they fail to perpetuate knowledge, but they also promote cultural values that contradict American ideals of individualism, self-reliance, and equality.[57]

They demand that our children conform in a monolithic system that gives more opportunities to those who are rich and privileged than to those who are poor and disadvantaged. Schools force-march our children like three great armies, some bound for opportunity, most bound nowhere.

Promising Change

Fortunately, this all can change. In fact, two promising patterns are emerging piecemeal across the nation. In the first, some education reformers are rejecting tracking and other practices that vary learning expectations for students according to their rank on a bell curve. Instead, they advocate high standards for all students. Schools, districts, states, and a variety of national professional groups are designing standards for what all students should know and be able to do when they finish school. Because this practice shifts the focus of education from process to results or outcomes, educators often call it outcomes-based education. Oregon adopted an outcomes-based plan that will replace the high school diploma with two certificates of mastery. Beginning in 1997, students will be expected to master a common set of performance standards. Through essays, projects, and presentations, they will be expected to show they can write well, reason, solve mathematical problems, understand scientific principles, and speak a second language. They must do this in order to graduate from high school. They will be allowed to earn their advanced certificate in a variety of ways, ranging from taking traditional college-preparatory courses to on-the-job learning in an apprenticeship.

The practices of setting high standards for all students is necessary but not sufficient to transform our schools. Students also must be allowed to meet those standards at their own paces and in their own ways. We should not expect all students to march lockstep through the system as they are forced to do in the more homogeneous society of Japan. Such a rigid system cannot easily accommodate the diverse cultural, racial, and economic backgrounds of American children. While all students can reach high standards, some will need more time to do so than others. Schools must, therefore, transform their age-based, group-oriented structures into more fluid, individual-oriented frameworks such as the staircase model used by swim and ballet schools.

This change also is beginning to happen in a second pattern unfolding across the nation. Schools are eliminating grade levels, abandoning tracking, and using computers and community resources to create more varied and individualized learning experiences for their students. Each of the 400 students in the alternative Open School in St. Paul, Minnesota, for example, has an individualized schedule that puts him or her in mixed-age classes. Paint Branch Elementary School on the outskirts of Washington, D.C., has been operating without grades or grade levels since 1987. Kentucky requires schools to eliminate primary grade levels, and Oregon has recommended that its schools do the same. Yet without high standards, these more flexible, individualized school organizations also will prove insufficient. Both high standards and more flexible school organizations are needed to rebuild schools that work for all children, that reject practices based on bell-curve assumptions. Both are needed to conquer the Bell-Curve Syndrome.

While she was still at the state Department of Public Instruction in Raleigh, Betty Wallace concluded schools needed this combination of standards and flexibility. Without these changes, she decided, American schools could never hope to produce a generation educated well enough to sustain a robust American culture in the next century. One day in the winter of 1989, she stood at the window of her third-story Raleigh office and gazed at the historic grounds across the street. There stood the stately granite Capitol building, built like a fortress before the Civil War. It looked sturdy enough to last a millennium. Out front a Confederate soldier perched proudly, timelessly, atop a towering pedestal. Wallace had devoted a career reaching this commanding view. Yet she could see that she could no more change schools from there than she could make that stone soldier step down off his pedestal. She felt unfulfilled, in the center of a massive bureaucracy committed to preserving things as they were. Change was intolerable there. She'd have to return to the trenches, a difficult move for a single mother with a son about to enter college. Life was secure and easy there. Leaving was risky. Even so, she began searching for a school district so desperate for change that it would allow her to sever its ties to the bell curve.

CHAPTER 3

▼

How the Bell Curve Invaded Public Schools

The roots of the American education system's preoccupation with the bell curve reach deep into previous centuries. Adventurers and religious pilgrims in the New World plowed the soil that nourished those roots. From their very beginning American schools have sorted children by class, expecting more of some than of others.

In Colonial settlements of Virginia, education was reserved largely for the rich who attended private schools, often in the mother country. Only a handful of schools bothered to teach poor children the rudiments of reading and writing. In New England, religious colonists also sorted children by class for different educations. Most boys and girls attended small town schools operated in churches and homes and were often taught by women. After learning enough reading and writing skills to allow them to understand Calvinist doctrines and the laws of the colony, most youngsters entered apprenticeships or went to work on farms. The aim of education was primarily religious. Most teachers used the *New England Primer,* which included an alphabet, spelling words, creeds, the Ten Commandments, Psalms, and other Bible verses and religious doctrines that children were expected to memorize. This schooling also had social aims—not to empower individuals, but to teach them to submit to the laws of religion and government.

Privileged children, however, attended grammar schools, which emerged in the early 1600s in New England to prepare the next generation of leaders, primarily clergymen. This education (reserved for boys) was more academic and abstract, a classical education that would help them fit the sixteenth-century Renaissance ideal of the educated leader. It would confer status. Boys studied Greek and Latin, Bible Scriptures, and the selected works of Plutarch, Seneca, Aristotle, Cicero, and Plato to help them learn civic character and qualities of leadership. The grammar school typically offered a rigorous, seven-year academic education that would prepare students for college, the first of which in America was Harvard College, founded in 1636. By the end of the century, thirty-nine grammar schools operated in New England. Even at this infant stage, American education was assuming two key and enduring features: It was a class-based, two-track system that prepared some students for college and most for work. It also was geared primarily to serving group and social rather than individual needs.

As a new nation emerged over the next century, society began to see broader social possibilities for education. New thinkers identified tyrannical qualities in schools that used religious doctrines to teach submission to authority. Scientists and philosophers of the age, such as British thinkers Joseph Priestly and John Locke, saw education and free thought as a source of liberation and a path to social prosperity. By giving more people access to free education unfettered by religious doctrine, society could rise above poverty and the crime and despair it fosters. The connection between knowledge and liberty surfaced repeatedly in the zealous essays leading to the American Revolution. In 1765 John Adams wrote:

> Let us dare to read, think, speak and write. Let the dialogues, and all the exercises, become the instruments of impressing on the tender mind, and of spreading and distributing far and wide, the ideas of right and the sensations of freedom. In a word, let every sluice of knowledge be opened and set a-flowing.[1]

Few appreciated the power of education to transform lives more than Benjamin Franklin. If education could lift him from the merchant status of an apprentice printer to scientist, statesman, and founding father of a new nation, then surely, he reasoned, it could help all citizens and, ultimately, society. He proposed libraries as one means of giving common people access to knowledge. He also advocated the creation of academies that would give students both practical "most useful" knowledge along with classical, cultural, and moral education. Such academies soon began to spring up in the New World as forerunners to the modern high school. In Vance County, North Carolina, The Granville Hall Academy was operating by 1771, and the Williamsborough Female Academy opened in 1780.[2]

As the first academies emerged, so did new ideas about the purpose of education. New thinkers in this Age of Reason were challenging Protestant notions of Original Sin, that man by nature was stained with evil and needed to be taught to suppress pride and cultivate obedience. Instead, thinkers began to see children as neither good nor bad by nature. Young people were like clean slates to be written upon, raw clay to be molded; this notion continues to surface today as teachers talk wistfully about molding young minds. These notions fostered the beginning of the nation's move toward mass education. While the nation's founders viewed education as a means to personal liberation, others began seeing it as a tool for social engineering, for improving, ordering, and ultimately perfecting society.[3]

Visions of education as a source of personal liberation on the one hand and as means of social improvement on the other created a persistent tension in American schools. The first view focused on the individual. The second focused on the group and would prevail with the rise of nationalism following the Revolutionary War. Authorities who embraced this group-oriented view of education would become interested in using the bell curve as a tool for social engineering.

Before schools could become useful to the nation's first social engineers, however, they had to be organized. By the early nineteenth century, formal education continued to be a hodgepodge endeavor, and most Americans expected merely that their children learn the rudiments of reading, writing, and arithmetic. Schoolhouses paid for by local taxes spread over the New England landscape, but they were more scattered elsewhere in the country, where they were funded from a mix of tax, private, and church sources. Schools were still hard to find in the farthest reaches of the South and West. North Carolina leaders estimated that the state had an average of about three school-age children per square mile in 1837.[4] Children went to school when they could break away from duties on their farms, usually during winter. Schoolhouses typically were small, poorly kept, and run by young, unmarried schoolmasters who viewed teaching as temporary work until they could find real jobs in crafts or farming. They taught children ranging in age from two to their late teens. Most white American children between ages five and fifteen spent anywhere from a few weeks to two months in school each year. This informal combination of mixed-age grouping and flexible scheduling made group instruction nearly impossible, forcing teachers to give children individualized lessons.

In the South, slaves were intentionally kept unskilled and illiterate. Some Americans did not go to school at all, and illiteracy was common in the hinterlands. Nevertheless, by 1800 Americans were more literate than citizens of most nations of Western Europe. They didn't read much, though, because books were expensive and often scarce. Even in the countryside of Massachusetts, no more than one household in ten or twelve received a newspaper.[5]

While small schoolhouses would dominate rural education well into the twentieth century, larger networks or systems of schools already had been organized by the early 1800s in Massachusetts and were beginning to emerge in other American cities. During this time, a variety of private charity groups, such as the New York Free School Society, were established, and they began opening schools to bolster the weak families of poor children. The primary purpose of these schools was to improve society by reducing crime and poverty and socializing children for an industrious way of life.[6] Toward that end, the societies began building the nation's first factory-model schools based on a system developed by Englishman Joseph Lancaster. These schools would serve as many as 1,000 children in a single room with a single schoolmaster seated at one end. With classes of this size, order in the classroom was a requirement. We can thank Lancaster for such gems of wisdom as "A place for everything and everything in its place."

Education historian Joel Spring describes in his book *The American School* one Lancaster school depicted in an engraving. This school in Pennsylvania was designed for 450 children. The teacher sat at the head of the room on a raised platform, like a king on his throne, with his subjects arranged by ranks below him. Three rows of student monitors sat in front, facing pupils, who were divided into three sections, each of which answered to one group of monitors. The monitors, taking their orders from the master, would each deliver lessons to a small group of students, so that nine lessons would be going on at once. Even educators of the period saw the similarities between the Lancaster school and the factory. One French writer called it a "manufactory of knowledge."[7]

The Lancaster schools emphasized basic skills and the virtues of submission, order, and industriousness, which children would need in the workplace. These objectives resembled those of colonial New England—the goals eighteenth-century thinkers called tyrannical. There was not much room for individuality in these early factory schools. They appealed strongly, however, to social leaders looking for ways to educate all children for social ends. The most prominent and influential of these leaders was a New England lawyer named Horace Mann.

Mann, born in 1796, seemed to embody the changing theologies and ambitions of his day. He rejected the harsh Calvinist home he grew up in as a "pall of blackness" and adopted a more positive Unitarian worldview. He set out to redeem society through law. He took a degree at Brown University, was admitted to the Bar in 1823, and served in the Massachusetts State Legislature between 1827 and 1833, during which time he helped create the Massachusetts State Board of Education. He came to believe that education would make a better tool than the law for pounding society into shape. He became the secretary of the Massachusetts State Board in 1837, which put him in a powerful position to advocate over the next twelve years for a common education for all children. Mann was particularly interested in using schools to shape children's moral and political beliefs and to foster a common social class. Schools, as Mann saw it, were to be used like huge blenders, taking in children from all religious, political, and economic backgrounds; mixing them into common dough; and turning out batches of good, productive Americans.

"Education then, beyond all other devices of human origin, is the great equalizer of men—the balance wheel of the social machinery," Mann said in his twelfth, final, and most famous report to the Massachusetts Board of Education in 1848.[8]

The common school movement expanded teaching as one of the few career options for women. By 1869, nearly two thirds of the nation's 201,000 professional teachers and librarians were women.[9]

The movement unfolded slowly and served more to standardize schools than to expand education opportunities. The percentage of people under twenty attending school in Massachusetts actually declined between 1840 and 1880. Further, the focus was on elementary education, and most American children continued to learn little more than basic skills. Finally, there was still little room in American schools for black Americans, most of whom remained slaves. For that "revolting barbarity and shameless hypocrisy," observed one well-educated black American named Frederick Douglass, "America reigns without a rival."[10]

The Graded School

The common school movement's most familiar and significant legacy first appeared in Boston in 1848, the same year Mann delivered his last report to the state board. John Philbrick of Quincy School drew national attention with what was considered at the time a radical change. He opened America's first grade school. Instead of putting all children in one big room, he divided them by age and put them in separate smaller rooms, what one educator of the day called an "egg crate" arrangement. The school had four floors, the first three divided into classrooms holding fifty-six students each and the fourth holding an assembly hall. It also had a separate office for Philbrick, the school's principal teacher or chief administrator. Here stood the basic framework of the modern elementary school.

The school was modeled after the rigid, highly structured Prussian education system. Many American educators, including Horace Mann, were fascinated by the factorylike order and precision of Prussia's schools. They seemed to offer the perfect solution to managing the mass education system Mann envisioned. By organizing children in smaller groups by age, the teacher could "address his instructions at the same time to all children who are before him," Mann said, after returning from a visit to Prussia. In effect, this allowed teachers to use the same mold to shape every mind in the classroom. And if teachers worked together using a standardized lesson plan, they could use the same mold on all children. This could produce the homogeneous, classless, common American generation Mann dreamed about. This vision of mass education would never lose its appeal among American educators. And the mold they eventually would use to shape young minds would have the shape of a bell curve.

Even Mann could not have predicted the powerful grip this system would have on American education over the second half of the nineteenth century. Grade schools spread across the country like new farms. Once grades were established, curricula and textbooks followed. Once this standardized system began to emerge, nothing that followed could change it fundamentally. In their zeal to educate groups of children on a mass scale, education leaders became absorbed with the management and standardization of schools. Indeed, education leaders seemed to consider student learning a secondary concern. William T. Harris, a U.S. commissioner of education, wrote in 1871, "The first requisite of the school is Order: each pupil must be taught first and foremost to conform his behavior to a general standard."[11]

After the Civil War, schools took a more defined and uniform structure of eight levels or separate grades. North Carolina opened its first grade school in Greensboro in the fall of 1870. It included five rooms and a chapel, a principal and three teachers, and 200 children in eight grades. More grade schools quickly emerged across the state during the next decade.[12] Some eight-grade elementary schools still survive today. As the number of grade schools increased across the nation, they were organized into districts administered by superintendents and governed by local boards. Legislatures created state superintendents and state boards of education, charged with ensuring that all children have access to a uniform system of common schools. At the federal level, a Federal Bureau of Education was established in 1867 with Henry Barnard as the first commissioner, a post largely ignored to the present.[13]

A reading textbook series written by William McGuffey

specifically for common schools symbolized and reinforced the emerging national system of uniform education. McGuffey designed his books to teach children moral lessons while helping them learn to read. The books, first published in 1836 and sold into the 1920s, included historical sketches, poems, animal stories, spelling lessons, and religious selections, such as The Lord's Prayer. About 7 million copies of the books were published in the first fourteen years. The number grew to 40 million over the next two decades. The book became most popular between 1870 and 1890, when 60 million copies, roughly one per citizen, were sold.

By late in the century, however, social leaders still worried about the large number of children who had not yet been brought under the mold of the common school movement. Educational opportunities still varied for American children. Many attended one-room schoolhouses when they could on a seasonal basis; others went to private schools; black children attended poorly funded segregated schools; and many children rarely attended school at all. American Indians were forced onto reservations throughout the West, where they were allowed a meager livelihood with no provision for education. Slightly less than half of North Carolina's 370,000 school-age children were attending school in 1874.[14] Educators were especially concerned with the lack of standardization among the academies and high schools, which were scattered across the country like wild horses. By 1850 there were more than 6,000 academies nationwide. Vance County alone had at least a dozen. These academies and high schools collectively served a minority of American youth, however, and their rigor and standards varied widely. Yet most of these schools set challenging expectations for all students rather than for just some. The purpose of education was to discipline the mind—what educators today might call thinking skills—through the mastery of core subjects. This was expected of students whether they were bound for college or work.[15]

At the turn of the century, the National Education Association (NEA), then a professional group rather than a union, assembled ten of the nation's leading educators to develop a plan to give high schools and academies a common curriculum. Not only were these schools producing graduates with varying levels of learning, but the nation's higher education institutions also lacked any semblance of uniformity. Freshmen at Harvard were performing at levels above graduates at other colleges.[16] The NEA panel, called the Committee of Ten, included U.S. Commissioner of Education William T. Harris and was chaired by Charles W. Eliot, president of Harvard. The group began its work in 1892 and produced a plan that defined the modern high school curriculum, though its primary purpose was to establish uniform admission requirements for colleges and universities. The committee considered demanding less of students bound for work rather than college, but after heated debate, it decided to set the same high academic expectations for all students. They all would be expected to take a minimum of four years of English, four of foreign language, three of history, three of mathematics, and three of science—requirements few modern high schools meet or many college admissions offices demand.

The plan's strength lay in its high expectations for all students, but it was flawed in requiring all students to meet them in the same way. "Every subject which is taught at all in a secondary school should be taught in the same way and to the same extent to every pupil," the committee wrote. This demand for conformity discounted individual differences among students. To divide the day into roughly one-hour periods per subject implied that each subject carried equal weight and that each student required the same amount of instructional time to learn each subject. This system ignored what students might already know or how they learned. It made no adjustments for a student well versed in literature but weak in math, who might more logically spend two hours a day on mathematics and skip literature altogether.

This structure also failed to recognize that just because a student takes, or even passes, a course in a given subject doesn't mean he or she has learned it. That oversight has grown into a serious problem in high schools today. Students pass their high school courses and win admission to college. Once there, however, they must take remedial courses to learn what they failed to learn in the courses they passed.

As high schools began adopting the Committee of Ten's curriculum and standards, they also began to see rapid growth. At most, about one in five teenagers attended some form of high school during the latter half of the nineteenth century, and a much smaller percentage graduated. About 203,000 students attended 2,526 public high schools nationwide in 1890. By 1900 the figure had doubled to 519,000 students in 6,005 high schools. Compulsory education laws and a rise in immigration began driving enrollment up sharply. Enrollment climbed to 1.1 million in 1912, and that figure doubled within eight years. But even by 1920, only 28 percent of youngsters between the ages of fourteen and seventeen were in high school. That percentage steadily swelled to 47 percent by 1930, when high schools enrolled 4.4 million students. A decade later, two out of three youngsters between the ages of fourteen and seventeen were in high schools. Total enrollment reached 6.5 million students.[17]

With this growth, a standardized, graded, mass education system, what education historian David B. Tyack called "The One Best System," became firmly established. Textbooks were written to match grade levels, and district and state curricula and national tests reinforced the structure. So did schools of education formed in universities to prepare teachers for specific subjects and grade levels. Schools opened offices for a hierarchy of people to run the bureaucracy—superintendents, principals, assistant principals, supervisors, deans, attendance officers, and clerks.

"Standardization became the magic word," writes Spring. "Administrators were preoccupied with standardizing student forms, evaluations of teachers and students, attendance records, personnel records and hiring procedures."[18]

In Oregon, Frank Rigler devoted his tenure as superintendent of Portland School District from 1896 to 1913 to perfecting this standardized education machine. He met with teachers on Saturdays and went through their textbooks page by page, telling them what questions to ask and how to answer them. People in the community said he could sit in his office and at any given moment know precisely what textbook and page teachers were working from.[19]

Perhaps nothing symbolized the uniform quality of the American education system more than rows of desks bolted to the floor and facing a blackboard. A school architect in New York City designed the standardized classroom plan: forty-eight bolted desks for grades 1 through 4, forty-five desks for grades 5 and 6, and forty for grades 7 and 8. One education researcher estimates that between 1920 and 1940, 80 percent of the desks in secondary schools were bolted to the floor.[20] In their quest for uniformity, educators became more concerned with how students learned than with what they learned. They focused on the process of schooling rather than the outcomes, just as most schools do today. This path led them to the bell curve and its power to help them manage this increasingly monolithic system of public education.

It also led schools away from any serious prospects of individualizing instruction. Individual ambitions would be buried in the broader social ambitions of public education. Children who seized the liberating power of knowledge did so at the price of great conformity. And that was a price many—in fact, most—students were either not able or not willing to pay.

Backlashes

Uniform, group-oriented education, with its rules and rigidity, has always grated against American individualism. The stern, grim-faced, knuckle-cracking schoolmarm or schoolmaster quickly became a stereotype of the authoritarian American public school. It is not surprising, then, that we see a long tradition of the hero in American literature and movies defying the school and asserting his individuality. Consider the words of Mark Twain's Huckleberry Finn:

> I had been to school most all the time, and could spell, and read, and write just a little, and could say the multiplication table up to six times seven is thirty-five, and I don't reckon I could ever get any further than that if I was to live forever. I don't take no stock in mathematics, anyway.
>
> "At first I hated the school, but by-and-by I got so I could stand it. Whenever I got uncommon tired I played hookey, and the hiding I got next day done me good and cheered me up.

Huck embodies America's ambivalence about its uniform schools. He seems to see some merit in education, as he speaks proudly of his ability to read, spell, and do multiplication. But he also questions the practicality of what he is learning—"I don't take no stock in mathematics." And he finds the regimen so wearing that it's worth skipping now and then, even at the cost of a "hiding."

Huck, like most American children through most of American history, would drop out of school. Early in the twentieth century, as schools grew increasingly similar, their students became increasingly diverse with each wave of European immigration. Schools responded by attempting to make their foreign students more like their American peers. Immigrant children's names were anglicized, and schools promoted democratic principles and taught against radical ideas such as socialism and communism. This one best system, however, did not fit many children. Many preferred to work in sweatshop factories rather than endure the humiliation and rigidity of standardized schools. One Chicago school inspector in 1909 asked 500 children whether they would prefer to work in the factory or attend school; 412 preferred the factory.

"The children don't holler at ye and call ye a Christ-killer in a factory," said one child.

"What ye learn in school ain't no good," said another. "Ye git paid just as much in the factory if ye never was there."[21]

Only a fraction of students stayed through high school. In that same year one statistician showed that Chicago enrolled 43,560 pupils in grade 1 but only 12,939 in grade 8.

"The general tendency of American cities is to carry all children through the fifth grade, to take one half of them to the eighth grade and one in ten through high school," the researcher concluded.[22]

One countercurrent to the crushing conformity of standardized schools, however, flowed well into the twentieth century in the one-room schoolhouses scattered across the countryside. In 1920, rural children were still taking their lessons in 200,000 one-room schoolhouses. A graded system was not practical for these schools, because students of all ages filled the one room. By necessity, teachers were forced to individualize. In these schools children could advance through mathematics, history, and literature at their own paces. They learned what they were ready to learn rather than what the system prescribed for children of their age or grade level. Older children tutored younger children. Many of the reforms currently being proposed in American education, such as mixed-age grouping and small-group learning, are practices once found in the one-room schoolhouse.

John Dewey, a prominent educational philosopher of the first half of the century, proposed these practices too. He saw big, standardized schools just as dehumanizing as the factories and urban centers emerging in the country. He believed schools did not have to be so alienating. Instead they could serve as community centers where children could cultivate a sense of place and confidence in the world. Like Benjamin Franklin, he saw learning as a source of great personal liberation and empowerment. At the turn of the century, Dewey opened a Laboratory School at the University of Chicago where he could test his views. Unlike most schools, his would focus on helping individual students find their place in the larger world rather than assigning them a place. He emphasized lessons tied to student interest and community life. He engaged students in group work, projects, and hands-on learning based on experience rather than abstractions. Nursery students would learn to count in his school by setting out forks to match the number of children for snacks. Six-year-olds would make model farms and explore the relation of climate to farm production. Older students studied the historical development of civilization, always learning through doing.[23]

Dewey's proposals for a more individualized and fluid system of education gained acceptance after World War I in what was called the progressive movement. The Progressive Education Association was founded in 1919, and its first honorary president was Charles Eliot, the Harvard president who belonged to the Committee of Ten. By 1938 *Time* magazine was writing a cover story on progressive practices. But the practices Dewey had advocated never reached many classrooms. Teachers who wanted to use his small-group methods immediately faced the problem of their bolted-down desks.

Many education historians believe that the progressive movement strayed far afield of Dewey's ideas by the second quarter of the century. They say that schools put less emphasis on academics, a move Dewey had never envisioned. One influential apostle of progressive education, for example, was William Heard Kilpatrick, a professor at Teachers College in New York. Kilpatrick rejected the study of subjects in favor of letting children decide what they should learn in school. Learning was to be fun, which usually translated as free of books or anything academic. By 1930 Kilpatrick and his supporters had put progressive education on its anti-intellectual track. Unlike Dewey, who envisioned the child's learning path extending from self to traditional bodies of knowledge such as literature, history, and sciences, Kilpatrick charted a course that led pretty much wherever the child decided to go. Other progressives embraced the notion of using schools for collective social action aimed at improving institutions and human relations. In 1945 a vocational education leader named Charles Prosser estimated that 60 percent of U.S. teenagers lacked the ability to benefit from academic or vocational programs. He and others who shared this then-popular view of the weak-minded teen supported more nonacademic life adjustment courses in the high schools. Students would learn practical skills in health, family living, and home economics courses. They would learn how to sew, cook, buy goods, and balance checkbooks. Only the college-bound were expected to roam into the worlds of physics or Shakespeare. The U.S. Department of Education and all the major education associations advocated this life-adjustment mission, which became part of a general education track public schools have yet to abandon. Americans find it hard to decide what to expect from their schools, say education researchers Harold Stevenson and James Stigler.

They write, "One reason [Americans] are unwilling to define the goal of education narrowly as academic excellence is that they believe that only some children are capable of achieving it."[24]

In fact, public education's social mission has continued to expand to child care, AIDS prevention, driver's training, and drug and alcohol prevention. Progressive education, though born to free individuals from the crush of conformity, eventually became part of a system geared to manipulating the masses. The progressive movement contributed to the general education track and reinforced the belief that some students didn't have the ability to grasp an academic education. It helped justify sorting students and using the bell curve to do so.[25]

The Pseudoscience of Sorting

One positive feature of the common school movement was its attempts to extend equal expectations for all children, an ideal upheld by the Committee of Ten. Unfortunately, not all students would meet those expectations. This was not because they couldn't reach them, but because standardized schools required that all students meet them in the same way and at the same age. Still, educators began to blame schools' mixed academic results on variations in student ability rather than on the rigidity of mass education. To support this view, they pointed to Charles Darwin and his theory of natural selection and survival of the fittest. Darwin's theory would lend support to efforts early in the twentieth century to begin classifying children on the basis of intelligence or perceived ability.

In 1809, about a half century before Darwin published his *Origin of Species,* the German mathematician and astronomer Carl Friedrich Gauss published the law of normal distribution, or the bell curve, in *Theoria Motus.* Darwin gave educators an explanation for why some students fared better than others in standardized schools; Gauss gave them a way of showing just how students differed. The two researchers gave educators the scientific authority they needed to justify sorting students for different destinations. Educators would use Gauss's bell-shaped curve in classifying students by intelligence or, in Darwinian terms, separating the academically fittest from the less fit.

It was not long after the Committee of Ten rejected varied expectations for students that education and community leaders began to demand them. Not all students were headed for the same destination, they argued, and so they should not all be required to take the same academic courses. Few thought individualizing education was practical in a mass education system, but the idea of separate tracks for students bound for work and for those bound for college had broad appeal. Ironically, critics said the Committee of Ten's plan was elitist in not offering a special track for students not going to college, which often meant going to fill an unskilled job in a factory. In the tradition of the common school, elitism was what the committee was trying to quash.

Nevertheless, the NEA established a new committee in 1913 called the Commission on Reorganization of Secondary Education, which issued a final report five years later. The report, titled the "Cardinal Principles of Secondary Education," recommended that American high schools become comprehensive institutions offering different courses of study to serve the varying ambitions of different students. For many students, the committee reasoned, academics was secondary to more practical instruction in vocational fields such as agriculture, business, industry, and homemaking. The commission said schools should allow individual students to find their place in society. Some education historians, however, argue that the system was designed to prepare human capital for the large-scale corporate state and to preserve class distinctions.

Whatever the intent, the system undermined the strongest feature of the Committee of Ten's plan—high expectations for all students. Now academic demands were allowed to vary. They remained high for the college-bound students, who were still a minority and tended to come from families that could afford to send their children on for further education. Most students would take less rigorous and more practical courses designed to prepare them for a workplace that did not demand, and in some cases discouraged, high academic skills. They took social studies instead of history, clerical courses instead of English, and no foreign languages at all. Some of these courses would evolve into basic and general-education tracks that have never led anywhere.

If this system ever had the potential of evolving into a student-centered, individualized one, that chance vanished with new notions of scientific management. Instead of allowing students simply to choose their destiny, educators began sorting students and, in effect, choosing their destiny for them. Rather than helping young people reach their aspirations, schools began limiting their ambitions. A new elite of public administrators, efficiency experts, and social scientists set out to design and operate the scientifically managed school.

During the second decade of the century, educators quickly embraced mass production as a good model for mass education. Frederick W. Taylor, the time-and-motion guru of the era, heavily influenced the hierarchal management organization of industry and schools. Taylor believed scientific principles could be used to make factories more efficient and workers more productive. He argued that management should control decision making and the workers' responsibilities should be reduced to simple tasks on an assembly line. Schools could be organized like factories with students moving through an assembly line. Administrators could control the lessons, textbooks, and curriculum. Teachers would be like assembly-line workers, delivering prescribed lessons from textbooks. They also could be standardized and used as interchangeable parts, easily moved from one classroom or school to another without disrupting the continuity of the instruction machine. Using this system, the modern comprehensive high school could put students on different assembly lines, or tracks.

Intelligence tests gave educators the tool they needed to sort students into varying education programs. The tests were first used on a massive scale during World War I to help classify 1.7 million U.S. Army soldiers. During this period, psychologists developed a variety of intelligence tests. They also developed arrogant assumptions about the power of their tests and drew elitist conclusions about test results. For example, Henry Herbert Goddard, who helped develop the test used by the army, argued in the 1890s that people of lower intelligence belonged in the simpler agricultural world of the countryside. After World War I he also proposed the people scoring in the top 4 percent on intelligence tests should govern the other 96 percent. Many psychologists concluded that the immigrants from southern and eastern Europe had low levels of intelligence and were reducing the general intelligence level of the country. Lewis M. Terman, who developed the intelligence quotient (IQ) scale, subscribed to this belief, writing in 1922 that immigrants from southern and southeastern Europe were "distinctly inferior mentally" to the Nordic and Alpine strains from northern Europe. Terman also helped revise the original test developed by French psychologist Alfred Binet into what is now known as the Stanford-Binet test. In the early 1920s Carl Brigham, who developed the Scholastic Aptitude Test, also sorted ethnic stocks by intelligence, ranking black Americans at the bottom.[26]

Educators in the early part of this century associated intelligence with ability and used intelligence tests to preserve an elitist system.

American schools were in effect "promulgating a doctrine of native intelligence," writes Spring: "What this means is that the early measurement movement reinforced social-class and ethnic differences by claiming they reflected differences in intelligence, but at the same time, it discounted the role of the school in doing anything about these differences."[27]

With the advent of intelligence tests, a new industry emerged. Like textbook publishers, private testing companies began producing achievement tests that could be used across the country. The tests typically measured basic reading and writing skills deemed appropriate for each grade level. They also were norm-referenced, judging a student's performance against the average of all students taking the test.

By 1925 the bell curve formed the mold for modern public education. Teachers and textbooks geared their lessons to the average student as described by bell-curve norms on standardized tests. Those performing high enough above average were tracked into higher reading groups in elementary school or into honors courses in middle and high schools. These students had a shot at college, but most did not. Students who scored at or below the norms would be tracked into remedial and basic academic classes and into shop, agriculture, home economics, and business courses. The bell curve determined destiny.

"The whole American education system, as I now see it, is dedicated to throwing bell curves around kids," said Marc Tucker, chairman of the Center for Education and the Economy in Rochester, New York. "Psychologists of the 1920s told us that intelligence is normally distributed on a bell curve, and they also told us that achievement is a direct function of intelligence, and therefore, it follows that achievement is distributed on a bell curve. Our whole system is designed to sort those kids out."[28]

After World War II, the sorting became more refined as more students stayed in high school and the profession of guidance counselor emerged. The proportion of seventeen-year-olds who graduated climbed from one in three in 1930 to nearly two in three by 1950. The number of counselors grew at a faster rate than students during the 1950s and 1960s. The proportion of high schools with full- or part-time guidance counselors climbed from 17 percent in

1951 to 65 percent in 1966.[29] As their name implies, one of the primary jobs of these new professionals was to help students navigate the increasingly complex and nonacademic curriculum of the comprehensive school. To help chart these courses, counselors drew on test scores distributed on a bell curve. There was nothing personal about this system. Each counselor was responsible for tracking hundreds of students as if sorting books for shelves.

Instruction continued to be geared to average group needs rather than individual needs. Tracked instruction was group-focused, geared to the average performance of students within the track. But even group needs began to change significantly during the 1950s and 1960s as a growing proportion of students stayed in high schools. Further, black students—long relegated to a separate but poorer and inferior segregated school system in the South and other parts of the nation—won legal access to the majority school system in 1954 with the landmark U.S. Supreme Court decision in *Brown v. Board of Education of Topeka*. They won actual access during the Civil Rights movement of the 1960s, which brought court-ordered desegregation and mandatory busing. Efforts to give all students equal educational opportunities increased the cultural and economic diversity of American schools. As numbers of students increased, average test scores dropped, a typical phenomenon with national, norm-referenced tests. Because instruction was geared to these norms, however, academic rigor also fell.

The Soviet Union alerted Americans to the declining quality of their schools in 1957 when it beat the United States into space with a satellite. Alarmed political and education leaders concluded that the nation's security was being threatened by its own diminishing brain reserve. James B. Conant, a former U.S. ambassador to West Germany and also a former Harvard University president, stepped forward to offer a solution to the crisis. He received a wide and grateful audience.

Like many leaders before him, Conant viewed public schools with the eyes of a social engineer. He successfully advocated for larger, more efficient high schools and school districts, launching a consolidation movement that continues to the present. For that alone, says Gordon L. Swanson, an education professor at the University of Minnesota, Conant deserves to be named a charter member in public education's Hall of Shame. In three decades, American school districts were reduced from more than 100,000 to only 15,000. More than one-fourth of today's high schools enroll more than 1,500 students.[30]

Conant had an even more devastating influence on education, however, in his promotion of rigid ability grouping. In *The American High School Today*, published in 1959, Conant proposed a more rigorous academic curriculum, especially in science and mathematics, but only for the nation's best and brightest. He recommended that high schools require four years of English, mathematics, and foreign language and three years of science and social studies for those students who scored in the top 15 percent on intelligence and aptitude tests. Those in the top 3 percent should get advanced tutoring and special classes. Slower students ought to be trained in trades leading to real job opportunities in their communities. And the very slow readers should be assigned to special teachers with special textbooks. In *The Last Little Citadel*, Robert Hampel notes that unpublished correspondence between Conant and the president of the Educational Testing Service, one of the nation's leading test makers, reveals Conant's near obsession with ability grouping and his low regard for the ability of most students. Conant believed academic subjects were out of reach even for average students, who would be happier learning vocational skills. He questioned one school that enrolled 40 percent of its students in physics, suggesting the course must be watered down if more than 15 to 20 percent of students were taking it. Students with an IQ below 90 should be encouraged to drop out of school. Hampel writes:

> He yearned for strict and dependable measures of native aptitude as the surest basis of grouping, worried about blurring the distinctions between the academically advanced and the less talented. Conant assumed that any problem with grouping would concern efficiency; justice was never a consideration. He never questioned the right of adults to maneuver students. . . . Like most school people, he did not apologize for the sorting and slotting done in schools.[31]

Conant's influence cut tracks deeper into the comprehensive high school. Academic lines separating students became sharper. One student might graduate knowing trigonometry, chemistry, English literature, world history, and German, while another would graduate with minimum skills and little knowledge beyond personal finance, business English, and bricklaying. Conant's plan again encouraged educators to chart the future of high school students by using test scores plotted on a bell curve.

More Backlashes

The comprehensive high school's rigid, more refined attempts to manipulate and engineer the destiny of children did not escape sensitive eyes. The countercurrent of individualized education that once coursed through the one-room schoolhouses and Dewey's Laboratory School ebbed in the shade of mass education but never died. In the 1960s, it regained vigor. Like leaders of generations before them, champions of civil rights and other causes used the schools to carry out integration and other social reforms. A group of critics who reacted against mass education's dehumanizing authority emerged. Books such as *Growing Up Absurd* and *Compulsory Miseducation* by Paul Goodman, *How Children Fail* by John Holt, and *High School* by Frederick Wiseman all portrayed schools as prisons that demand conformity and crush curiosity and creativity. In the tradition of John Adams and Huck Finn, they argued that education should liberate rather than suffocate children. They argued for freedom. A. S. Neill gave the nation an example of what the critics were advocating with his best-selling *Summerhill,* an account of a progressive private school operating in England that emphasized student freedom and individualized instruction.

Many American schools in the late 1960s and 1970s experimented with more individualized systems, though most attempts amounted to little more than tinkering. One popular approach was to remove classroom walls and give students the freedom to move among a variety of learning centers, such as an art corner, a reading station stocked with books, and a science area equipped for experiments. Teachers were not trained for this system, however, and continued to rely on traditional practices of group instruction based on textbooks. The absence of walls only made their job more difficult. Neighboring classes continuously distracted students. It was like trying to hold class in a shopping mall. Soon teachers began demanding partitions, and before long, permanent walls once again separated classes.

However, the reformers' call for more freedom and relevancy had subtle yet widespread and significant influences on education. Schools became more relaxed. They scrapped dress codes, simplified rules, and looked for ways to make school more fun and interesting. Students wrote short stories instead of essays. They took elective courses such as science fiction in place of traditional English courses. Teachers were more cautious about damaging student self-esteem by giving them low grades or by bloodying their papers with red-ink corrections. While not all bad, these changes produced two troubling results: a rise in discipline problems and a drop in academic achievement. Polls showed poor discipline topped the list of concerns among parents during the 1970s. And high school graduates were making headlines by suing school districts for failing to teach them how to read. Even college-bound students were losing academic ground. Their scores on the SAT college entrance exam declined.

This time instead of the Soviets, a commission serving President Ronald Reagan alerted the nation that its schools were in trouble. In 1983 the commission issued *A Nation at Risk,* warning that problems in education jeopardized the nation's economic future and security. Leaders also were seeing the first signs of a shifting economy. Mills and factories were closing because of foreign competition; computer technology was emerging everywhere in the workplace, even on the American farm; and high-paying jobs for high school graduates were becoming scarce. The commission's report jolted the nation like a double espresso.

Failed Reforms

With a sense of urgency, leaders in every state began developing plans for school renewal. Improving schools became a priority among governors, legislators, and business leaders. Forty-two states, including North Carolina, raised their graduation standards;

thirty-nine states upgraded teacher standards; all launched dropout prevention programs; and the number of states with statewide testing programs climbed to forty-seven. Seventy percent of high schools adopted stricter attendance and conduct requirements and higher grade requirements for students wanting to participate in sports and activities. Tennessee governor Lamar Alexander, who would become U.S. Secretary of Education under President Bush, pushed for a plan to improve teacher quality using the incentive of merit pay. South Carolina expanded testing and offered schools rewards of money and the threat of state takeover depending on whether their test scores climbed or fell.

Almost without exception, this flurry of school improvement efforts involved shoring up the existing system. Few leaders were proposing more fundamental changes. No states challenged grouping children by age or sorting them by ability. Few questioned what education researcher Barbara Tye calls the deep structure of schooling: the physical uniformity of classrooms, tracking, grade levels, standardized curricula, a reliance on textbooks, an overall orientation toward control and group instruction, and the use of national norm-referenced test scores to measure success.[32] Few educators recognized how their uses of the bell curve undergirds this framework.

North Carolina's Basic Education Plan (BEP) was typical of school reforms in the 1980s. The eight-year plan, launched in 1985, was adopted by the legislature as a top-down, centralized effort to expand and improve the traditional structure of the state's mass education system. The plan called for pumping more money into the system over eight years so that all schools could afford guidance counselors and a full curriculum. The plan would add 11,500 teachers and 14,000 teacher aides to reduce class sizes. As envisioned, by 1993 the state would be spending an additional $700 million a year on schools so they could offer courses in art, dance, drama, music, foreign language, and physical education at all levels, beginning in kindergarten. Statewide testing would be expanded so legislators could measure the payoff on their investment.

The plan did expand opportunities for students, particularly in the poorer districts, such as Vance County, and the state saw modest gains in basic skills. But after four years and with half the plan in place, North Carolina's public education system still was faced with disappointing results. About one in four of the state's students quit before finishing high school, its seniors were posting the lowest SAT scores in the nation, and a third of those who went on to college needed remedial courses in math or English. In 1989 the BEP began to founder. Some leaders began to lose confidence in it. The state faced a financial crisis, and the legislature postponed paying the final installments. By 1992 the plan was in a shambles, and student achievement remained largely unchanged. By 1994 legislators rarely mentioned the plan, which was virtually forgotten by the public.

The Basic Education Plan was designed chiefly by Howard Maniloff, a former newspaper reporter from Charlotte who took a doctorate in education and went to work as assistant to Dick Spangler, chairman of the state Board of Education and later president of the state university system. After successfully lobbying for the BEP in the legislature (in July 1987) Maniloff took over as superintendent of Vance County Public Schools, where he hoped to watch his plan transform a poor, low-performing rural system. Vance County schools did see changes. They got more teachers and counselors so they could reduce class sizes. They began offering courses in elementary schools that they could never before afford, such as music, art, physical education, and Spanish. The problem was that these courses competed for time with basic academic courses. Student academic performance on national norm-referenced tests actually declined. Vance County's scores ranked near the bottom in the state. They were so low that the state Board of Education in 1990 named it one of the state's three worst. The board warned the district that it faced state takeover if it did not pull up its scores within two years.

Howard Maniloff, the father of what many had called the most ambitious and expensive school reform effort in North Carolina history, found himself heading one of the state's most pronounced failures. He resigned in 1991.

Betty Wallace stepped in to replace him. She had long considered the BEP doomed because it failed to address the problems of mass education governed by bell-curve assumptions about student achievement. Her plan would focus on serving the individual rather than the group, on outcomes rather than process, on high standards for all, not just some students. The school factory would go the way of the crumbling cotton mills. She intended to give all children the knowledge they would need to climb out of poverty and lead fulfilling adult lives. In the poor rural South, Wallace aimed to revive the revolutionary tradition of John Adams, Benjamin Franklin, and John Dewey by destroying the Bell-Curve Syndrome.

CHAPTER 4

▼

NEW PATHS FOR VANCE STUDENTS

Betty Wallace took her first swat at the bell curve only days after she arrived in Vance County.

She stopped by Northern Vance High School to meet Principal Wayne Adcock and found him and his two assistant principals, George Grissom and Trudy Tidwell, huddled over a stack of test scores and schedules spread across a table. Wallace introduced herself and asked the administrators what had them so occupied. They were scheduling seniors into advanced, general, and basic courses in the core curriculum, they said. In other words, they were tracking. Here was the enemy staring Wallace in the face: three administrators calmly sorting expectations for hundreds of children.

"What are you using for criteria?" asked Wallace.

Adcock said they used the student's eighth-grade scores in reading and mathematics on the standardized California Achievement Test. Wallace winced. Could they really be using norm-referenced test scores to determine the education and future for students four years after they had taken the test? Adcock, who'd been a principal for years, observed that once students were sorted into a track as freshmen, they typically stayed in it. These tracks tended to reflect racial divisions, Tidwell said. With few exceptions, all of the advanced classes were white, and all the basic classes were black.

"Doesn't that strike you as strange—that we would have a segregated school system, segregated within the walls?" asked Wallace.

Yes, agreed the educators, it was a problem. They didn't like it. Tidwell understood how tracking hurt students because she was deeply knowledgeable about how children learn mathematics. Wallace later moved her into the central office to revamp the district's math curriculum, which eventually led to dramatic districtwide gains in student math performance. Wallace also put Tidwell in charge of overseeing program evaluation for the district's entire reform effort. Tidwell and the other administrators had continued to track children because Vance County school board policy required them to.

Yet while the board did require the high school to offer advanced courses, it didn't mention basic ones. So Wallace asked the administrators if they could scrap the basic track and move its students into the general track. They readily agreed to do so. Adcock also agreed to call the principal at Southern Vance High School and ask him to do the same. Thus, in her first week on the job, Wallace raised academic expectations for hundreds of seniors. The small deed made her all the more eager to wipe out the Bell-Curve Syndrome in Vance County.

She planned a two-pronged attack. First, she would end the practice of using grades and test scores to compare students and sort them for differing academic expectations, instead using learning objectives to set high academic expectations for all students, not just those deemed advanced. Second, she would restructure the district so students would have freedom to meet those expectations in varying ways at varying paces. For starters, she would eliminate grades and grade levels districtwide, save in the two high schools.

Wallace was about to reorganize an entire school district in a way unfamiliar to teachers, students, and parents. She knew of no one in public education who had attempted to make such deep structural changes on this scale or at this speed.

Building High Standards

Her first job was to set academic goals. If Vance County was going to set high expectations for all students, someone had to decide what those expectations were going to be and how they would be measured. Academic objectives needed to be clear, not only to teachers, but also to parents and, most important, to students. The better everyone understood where they were headed, the easier it would be for them to get there.

Wallace had few examples to draw from. As mentioned, when

schools do set academic goals, they usually aim low, focusing on rudimentary skills in reading and mathematics. What's more, they focus on group averages and test results that tell more about how children compare to others the same age than about what they actually can do. Wallace wanted to give parents a clear picture of where students were headed and how well they were progressing. She wanted to show them what kind of book their children could read and understand and how well they could write an essay or solve a math problem.

Though she wasn't fully aware of it, Betty Wallace was on a search shared by colleagues across the country in the most serious reappraisal of education standards and testing to emerge in the nation in more than sixty years. A growing number of leaders in the field of education were looking for ways to set high, not minimum, standards. And they wanted these standards to mark the academic stretch expected of all children, not just some. Wallace recognized that all children would never meet expectations, wherever they were set, as long as they all were forced to do so at the same time. She needed to find a way to give children the freedom they needed to meet high standards at their own pace and in their own way.

She found the model she was looking for in the *Boy Scout Handbook*.

The Boy Scouts of America is an organization devoted to helping boys become fit and knowledgeable outdoorsmen and productive citizens. Toward that end, the organization has developed a staircase educational structure. It has defined a series of ranks or steps that boys can climb like stairs. The first step is Tenderfoot, followed by Second Class, First Class, Star, Life, and at the top, Eagle. There are clear outcomes describing precisely what boys must know and be able to do to reach each rank. To make First Class, a boy must meet fifteen objectives. He must, for example, demonstrate how to find directions during the day and at night without using a compass; identify or show evidence of at least ten kinds of native plants in his community; and demonstrate bandages for injuries on the head, the upper arms, and collarbone, and for a sprained ankle.

Whenever a boy meets an objective, a scout leader signs and dates a special form. When a boy meets all that are required for the next rank, he takes a final exam and goes before a board of review made up of scout leaders. Upon passing the review, he's awarded the new rank. While all boys must meet the same standards to advance, they can do so in their own way and at their own pace.

"You may pass any of the requirements for Tenderfoot, Second Class and First Class at any time," says the *Boy Scout Handbook*. "For example, if you fulfill a First Class requirement before you are a Second Class Scout, you may go ahead and check off the First Class requirement as complete."[1]

The system becomes even more fluid at the higher stages, where boys must earn a number of merit badges for specific endeavors such as swimming, sculpture, or woodwork. Each merit badge has a list of objectives. To earn a badge in geology, for example, a scout must, among other duties, collect at least ten different earth materials from his local area, discuss and define three classes of rock, and describe the major steps in the geologic history of a mountain range. Eagle Scouts must earn a total of twenty-one merit badges. Some are required, some are not. This allows boys to explore their own interests while still meeting the same high standards for Eagle rank. Boy Scouts can each follow their own paths up the ranks. No one fails. In this system, the *Boy Scout Handbook* points out, the biggest rewards are not the badges but what Scouts gain by earning them. "The skills you master, the wisdom you gain and the experiences you enjoy are what really count," it says.

Like the Boy Scouts, Vance County schools would judge students on specific objectives, Wallace vowed. District educators would establish the outcomes they expected students to meet in order to get a diploma—the academic equivalent of Eagle rank. Unlike the Scouts, though, all students would be expected to reach this rank. Along the way they would encounter three benchmarks, each like a stepping-stone similar to the lower ranks in scouting. The first would establish objectives students would need to meet to graduate from the primary level. During their primary years, students would focus on mastering basic skills in reading, writing, and arithmetic. Once children mastered those skills—and not before—they would advance to the intermediate level, where they would begin using their new skills to harvest knowledge. To move on to middle school, they would need to master the intermediate benchmark learning objectives in the core curriculum areas. Similarly, they would have to scale middle-school benchmark objectives before entering high school.

This four-tiered structure would correspond roughly to grades kindergarten through 3, 4 through 6, 7 and 8, and 9 through 12. Students, however, could spend fewer or more years at each level, depending on their needs. Time could vary, but learning expectations would be fixed at the same high level for all students. Some students would move through the system faster than others, but most probably would take about as much time as ever. The difference would be that every single student would leave school with high levels of knowledge and skills. Children would be able to follow learning paths that suited them best as they advanced. Vance County would be structured like a four-story building with a network of staircases branching up through each level. Some staircases might wind their way up while others would be straight; some might be steep while others stretch over a more gradual grade, but they all would lead through each floor—primary, intermediate, and middle school—to the high school diploma at the top. Students would be urged to take flights of stairs that were as steep and direct as they could handle. Undoubtedly, most children would climb steep staircases in some subjects and winding, more gentle slopes in others. Teachers would be their guides, making sure they all kept moving up paths that were challenging but not overwhelming. Wallace called her plan Guided Learning through Outcomes-Based Education, or GLOBE 2000.

Wallace's immediate problem in setting learning objectives was time. She could not afford to wait years for her staff to define learning goals in every subject at four levels. But they could, she reasoned, use the state's curriculum objectives as crude standards. The curriculum division of the state Department of Public Instruction, where Wallace had once worked, had developed a seventeen-volume Standard Course of Study outlining learning objectives for every subject at every grade level. Vance County could narrow and simplify those objectives to describe what skills and knowledge students would be expected to master at each of the system's four levels.

In the fall, Wallace assembled 104 teachers from across the

district to convert the state curriculum into learning objectives for communication, mathematics, science, social studies, and geography at each of the four levels. They tried to keep the objectives as plain and simple as possible. The district reproduced them on colored GLOBE 2000 cards for each subject so parents could post them on their refrigerators and check off objectives as their children mastered them. Once a child mastered all the objectives at one level, he or she could move on to the next.

At the primary level, for example, students faced three or four arithmetic objectives under each of seven categories: patterns and sequences, geometry, numeration, computation, measurement, charts and graphs, and problem solving. Some of the objectives required students to show they could add and subtract three-digit whole numbers, multiply numbers 1 to 10, use objects and pictures to create graphs, and demonstrate a variety of ways to solve problems.

Students would begin working on these objectives their first year of school. Instead of report cards, they would get quarterly reports showing which objectives they had mastered. There would be no letter grades, no Ds and Fs. A child either learned the objective or didn't. These reports, therefore, would clearly show parents what their children had and had not learned. Once primary children mastered all of their objectives, whether it took a year or four years, they could move on to the intermediate level.

The academic demands for the four levels were not extraordinarily high, but respectable and challenging. They required all students to learn what the state expected of them by the time they reached high school—a goal that neither Vance County nor any other district in the state was meeting. While Wallace was not satisfied with these objectives—they were still too crude, complicated, and, in some cases, vague and dated—nevertheless, they marked a beginning. As students and teachers adjusted to the system, Wallace and her staff aimed to refine academic requirements until they were clear and rigorous enough to rival any in the nation. Following are the district's first GLOBE 2000 Middle School Communication Skill standards for writing, just as they appeared on the refrigerator check-off sheet:

Write in a Variety of Modes and for a Variety of Purposes

- Produce book reports/reviews

- Compose business and friendly letters

- Organize cause and effect paragraphs

- Create original poetic/prose compositions

- Write a personal narrative

- Develop a descriptive paper

- Compare two like/unlike ideas/objectives using webbing, charts or grouping

- Write point of view compositions

- Write persuasive compositions

- Write dialogue

- Demonstrate survival writing skills (applications, checks, test grid, telephone message)

- Use the writing process (prewriting, writing, rewriting)

- Write independently for a sustained time (15 minutes minimum)

Vance County teachers produced concrete, practical objectives such as these for each benchmark.

Measuring Standards

Betty Wallace recognized that developing practical, accurate, and fair ways of measuring whether Vance County students were meeting the learning objectives would be as important as the objectives themselves. Sloppy, narrow, or shallow measures could make the learning goals meaningless. National norm-referenced tests were out. Wallace joined a growing number of political and education leaders across the country who were looking for better ways to measure learning—ways that foster in-depth, rigorous instruction rather than the shallow, watered-down type.

"They seek tests that are valid in the sense that they 'measure' qualities we desire rather than items that are but tokens of those qualities," writes Theodore R. Sizer, education professor at Brown University and one of the nation's top experts on high schools. "These leaders are concerned that what is measured should be the real power of a child, that child's enduring habits, not just what he has prepped for passing a test."[2]

Researchers now believe that all teachers should adopt evaluation methods similar to those used by the art teacher who looks at paintings to judge a student's mastery of perspective or the wood-shop instructor who surveys a coffee table to gauge a student's craftsmanship. Students in academic courses could be evaluated similarly on the basis of projects, essays, presentations, and portfolios of their work collected over months or years. Educators call this performance or authentic assessment. Advocates say it fosters in-depth instruction rather than drill-and-kill busywork and appropriately shifts the focus of evaluation from group averages to the work of individuals.

It also relies heavily on teacher judgment, which can vary widely. Performance measures can be turned into consistent standards, however. North Carolina, Oregon, and other states have proven this with writing tests that employ hundreds of teachers to score essays, using well-defined scales. In Oregon, each year students in grades 3, 5, 8, and 11 have three hours to compose an essay on a small selection of broad topics. The exam is scored by two judges who use a well-defined five-point scale. If the scores of the two judges disagree, a third is called in to evaluate the work. This process provides statewide consistency, something you don't find with grades and most other traditional forms of student evaluation. The state could make its writing exam a performance standard by requiring students to score a 3 or better to advance.

Performance standards are used in licensing and certification exams for a variety of other practical and professional endeavors in American life, such as practicing law and medicine, scuba diving, wiring houses, accounting, fixing elevators, piloting airplanes, and making jewelry. The most common are state driver's license exams. To drive, people must show they know the rules of the road by taking a written test. Then they must perform—show they can apply their knowledge by driving a car.

Professional education groups in every academic discipline are developing exams to measure performance. In some cases, they also are developing guidelines or scoring scales that will give teachers a consistent way of judging students. Eventually these groups will define, say by a point on the scale, what they consider an acceptable level of proficiency. That level will become the standard, the bar that students must clear to meet a given objective or goal.

Foreign language is one of the few disciplines that built a scale to judge proficiency years ago. The American Council of Teachers of Foreign Language issued guidelines in 1986 that "identify stages of proficiency" in any language. The researchers who developed the guidelines wrote these "are not intended to measure what an individual has achieved through specific classroom instruction but rather to allow assessment of what an individual can and cannot do, regardless of where, when or how the language has been learned or acquired." The foreign language guidelines describe four stages, and in some cases substages, of proficiency in speaking, listening, reading, and writing. Low-intermediate speakers, for example, can ask and answer questions, initiate and respond to simple statements, and maintain face-to-face conversations—although in a highly restricted manner and with linguistic inaccuracy. They also can order meals, ask directions, and make purchases. Superior speakers can participate in most formal and informal conversations on practical, social, professional, and abstract topics, can support opinion, and can hypothesize. Using these definitions, teachers on opposite coasts can judge the foreign language proficiency of students with reasonable consistency.

Professional groups in geography, art, and mathematics have drafted proposed national standards that define what students should know and be able to do at certain points, usually described by grade level, in their education journeys. Geography standards will require students not only to show where the Nile River is, but also to describe how it influences the region and its people. Art standards will require all students to be able to play a musical instrument, create a dance, and stage dramatic material by the time they graduate from high school. Mathematics standards expect high school students to demonstrate they understand algebra, geometry, trigonometry, statistics, probability, and the conceptual underpinnings of calculus.

The National Council of Teachers of Mathematics has proposed tasks to measure whether students meet math standards that go far beyond simply solving equations. The council's evaluation system requires students to keep problem-solving journals, write essays, propose theorems, and solve open-ended questions with a variety of possible answers. The council, for example, proposes that high school students be required to tackle tasks like these:

- You are considering purchasing one of two cars, both four years old. One car costs $3,000 and gets 20 miles a gallon. The other costs $4,500 and gets 35 miles a gallon. Which car is the best buy if you plan to keep it two years?

  Rather than answering this question students are expected to show what additional information they would need to answer the question. They need to identify the missing information and the likely estimates for the missing quantities.

- Using an electronic spreadsheet, demonstrate that if 1 gallon of deicer fluid is added with each fill-up of a fuel tank, a limit of 2 gallons of deicer in the tank at the fill-up will eventually be reached. Assume that the driver habitually fills the tank when it is half full.

- Roger doesn't believe that adding the same number of points to each student's test score will increase the average score by that same amount. Write a valid argument to convince Roger that this is true.[3]

To handle problems like these, students are going to have to know more than the basics of mathematics.

Vermont has led the nation in actually scrapping norm-referenced national tests for more meaningful performance exams. All public school fourth to eighth graders save their best written works and math problem-solving works in portfolios for state assessment each spring. On one warm October day at Gertrude Chamberlin Elementary School in South Burlington, for example, Sara Fuller flips through the work she chose for her writing portfolio the previous spring. The gray-eyed, freckle-faced fifth grader is surprised, she says, at what she is capable of doing. She proudly describes the outline, multiple drafts, and artwork accompanying the original myth she submitted as her best written piece. It opens, "Spring, who has dark hair, blue eyes and likes to wear green, was walking in the woods." Sarah included a short note to her judges explaining why she chose this piece. "It's short but neat," she wrote. "I've worked hard to make it nice and neat for people to read."

Her classmate, Susan Lambert, sifts through her portfolio, showing a story about Christmas in Virginia, a biography of Martin Luther King, Jr., and a report on the New England cottontail rabbit. Susan says she loved making her portfolio. "I just wish it could be bigger," she says.[4]

Sarah and Susan show an affection and pride for their work and performance that few children express for national multiple-choice basic skills tests. Further, five minutes with these portfolios would give any adult a good picture of how well these children can write and think.

Unfortunately, Vermont has not been able to shake the bell curve. The state goes through an expensive and cumbersome process to grade portfolios and compare them to others prepared by students of the same age. So about half of the state's students will be left feeling their work is below average—hardly a reward for earnest work.

The private Waldorf schools, founded in Germany seventy-five years ago by a philosopher named Rudolf Steiner, have long judged students on performance. However, these schools, which are scattered around the world, do not use grades. They ignore the bell curve, and the benefits are apparent. One fall day at the Waldorf School in Portland, Oregon, eighth graders in Dolores Julien's room write short biographies of the French king Louis XIV with neat, cursive handwriting in handmade books. They paint portraits of the monarch and decorate the borders of their pages with elaborate designs as if they are making medieval scrolls. They get no grades on their work. So why do they do it?

"You feel satisfied that you have completed a book that is beautiful," says Angela Burke, a student in Julien's class since third grade.[5]

Like Sara and Susan in Vermont, Angela and her classmates were finding rewards in their performance, in learning and creating works of writing, rather than in abstract grades. Unlike Sara and Susan, however, they did not face prospects of having their work judged on the basis of how it compared to that of other students. Instead, they were expected to do their best, to meet a standard, albeit a vaguely defined one, of excellence. So all Waldorf students are rewarded for their work, while only some Vermont students are. Waldorf schools instill a love for learning in children that eludes the more judgmental and punitive public schools.

Betty Wallace and her staff would take the Waldorf approach, using portfolios, essays, presentations, interviews, perhaps even review boards like the Boy Scouts use, to measure whether students were meeting learning goals. Other measures might be as simple as a short interview with a primary student to see if the child could count by tens to 1,000 or a yearlong journal to determine whether an intermediate student could organize information and judge the merit of ideas. Through multiple measures, Vance County teachers could paint detailed portraits of each child's knowledge and skills, of what each had learned and needed to learn. Teachers also could draw on some objective measures developed by the district and the state Department of Public Instruction. Multiple-choice tests could be valid and efficient measures of some areas of knowledge and skills. Anyone who has taken the Scholastic Assessment Test knows they can be rigorous. In grades 3, 6, and 8, Vance County could use the state's writing and end-of-grade tests, which are designed to match the state curriculum.

As much as possible, Wallace's staff tried to set learning expectations at the proficiency levels teachers associated with specific grades. The primary learning objectives were set at the level of what students typically were expected to know and be able to do by the end of the third grade. Similarly, the intermediate benchmarks were geared to the end of sixth grade, and the middle school benchmarks matched the end of eighth grade. This gave teachers some familiar bearings and gave some measure of consistency to benchmark proficiency levels districtwide. Teachers could tap the professional judgment of colleagues whenever they had any doubts about whether a child was sufficiently proficient in a particular area. Wallace knew that standards set roughly at grade level were average and mediocre, but she felt that initially, meeting even mediocre standards would mark a gain for Vance County students.

Children would have the option of being tested for particular learning objectives whenever they felt ready. Instead of sending parents quarterly grade reports, teachers would send them summaries of the learning objectives their children had mastered. These would be true progress reports. Teachers would find this new, more complicated evaluation system clumsy at first. Even so, it would encourage them to expect far more of children than a mastery of basic skills. Vance County would apply new proficiency definitions for performance standards in various subjects as national researchers developed them. As time passed, the district's standards would climb and the ways of measuring whether students met them would become increasingly consistent and refined.

Why Should Teachers Make the Change?

Nothing troubles American teachers more than low student motivation. Problems with status, salary, working conditions, and hours pale against this enormous obstacle. If parents cared more about education, teachers lament, their children would not be so hard to teach. Indeed, motivated students who embrace the high priority their parents put on education do well in just about any school, including an American one. The high academic achievements of recent waves of non-English-speaking Asian immigrants have demonstrated that fact across the country. That is why some education leaders say the United States needs a cultural revolution to improve its schools. If American society placed more value on education, they reason, student achievement would improve. The only way to make Americans widely cherish education, however, is to produce a highly educated generation that would instill that value in its children. But how to produce that first generation?

Indeed, the prospects of imbuing students with enhanced academic drive seem dim, particularly in places like rural North Carolina, where the stream of poverty and school failure runs wide and deep. Educators in this region try a variety of strategies to motivate students and improve their self-esteem. They offer group counseling, student-of-the-month awards, and classes on values, choosing careers, and avoiding drugs. They plaster their walls with student work, posters, goals, and motivational slogans such as "Only Your Best Is Good Enough." They invest in well-stocked libraries. But students don't respond. Few read their assignments, let alone read for pleasure. Some teachers resort to video versions of literary works as well as "high-interest, low-ability" books and even pizza and candy to motivate students. Social studies teacher Stanley B. Gelbhaar at Charity Middle School in Duplin County sometimes allows students to draw pictures instead of write reports, not an uncommon practice.

"They can express themselves in a drawing a lot better than they can on a piece of paper," Gelbhaar says.

When teachers try to raise expectations and push their students, they face what is tantamount to mutiny. Michael W. Kegerreis, a math teacher at East Duplin High near Beulaville, said he was shocked the first time he handed a sheet of story problems to his math students. A tap, tap, tap spread across the room like falling dominoes as students slapped pencils down on their desks in defeat, refusing even to give the problems a try. At Southeast Halifax High School—which lies in a county neighboring Vance—Louise A. Robinson faces the challenge of teaching Shakespeare to students who struggle with elementary schoolbooks. Even assigning them a short story to read over the weekend is an exercise in futility.

"When they come in Monday, 90 percent of them will not have read it," she says. "It gets worse every year. Definitely worse. They get less motivated. They are less prepared to work."[6]

These rural North Carolina teachers are wrestling with victims of the Bell-Curve Syndrome. Students have lost their fire for learning after enduring years of unfavorable comparisons with their peers and of ill-fitting, impersonal, often irrelevant group instruction.

Research shows that students lose heart in traditional schools because of disincentives rooted in the bell curve. Edwin Farrell of the City College of New York enlisted a group of students to help him study the forces influencing high school teenagers. Students consider school boring, Farrell discovered, in part because it seems irrelevant to the social pressures they faced in trying to establish their identities and place in society. More interestingly, students distinguished boring classes from more interesting ones on the basis of the process, rather than content. Classes students considered boring were heavily coercive and punitive, led by teachers who confronted them each day with worksheets, tests, comments, and routines that reminded students they probably would continue to fail. In other words, they found classes boring that repeatedly highlighted their low status on the bell curve. Students naturally preferred teachers who conveyed a less judgmental tone. Monica Richards, a middle school English teacher in Kentucky, drew similar conclusions after doing a research project on motivation with her lowest-achieving, most alienated class. Students said the top inhibitor to motivation was "comparing me with another student in class," followed by "picking out a certain group of students as pets," "lack of trust in students," and "a teacher who always 'cuts you down.' " Again, students declared they detest judgmental comparisons.[7]

These findings support Betty Wallace's view that the key to sustaining student motivation lies in protecting them from the demeaning forces of the Bell-Curve Syndrome. All students were capable of meeting Vance County's new standards, and in a flexible system that adjusted to their needs, they would.

Children enter school with a natural motivation to learn. Deep down, says Peter Senge, a consultant heavily involved in school reform, we are all learners.

> No one has to teach an infant to learn. In fact, no one has to teach infants anything. They are intrinsically inquisitive, masterful learners who learn to walk, speak and pretty much run their households all on their own. Learning organizations are possible because not only is it our nature to learn but we love to learn.[8]

By abandoning harsh instructional and evaluation practices based on the bell curve, Vance County schools would create a responsive and inviting environment rather than an impersonal, coercive one. Children would not have to worry about poor grades and demoralizing comparisons. They would clearly see their mission, have every reason to pursue it and no reason to remain idle. They would find their reward in their work, in what they learned and produced, and in their advancements, rather than in abstract grades. Being free to advance whenever they were ready would give them real power over their destiny. Gaining knowledge and skills would affect their status. The more they learned, the better their status, just as in the adult world. Since all, rather than just some, would have this option to success, it is fair to assume they would all take it. People enjoy doing what they succeed at. Success breeds success and self-respect. The farther children advanced in Vance County's new system, the more inclined they would be to press forward. By contrast, the consequence for idleness would be stagnancy—an option few children will choose, particularly when they see others advancing. Unlike the traditional system, Vance County's new framework had the right learning incentives.

A Staircase to Success

Wallace and her staff concluded that they could use two basic strategies in building a flexible school system that would be responsive to individual student needs. The first is to group students by achievement levels in a staircase structure, allowing children to move from one level to the next whenever they are ready. This is the method used by swim and ballet schools. The second strategy is to use a variety of techniques—including computers, projects, community resources, and peer tutoring—to individualize instruction within a group. This might be viewed as the one-room schoolhouse approach. The staircase structure provides a more logical way of grouping children for common lessons, but it can be combined with the schoolhouse strategy to provide even more flexibility and individualization.

One way to organize a staircase structure is by subject. A school, for example, might have five levels of math leading to the primary benchmark: the first focusing on numbers, counting, and geometric shapes; the second, on mathematical classifications, patterns, relationships, and sequences; a third on measurements; a fourth on problem solving; and a fifth, on data collection, graphing, and interpretation. Students could move up these steps at their own pace. One might make the trip in one year, another might take three, but all would be expected to reach the top. They would move up a similar flight of stairs in reading, science, and other subjects, depending on the practical limits of scheduling.

Traditional grade levels resemble the staircase structure in some ways; they differ in two critical ways. First, children occupy each step according to their age rather than their educational needs, and many, consequently, are not where they belong. Second, they advance only in unison once a year rather than whenever they are ready.

Paint Branch Elementary School on the outskirts of Washington, D.C., has been operating in a staircase structure without grades or grade levels since 1987.[9] All of its students leave the school with solid skills in math and reading. Though they advance at varying paces, every child ultimately reaches the top step and achieves at high academic levels. One of Principal Linda Dudley's biggest concerns is that she must send her children on to conventional graded middle schools that teach skills and topics her students already have mastered. One graduate skipped middle school altogether. Paint Branch children are used to advancing to higher academic levels whenever they choose. Early in the 1991 school year, for example, eight-year-old Miriam Berdichvsky was already thinking it was time for a promotion.

"If it is too hard, I'll move back," the shy girl told her principal, who was all for the move.

Students at Paint Branch are grouped according to their academic needs rather than their ages. Children learning the alphabet are in one group; those learning to read words are in another. The ages, cultural, ethnic, and economic backgrounds may vary among students in a group, but they share common educational needs. Even within the group, teachers are searching for ways to further individualize. Children in a reading group, for example, may be encouraged to independently read books of their own choosing or write stories. They then meet as a group to share what they read or to edit one another's writing. The fact they are all working at about the same proficiency level, teachers say, makes them easier to teach.

Dudley and her staff decided on this more fluid structure after a weekend retreat in 1987. Since the change they have seen dramatic changes. No child flunks at Paint Branch. When there are no grades, there is no way for a child to repeat a grade. No child is frustrated by assignments too difficult or by lessons already learned. No one is led away for remedial work or special lessons for the exceptionally bright. Every child succeeds. This success inspires learning, quashes discipline problems, and pushes Paint Branch student achievement high every year.

"Motivation is very high because they really do see everyone making it," said Dudley, a no-nonsense leader with a doctorate in education and a reputation for innovation. "Once children understand they can do it, they will do it. A child doesn't opt to stay behind."

Paint Branch's success is all the more remarkable because the school is not simply drawing affluent, middle-class students who have already learned to read in preschool. Nearly a third come from low-income homes on the outskirts of Washington. Many live surrounded by violence; many have seen someone shot in their neighborhood. By the middle of the 1992–93 school year, the principal reported, she had attended seven funerals for shooting victims related to children at her school. One fifth grader transferred to her school in February after seeing his father shoot his mother, then himself. Even in the wake of this trauma, the boy chose more challenging academics over boredom and was soon doing mathematics usually reserved for seventh graders.

Dudley has no doubts that eliminating grade levels is the chief reason student performance has climbed at Paint Branch. Ironically, because the school does not rely on the bell curve to organize instruction, its students all fall on the high end of the bell curve when they are compared to other students of the same age on norm-referenced tests. But Paint Branch doesn't care how students compare to others of the same age. Instead, teachers focus on whether students are learning the school's knowledge and skill objectives. The school, for example, wants to see every student become a fluent and devoted reader by the time he or she leaves. Teachers can measure this objective every day by listening to students read and by watching their reading habits. All students meet this objective.

"There is not a child down there who does not enjoy reading," Dudley said, nodding toward the group of students who must move on to another school next year because of their ages.

The students do equally well in math. Before they leave Paint Branch, most students are learning introductory algebra—a subject other American children encounter later in middle school, if then.

Paint Branch teachers have built a complicated organization to give students the freedom to advance at their own pace and to some degree along personal learning paths. The 600 students are divided into four groups, each led by a team of teachers. The groups represent four broad steps spanning an academic spectrum that would traditionally be kindergarten to sixth grade, though some advance farther. In the primary team, for example, seven teachers are responsible for 150 students, most between the ages of six and nine. The teachers group the students into homerooms based on reading levels but will regroup students as needed for mathematics, science, and other classes.

Students have a say in when they move to a higher team and in setting academic goals for themselves. Ben Sedlask, seven, who would be a second grader in a conventional school, already has moved to the intermediate team, which includes students through age ten. He has the option of moving still higher because he is ready for mathematics traditionally offered to sixth graders. But Ben is comfortable with his team and has decided he will stay and work more on reading and writing, subjects in which he is not as advanced. Paint Branch teachers are trying to find paths through their scheduling jungle that would allow students like Ben to work with one team in one subject and a different team in another.

By the time they reach the third team, simply called the West Team, students have solid reading skills and are grouped according to their levels in math. Reading is totally individualized for the highest group, the East Team, which is composed mostly of ten- and eleven-year-olds, but the students still work in groups on math. About a third of the team is ready for algebra as the school year begins.

This is not a system of ability grouping. Students are fluidly grouped and regrouped on the basis of what they know and need to learn. But they all are expected sooner or later to acquire knowledge and skill levels that most schools would consider out of reach for poor children. Some Paint Branch students stay at the primary level as long as four years. But once they master the basics, often they advance quickly, skip groups, and catch up with other students their ages.

Students who typically become misfits in conventional schools—the exceptionally bright, slow learners, children with learning disabilities, and others who do not fit bell-curve norms—all seem to fit in at Paint Branch. Students who take Ritalin to control hyperactivity or attention deficit disorders often can give up the drug after a few weeks at the school. In 1987 the school enrolled 300 children, 40 of whom were in special education. Five years later the school enrolled twice as many students, but only eight are classified in special education. And since Paint Branch treats them just like everyone else, these students do not know the system has given them special labels.

Paint Branch is not a quiet school because teachers often have students working in groups on projects or tutoring one another. Rather than the clamor of chaos, however, a pleasant bustle of purpose rolls through the school, similar to what you would find in a busy post office or any thriving marketplace. Children are too busy and engaged to create discipline problems. They're learning.

In the intermediate wing one morning, about sixty children gathered on a rug to hear one teacher read them a story (freeing the other teachers to make plans for later in the day). Among them were Rahman, nine; Ronald, ten; and Kyle, eleven—formerly severe discipline problems at other schools. More challenging academics and the company of mature students is usually all it takes to settle down misbehaving children, Dudley said.

The school's unusual structure fosters other innovations. To work together, teachers often remove the walls separating their classrooms and launch projects that integrate various subjects. Last year, for example, intermediate students spent weeks at a nearby stream, studying how it was being polluted and affecting Chesapeake Bay into which it drained. Lessons in mathematics, geography, history, science, and reading were all rolled together through the project.

Students on the team took first and second on group projects for fourth graders in the district's science fair. The first-place team, dominated by students who would typically be third graders, decided on its own to study the effects of color on heat absorption. The children painted aluminum cans, filled them with water, put them in the sun, measured the temperature increases, and charted the results. The competition was scrapped the following year because the quality of projects from other schools was so poor.

Paint Branch Elementary has abandoned the bell curve and nearly eliminated the Bell-Curve Syndrome. There is no tracking, no under- or overachievers, no failures, no losers, none of that collection of symptoms that make up the syndrome. The disease is dead, and the joy of learning thrives.

Dudley and her staff are drawing on one-room schoolhouse strategies to push the school structure farther from group instruction toward individualized learning. During summer school, her teachers are exploring ways to give students nearly full control over their learning by allowing them to pursue independent study projects.

"We are creating new teaching techniques as we go," said teacher Laith Keane. "My brain never stops anymore. This is the way school should be."

Expanding the Classroom

Children can learn in individualized ways within groups, even diverse ones, as they did in one-room schoolhouses, but not without more options than lectures, worksheets, and textbooks. Group lessons must embody individual choices. A group of students of varying ages, skills, and knowledge, for example, could explore the history and culture of the Cherokee Indians in America by each investigating what interests him or her most about the Cherokee. Each could do research and write about what is learned, whatever his or her skill levels in reading and writing. Class members could then share what they learned through written and oral presentations. In this way students can learn and hone their skills in highly individualized ways while still being part of a group, whether the group is based on age or achievement levels.

Vickie C. Lineberry and other kindergarten teachers began using these practices years ago at Frank Porter Graham Elementary School in Chapel Hill, North Carolina. The teachers design lessons to fit each child as he or she moves among various learning centers within the classroom. While some students read, others learn colors, and still others build a terrarium. Some kindergartners, Lineberry said, are like average three-year-olds, others like average eight-year-olds. Three in one class, for example, can read, and several more are ready to learn to read, while eight others know neither numbers nor the alphabet. Even so, they still can enjoy working together in small groups on fun projects. A group might, for example, make a model of a town. Those able to write could label the streets while those who cannot could mold houses out of clay.[10]

In addition to using learning centers, projects, and trade books in the classroom, teachers also have a wealth of choices outside the classroom—such as museums, institutions, and businesses—where children can learn in the context of their own community. And teachers can tap computer and video technology to give children access to knowledge.

In the one-room schoolhouse, teachers could not take students into a laboratory to practice science with beakers, mail-order frogs, and dissecting needles. So they took their students outside, into the laboratory of nature, to explore science as it revealed itself in the layers of stone on the face of a cliff, the roots of a windblown tree, the meander of a lazy stream, the lakeside tracks of a raccoon, and in a thousand other haunts and hollows. Teachers also tapped their communities for information. They might, for example, take students to a political rally, a town hall meeting, or a trial to study government. Students were encouraged to look beyond the classroom and textbooks for knowledge.

Today a growing number of teachers are encouraging their students to do the same. At Chapel Hill High School in North Carolina, Fred Kiger takes his history classes to Civil War battlefields such as Gettysburg and Antietam.

"History can be black or white," he said. "I want to color it. I want 'em to live it. I want 'em to feel it. I want 'em to smell the smoke, to feel and see the casualties. . . . I'm probably a lousy text-book teacher."[11]

Dan Tilson, 1992 Oregon Teacher of the Year and a fifth-grade teacher at Eastwood Elementary School in the logging community of Roseburg, turned forty-four acres near the school into an outdoor classroom that includes trails, a wetlands, and a fish hatchery. He and his students are using the hatchery to restore fall Chinook salmon runs to a creek near the school. Tilson can easily tie lessons in science, history, reading, and writing to the outdoor project.

"It makes learning more real for students," he says.

Teachers at Dag Hammarskjold School No. 6 in Rochester, New York, have expanded their classrooms to include the entire Genesee River Valley, which spreads from the city south into western New York. The school sends its students on 400 study trips into the valley each year. During early fall of 1991, for example, the fifth and sixth graders spent a week in the 64,000-acre Allegany State Park one hundred miles northeast of Rochester.

Their school day begins at dawn with a bicycle ride along park trails that lead the students past deer, rabbits, and other wild animals. Later the students look through microscopes at the strange world living in a drop of pond water. They use compasses to find their way out of the woods. They visit museums, identify plants, and study the park's geological history. They read about what they see and record their impressions with entries in journals and drawings in sketch pads. As their school hours stretch into darkness, they gaze at the planets and then gather around a campfire. There, as forty pairs of eyes stare dreamily into the flames, a Seneca Indian tells the old story of how the hermit thrush robbed the eagle of a beautiful song.

Teachers discovered they can teach almost anything and tie it to the Genesee River and the wide valley it cut. The school chorus was rehearsing songs about the region for its Christmas program. The special education students have compared the heyday of Seneca Indian communities on the Genesee to the city of Timbuktu that emerged about the same time on the Niger of Africa. Students learn the nation's history by studying their own with visits to the homes and graves of famous Rochester residents such as Harriet Tubman, Susan B. Anthony, and Frederick Douglass. The project has built confidence and camaraderie among inner-city children living in one of the worst neighborhoods in Rochester for drugs, crime, and poverty.

The school has cut suspension rates in half. Attendance has climbed ahead of a dozen other schools in the district, to 93 percent. Test scores climbed 28 percent in reading and 24 percent in mathematics during the first two years of the project. Student attitudes about school improved during the same period, University of Rochester researchers concluded in a study. The enthusiasm of teachers and students, they wrote, "is almost palpable."[12]

Teachers in traditional schools find it easier to deliver their group-oriented instruction in the classroom than to take their charges into the world outside where the group is more difficult to control. The staff at Rochester's school No. 6 managed, but only with special grants and single-minded determination. Even then, most of the instruction continued to be group-oriented.

In an individualized structure like Wallace was trying to build in Vance County, however, teachers would find classroom walls confining and limiting. They would want options to help each child find a fitting learning path. They would seek the learning options beyond the classroom that traditional teachers would be more inclined to avoid. They also would be looking for ways, with or without money, to guide their students into the intriguing labyrinths of computer networks. How could they resist?

Learning Technology

David Barbee will never forget that morning in 1968 when he was showing a group of educators the individualized learning system he helped establish at Syfax Elementary School in southwest Washington, D.C. The group came upon a room where Barbee had set up reading machines designed to help children learn at their own pace. This was before the days of the personal computer. Learning technology was young, and the reading machine was crude. Nevertheless, it provided feedback to the learner, with written prompts of praise and reinforcement as the child advanced. The door was closed to the room, and Barbee peered through the window before going in. He was astonished by what he saw.

A single little girl sat at the machine. No one else was in the room. She had just completed an exercise, and she stood up, leaned forward, and embraced the reading machine in a big hug.

"You could see in that child an appreciation for that responsiveness," said Barbee, recalling the incident twenty-five years later. "That was powerful. It showed me the importance of the responsiveness of the environment for learning."

A child getting little response from teachers in a group-based mass education system found a machine that would give her some personal attention. Barbee, head of the Institute for Technological Solutions, an education consulting firm based in Washington, D.C., has been an advocate of individualized instruction throughout his career. He saw its power as a principal of elementary and secondary schools in Colorado. He developed an individualized system, for example, at Aspen Elementary School, where every child moved at his or her own pace.

"Every child was reading," he said.

The powerful new generations of personal computers can help children tap vast, inviting data banks of information and learning programs. They allow students to study precisely what they want to learn on demand. Barbee naturally turned to technological resources for education because they foster powerfully efficient, responsive, individualized multimedia learning worlds. These machines are like smart assistants there to serve at the command of the learner, he said.

"They will help us do our work for us," he said. "Whatever you can dream, you can do."[13]

A student curious about the neo-Nazi movement in Germany and Europe could quickly retrieve hundreds of articles from magazines and newspapers by sitting down to a computer equipped with a modem and printer. What's more, the computer can serve wherever the student's interests lead. If she wants to know more about Hitler, the roots of the pre–World War II Nazi movement, the Holocaust, or Anne Frank, the computer can retrieve that information within minutes, even seconds. Information technology, which is rapidly becoming less expensive and more accessible, can give the learner both documents and pictures, even moving and speaking pictures stored on digitized laser and compact disks. Children can use computerized encyclopedias that will not only tell them about Adolf Hitler, but also show him giving a speech or meeting with his generals.

International Business Machines Corporation (IBM) produced a software program on a single poem, Alfred, Lord Tennyson's poem, "Ulysses," to illustrate the potential of a model for restructured learning that the company calls knowledge navigation. A computer equipped with a laser disk and mouse provides the text of the poem and a rich menu offering a multitude of paths to explore its meaning, context, style, history, and applications. Learners can watch six different actors read the poem with different interpretations and see six literary professors give their interpretations of it. They can see how the poem compares to rap music and Haiku poetry, get background lessons on the Trojan war and Ulysses' life, and watch Bill Moyers and Joseph Campbell discuss the meaning of the hero. They can watch Ted Kennedy recite the poem at the 1980 Democratic convention. The options go on. The computer allows students, as Tennyson says in the poem, "To follow knowledge, like a sinking star, / Beyond the utmost bound of human thought."[14]

The IBM prototype requires expensive equipment, but similar systems are being developed that will cost far less. David Boulton, head of DIACOM Technologies, Inc., in Aptos, California, has created the software for what he calls a general-purpose electronic learner-oriented environment projected to cost about $200. Boulton has created a framework that allows learners to explore any body of knowledge in a variety of ways according to their "meaning needs." The computer system responds to a learner's curiosity, learning style, and achievement level.[15] A student might begin, for example, probing the Renaissance, run into Galileo, become interested in history of science, and end up watching Albert Einstein discuss his general theory of relativity. Like the IBM prototype, Boulton's system integrates sound, text, and pictures.

Boulton created his system after watching and recording three- to five-year-olds play Nintendo. He concluded that the electronic game engaged them with cycles of challenges, usually some menace such as attack bats in a castle, and a variety of solutions to overcome those challenges, such as trapdoors and weapons. The game steadily increased the speed and rigor of the challenges as the player developed skills and advanced from one level to the next. Boulton designed his learning system to engage students with challenges that they can solve by taking a variety of learning paths. Like Nintendo, it allows children to act creatively upon their frustrations.

Responsiveness is the key, Boulton says. The machine can respond to each individual's "meaning needs" with a scope and precision that classroom teachers could never find time for, he says. Students quickly begin suppressing personal needs for meaning in traditional classrooms, because their teachers can't possibly meet them. Gaining understanding in school is like trying to learn to swim in the desert, Bolton believes. To learn, the student must be immersed in the water of knowledge and feel it respond to individual probes and strokes. Without this water, there is no feedback, no way for learners to draw conclusions from their inquiries.

"Our education system is fundamentally, tacitly teaching us to ignore the core of our capacity for learning," Boulton says. "It is an insidious process we don't recognize."

Boulton is testing his system in two classrooms in the Cupertino School District near San Jose, California. His product is being developed to run initially on Macintosh, Apple II, and IBM-clone personal computers, but eventually he hopes it will become part of home multimedia systems and compatible with game machines such as Nintendo and Sega. As more and more people have access to this technology, a learning-oriented culture will emerge, Boulton predicts. Schools will specialize in team learning and dialogue, he says, and allow machines to provide the "one-on-one relationship between an individual and what he is learning about."

A growing number of educators like Boulton believe the primary mission of schools should no longer be to convey knowledge but to help children develop their capacity to learn. Children soon will be able to tap whatever knowledge they need just about anywhere.

Emerging plans to link television, telephone, and computer networks through fiber optic cables into information highways promise to put vast reservoirs of knowledge at the fingertips of the masses. The North Carolina government is contracting with the state's three biggest phone companies to connect the information pools of all government enterprises, including schools and colleges, by the end of 1995. This will allow a student in one school to tap a class in another and even ask questions of the distant teacher. Soon, researchers say, electronic information will be on tap in the average home. *Newsweek* magazine describes it this way.

> Simply put, the ultimate promise is this: a huge amount of information available to anyone at the touch of a button, everything from airline schedules to esoteric scientific journals to video versions of off-off-off Broadway. . . . consumers would be like information "cowboys," rounding up data from computer-based archives and information services. There will be thousands of "channels" delivered through some combination of cable, telephone, satellite and cellular networks. To prevent getting trampled by a stampede of data, viewers will rely on programmed electronic selectors that would go into the info corral and rope in the subjects the viewer wants.[16]

Lewis J. Perelman, a scientist and educational technology consultant, says the new wave of learning technology provides information at unprecedented speed and scope. More important, he says, it delivers to the learner information with the sight, sound, and, in the case of computer-simulated environments called virtual reality, even physical experience of real-world contexts. This produces, he says, "an unprecedented degree of connectedness of knowledge, experience, media and brains, both human and nonhuman," that teachers and textbooks cannot match.

"We have the technology today to enable virtually anyone who is not severely handicapped to learn anything, at a 'grade A' level, anywhere, anytime," he writes.[17]

That technology may make homework more important and learning at school more limited, observes Theodore Sizer of Brown University. "The differences among children could be far more readily addressed, and the school site could become a place more of tutoring, seminars and laboratory work than a place in which to pass on information," he writes.[18]

Departures from textbook-based group instruction to community- and computer-based individualized learning, however, demand new roles for both teachers and students. Children must become active learners. Education leaders can no longer view children as so many passive, empty heads, like bottles in a soda factory, waiting to have teachers dump knowledge into them as they pass. Students must take command of their learning, enter the rapidly growing garden of knowledge, and learn how to harvest whatever their heads need to carry. Teachers should be their guides, helping them cut suitable paths through this garden, whether that means a trip to the library, work on a computer, a hike in the woods, or a shift shadowing a county social worker. In Vance County, Wallace called this Guided Learning.

By rejecting group-oriented instructional practices, she hoped to create the more flexible system teachers and students need for Guided Learning. Clear, high standards would define their destination. Wallace was throwing open shutters and doors and letting new light into an old, musty house. No longer would teachers be forced to compare and sort children; no longer would students be forced to conform. They'd be free to explore a multitude of learning paths that could take them to the mountaintop of knowledge.

Wallace's Plan

Betty Wallace called her liberating plan a loose-tight organization. The tight part was the framework: performance standards and the elimination of grades and grade levels. It also included the many state and practical requirements that a public school system could not abandon immediately. In a purely individualized system, children would have full control over their learning. A school would be just one of many sources of knowledge. Children might choose to spend the morning at their personal computer at home, the day in the library, or the week on the job in an uncle's printing business. That kind of flexibility, however, would have to come with time. In the short term, Wallace would focus on burying the bell curve. At least at first, children could not choose their school, the hours they attended it, or the times when they would have to arrive, eat lunch, and depart. They would still face rules of conduct, attendance, and course work. Teachers would still need to keep records, monitor hallways, and coach plays and sports.

Within these constraints, however, teachers and students would have new freedoms that constituted the loose part of Wallace's plan. Schools would be required to remove any obstacles that kept students from advancing toward the benchmarks. Faculties at each school would be free to organize their schools and instruction however they saw fit to meet that requirement. The central office would focus on providing the staff training in individualized instruction, or Guided Learning. The plan would empower teachers, giving them more control over instruction and a role in shaping the Vance County education revolution. Wallace hoped empowered teachers would be more committed to carrying out change. Students would discover they had new authority too. They would be free to advance in school as fast as they could learn.

Freedom, however, would come more slowly to Vance County's two high schools. They were too deeply mired in traditional practices to dislodge themselves swiftly. They would have to deal, for example, with the tangle of college admission standards. Admission officers relied heavily on the bell curve, sorting students on the basis of their grade point averages, class rank, and scores on College Board entrance exams such as the Scholastic Assessment Test. The high schools would have to replace course requirements with learning outcomes that would satisfy the state Board of Education and college admission officers. Wallace decided to give the high schools one to two years to eliminate grade levels and reorganize as more liquid institutions with high graduation standards. Students eventually would be able to move through high school at their own pace. Once they met the required learning objectives, whether in two years or five, they could pick up their diplomas and move on to higher education in college or technical schools. They would all be qualified to do both.

Wallace envisioned high schools looking more like colleges. Students could take physics whenever they chose. An American literature course might meet just once a week while calculus would meet daily. If students already knew the material offered in a given course, they could skip it. They might prove their knowledge through various performance indicators such as portfolios, essay and short-answer tests, or oral exams before a faculty review board. Wallace hated that change in high schools would take so much time, but she had to be realistic. For the time being, she'd have to settle for the mammoth job of getting the rest of the district's students ready for high school.

The lower schools in the first quarter developed flexible structures for grouping children—all variations of the staircase structure. They grouped children with teams of teachers, each team representing a step or achievement level. Each teacher within a team taught a different subject. Most teams also sorted their own students by achievement levels. The language arts specialist, for example, would teach students grouped at one achievement level one period and others grouped at a different level the next. Children, then, climbed the staircase within the team before taking the larger step to the next team.

At all levels in all schools, teachers were encouraged to individualize instruction through learning centers, projects, community-based ventures, peer tutoring, and other practices of the one-room schoolhouse. Where possible, teachers also were encouraged to use computers and to blend subjects.

In a fluid system where children are being regrouped continuously, students will encounter many teachers, even in their primary years. This concerned Wallace. She knew some young children feel more secure working with fewer adults for an entire school year or, more ideally, for many years. This need could be addressed in part by trying to match children with the same team of teachers for several years. But that was possible only for some teams in some schools. So Wallace decided that each student needed an adult advocate who would carefully monitor his or her progress year after year throughout elementary school. Every school would divide its students among all of its professional adults—teachers, administrators, counselors, librarians, speech therapists, and so forth. Each of these adults would become an advocate for the same group of ten to twelve students year after year. The advocate would be responsible for ensuring that no group member strayed from a productive learning path.

Vance County educators summarized the plan in one mission

statement and nine goals that could be easily conveyed and sold to
students, teachers, and parents in the community. The mission
statement said simply. "Vance County School System is committed
to educating all children for productive global citizenship in the
twenty-first century." To fulfill that mission, the system would
adopt learning goals, embrace guided learning, abandon grades and
grade levels, designate student advocates, and set high expectations
for attendance and student achievement in core courses. Schools
also would cultivate student appreciation for the arts, vocational
skills, and healthful living. Each school would be encouraged to
enlist the help of parents and students in organizing as it saw fit.
The new structure gave everyone in Vance County a part to play in
delivering their teachers and children from the ravages of the Bell-
Curve Syndrome.[19]

Keeping Track

Like democracy, an individualized education system can be messy.
In many ways it is easier to manage a graded system, which is one
reason schools have been grouping children by age for the past 150
years. But an individualized system need not be as complicated as it
might seem, particularly with the aid of today's powerful and affordable computers.

The big advantage of an individualized organization geared to
learning goals is that it delivers teachers and students from the dark
consequences of practices rooted in bell-curve assumptions. There
is far less need, for example, to provide special remedial, gifted and
talented, and psychological services. An individualized plan such as
Vance County's makes room in the mainstream system for just
about every child. Administrators are freed from the headaches of
trying to find special services for large numbers of classified children. Paint Branch Elementary enjoys this benefit.

Second, a system in which children are continuously changing
groups as their educational needs change takes on a life of its own
that really requires no action from the central office. If a child, for
example, moves from one team of teachers to another, the transac-
tion is handled by the team, not the principal. As students move
throughout the system, teachers adjust and readjust. The school

organization is in constant flux but, at the same time, under professional control.

The main organizational challenge of the central administration is to keep track of where children are in the school and to chart their progress on their educational journeys toward the learning goals. For this job, Betty Wallace turned to the computer. An electronic record would be kept on every child. Each time a child fulfilled an objective, say understanding the elements of fiction, a teacher would record the achievement on the child's computer record. Any teacher or administrator could immediately call up a child's computer record and see how far he or she progressed toward the learning objectives. Eventually, as the system became more sophisticated, Wallace envisioned keeping samples and pictures of student writing, math problem solving, art projects, and other work—a sort of electronic portfolio—in student records. The computer also would be able to present student progress toward benchmarks with bar graphs that would give teachers and parents an instant glimpse of what objectives the student had mastered and what still needed to be learned.

Wallace was converting a system based on the old factory model of production into one based on principles of the modern high-performance workplace: just-in-time delivery, instant flexibility, and zero defects.

The Cost of Change

The Vance County Public School System operated on a general fund budget of about $35 million when Wallace took the helm in 1991. Two years later, after she had put most of her plan for change into place, the district was operating on the same $35 million budget. Wallace would win a $1.65 million grant from the state to help her carry out her school improvement plans, but that was offset by reductions in other state and local revenue. Still, she managed to overhaul the school system. It is a myth in public education that change or improvement must cost more money. It is also a myth that spending more will necessarily improve schools. Studies repeatedly have failed to show a relationship between school spending and student achievement. Between 1980 and 1990, the national average per-pupil spending in constant 1990–91 dollars climbed by $1,479, or 35 percent, to $5,748 with negligible increases in student performance.[20]

While there were costs associated with Wallace's attempt to pry Vance County schools away from old practices, these were offset by accompanying savings. A more fluid, outcomes-based system, for example, will reduce and eventually all but eliminate high school dropouts, which drives up costs. But it also will allow at least some students to move through the system in fewer years, reducing costs. On balance, Wallace concluded, the new system was cheaper largely because it used resources more efficiently. The district no longer bought hundreds of textbooks, for example, that failed to fit the needs of large numbers of children.

Probably the biggest expense in carrying out school change is preparing administrators and teachers to make the transition. Wallace was able to cover a large measure of these costs by using money the district regularly budgeted for ongoing staff development. She also drew heavily on her old employer, the state Department of Public Instruction, for free help. And she persuaded colleagues elsewhere in the region to share their expertise for nominal fees.

The other primary expenses of reorganizing into a flexible system with learning goals lie in developing standards, designing ways to measure whether students meet those standards, and tracking students. Schools also must invest in computers and more varied instructional materials when they focus on individuals rather than groups.

Many of these costs, however, can be covered with savings elsewhere. Much of the thousands of dollars a district like Vance County typically would spend each year on textbooks, for example, can be spent on books and computer supplies more suitable for an individualized system. In abandoning bell-curve assumptions about achievement, the system also can reduce costs associated with tracking and a variety of special education services ranging from federal remedial programs to gifted and talented classes. Because a flexible structure with high standards works better, discipline problems diminish, reducing costs of heavy supervision. Finally, teachers in individualized schools are more inclined to use community members, supplies, and settings to provide more learning options for their students. This, in effect, brings donated resources and help into the school system.

Extra money, of course, can help smooth the transition when a district embarks on deep structural change. But Wallace managed to carry out two difficult years of change without extra money. If she could do it in a poor system like Vance County's, most other districts in the nation should be able to do the same.

What About Those Children Who Don't Make It?

The big question all parents have about a system focused on high standards is, what happens if a child fails to reach them? Surely not all children will make it, they say. As we've shown in earlier chapters, generations have grown up in our culture believing that only some people are smart enough to do well in school. And the Bell-Curve Syndrome ensures that only some do. But eliminate the syndrome, set high expectations for all children, and they all will meet them.

An individualized, nongraded system eliminates the frustrations typical of the traditional system, improving children's attitudes and motivations to learn. The only children who will not learn in a system like this are those who suffer from brain damage or, in some cases, severe social problems that make it impossible for them to focus on their schoolwork. The large numbers of children unfavorably compared in traditional schools—those labeled slow or learning disabled—largely disappear in an individualized system. Nearly all children find their stride and a productive path to success that in itself is reward enough to push them on. As David Barbee said, every child became a strong reader in the Aspen, Colorado, elementary school where instruction was individualized. Principal Linda Dudley said that in five years at the ungraded Paint Branch Elementary School, she did not know of a single child who took longer than four years to become a reader and graduate to the second level. Some did so in one year. Further, she said, every single student who leaves Paint Branch can read and do mathematics on at least the level deemed suitable for average sixth graders and, in most cases, higher. This is true even for some children who would have been assigned to special education services in other schools.

Should a child stall academically, however, it becomes readily apparent in a system that focuses on individuals rather than groups. And with fewer students needing special help, the system has more resources to help those who do. If a school discovers a child is struggling in school because of abuse at home, for example, it can bring in intense help immediately—teachers, counselors, social workers, psychologists, and the child's advocate. The schools also can provide one-on-one help for any child who gets bumped off a productive learning path.

Even after a district parts with the bell curve, however, the effects of the past linger during the first years of transition. Students heavily wounded by the syndrome will lack confidence and drive and have trouble meeting high standards. Those used to being promoted each year with their age group will be inclined to look at themselves as failures if they do not advance as fast as their peers. The new habits and values of an individualized system will not prevail immediately.

This posed political problems for Wallace in Vance County. Some students reached the age when they traditionally could be expected to leave middle school, for example, but they had not yet reached the middle-school benchmarks. Holding them back until they mastered the objectives startled both students and their parents. The ages of students become more mixed, however, as a gradeless system takes hold. Then it becomes less apparent and important to students that others the same age are advancing faster, just as it is rarely an issue in the Boy Scouts. What does matter to students is that they master knowledge and advance. They will focus more on the learning objectives than on how they compare to their peers. Some children will be content to take longer than others to make their way up the staircase, but they all will make it. By the time they reach high school, they all will be prepared to read Shakespeare, study trigonometry, write persuasive essays, and handle other work at the high school level.

Even the best plan can go awry if improperly executed, however, and Wallace knew she didn't have much time. People would grow impatient with the turmoil of change quickly unless it yielded fruit.

CHAPTER 5

▼

LAUNCHING CHANGE IN VANCE COUNTY

Betty Wallace drove her gray Buick through a neighborhood served by Pinkston Street Elementary School. It was a typically hot, moist July afternoon, only days since she arrived in Vance County, and the air felt heavy. The car rolled down narrow streets lined with small, clapboard houses flaking paint like dry skin. Small yards were scuffed with patches of dirt. These were the homes of the district's most disadvantaged children.

Wallace imagined how, given the means, she would restore that neighborhood. She had moonlighted over the years fixing up old houses and reselling them for profit. She and her son restored several abused houses, the last located in the Five Points neighborhood of Raleigh. She would soon buy a neglected home under big pines on an acre in Vance County's upscale Country Club neighborhood with plans to do the same. I'd love to try some of my handiwork here, she thought as she glided by those withering homes of the Pinkston Street kids. She imagined them all painted in pastels, surrounded by junipers and fruit trees, enclosed by white picket fences topped with wooden pineapples and connected by brick walkways. It could be a wonderful neighborhood, she thought, a Southern version of Sesame Street.

Even then, it was in many ways a good place for children. Families were still important there, though more than half of them were finding it increasingly difficult to stay together. Neighbors knew one another. They talked, met on the streets and in the churches and businesses scattered through the neighborhood.

This community, however, also wrestled with more than its share of drugs, unemployment, and stress. Drug use and sales seemed to be growing more prevalent by the week, especially in the projects. Though warned not to, Wallace drove by the Beacon Light and North Henderson Heights apartments, government housing where many of the Pinkston Street children learned the names of drugs before they learned their colors, letters, or numbers. She saw little in those hard-edged, barren buildings that boded well for kids. They stood silent and empty; no one was outside in this heat. The scene seemed out of context, surreal, like a Salvador Dali painting. Wallace imagined one of Dali's clock faces melting over the metal second-story handrails of the apartment buildings. How different these sterile buildings seemed from the fertile timeless countryside that spilled away from Henderson in rolling green hills.

Pinkston Street teachers said some of their students were being employed as drug holders for adults. The kids carried drugs in case their parents' apartments or homes were raided. Some children also packed gold jewelry and rolls of $20 bills worth hundreds of dollars. Some of them knew how to distinguish between real and imitation gold. Teachers also saw children who were wounded by their parents' drug and alcohol abuse. These children develop slower, have trouble concentrating, and are often hyperactive.

Pinkston Elementary School was failing its many poor children with traditional educational practices that compared them to their more advantaged peers and relegated them to the dark side of the bell curve. Wallace was hardly surprised that they occupied the basement of academic performance. Seeing these bleak images of their lives in this worn neighborhood fed her sense of urgency. Traditional education would never help these children, she thought, but scrap the bell curve and they had a fighting chance, as would millions of other inner-city and rural poor children like them.

She stopped at the Buy-Rite produce market, picked out a sweet-smelling cantaloupe, took a place in the checkout line, pulled a copy of the *Henderson Daily Dispatch* off a rack, and pondered the headline: SUPERINTENDENT SEEKS MASSIVE SCHOOL CHANGE.

Well, I have gone and done it now, and there is no going back, she thought.

This is the way she felt when the doctor told her she was pregnant.

The poverty she had just witnessed in the projects posed enormous challenges for her and her plan, not only in hardening children, but in other ways, too. While the district had a new high school and a new elementary school under construction, many of its other buildings were old and substandard. There was no money to fix let alone replace them.

It was not always so. Tobacco and cotton entrepreneurs created the county's first public school system in 1899, and through World War II prominent business and civic leaders dominated the school board and county board of commissioners, which controlled local funding for schools. But after the divisive labor turmoil of the 1950s and desegregation battles in the 1960s, prominent residents played less and less of a role in the public schools. Control over the schools slowly slipped into the hands of small businessmen and small-town politicians who had little background in finance, planning, and policymaking. Public confidence and, subsequently, support began to erode as the local economy gradually declined. Since the mid-1960s, Vance County's per-capita spending on its schools ranked among the lowest in the state.

Wallace's central office was divided between two old, deteriorating buildings about a mile apart. Half her central staff, including Laura Joyner, her community relations director, were in a two-story, turn-of-the-century brick school with creaky oiled wooden floors. They called the building the Chestnut Street Annex. It had deteriorated to the point of being condemned, yet people were allowed to keep working inside. Bats living in the attic had stained the eaves and gutters with their droppings, which could not be removed because of the asbestos in the attic and walls. Wallace's office was in the other building, which early in the century served as a teacherage, a dormitory for local female teachers. In a small, second-story corner bedroom, she set up her office with a big desk and a computer, which she kept feathered with scores of yellow stick-em notes. The old air conditioner in the window was so noisy she had to turn it off to use the telephone.

Deep Traditions

To Wallace, the district's shabby buildings were not as daunting as its rigid traditions. During her first weeks in Vance County, she saw evidence of the Bell-Curve Syndrome everywhere. Group lectures and textbook-based instruction were the norm, principals admitted. Students of the same age were grouped together, they said, and taught the same thing at the same time from the same books as if all were at exactly the same point in their educational journeys.

Changing education in Vance County ultimately would depend less on buildings and money and more on committed teachers and principals, Wallace recognized. So during her first weeks on the job, she began looking for professionals willing to join her mission. She found plenty.

John Streb, principal of E. M. Rollins Elementary School, which served the district's most affluent students, warmed immediately to Wallace's proposal to eliminate traditional uses of the bell curve.

"Multiage classrooms would work better than what we have now," the tall, sturdy, former Green Beret soldier told her. He agreed that it made sense to narrow the range of achievement in each classroom to a workable span for each teacher. The range now was wide, with nonreaders mixed with students ready for middle school, all in the fifth grade. Teachers were growing increasingly frustrated as the economic and cultural diversity of the district continued to broaden, he said.

Carver Elementary principal William Mueller, whom Wallace soon brought to the central office as head of personnel and testing, was frustrated by the absence of technology in schools. He understood how computers could be used both as powerful teaching aids and management tools to individualize instruction. "There is a whole world out there, and we are not part of it," Mueller said.

L. B. Yancey Elementary School, one of the district's poorest schools in an industrial section of Henderson, had major problems, Principal Winston Kerley conceded. But the community clung to tradition like cotton on burlap.

"The expectation is that you improve the school, but you are not to change anything," a frustrated Kerley said with a sigh. "Would you believe that the greatest compliment paid this school in a decade has been that we cleared away a trash dump next door and graveled it for a parking lot? People could see that as progress, but progress in learning is harder to point out."

Many of the school's parents had had such bad experiences

themselves as students that they mistrusted the school and did not expect much from it for their children. General behavior problems in the 500-student school were growing so rapidly, Kerley said, that all children were getting less and less of what they needed individually.

"We just bowl down the middle, and hope the bright kids and the slower kids get a little of what they need," said Kerley, who, Wallace later learned, was a strong advocate for exceptional children.

After a two-hour talk with Kerley, Wallace was convinced she could count on Yancey Elementary's support in her crusade. Principal by principal, she scoured her school district for talented leaders whom she could put in key spots to help carry out her changes. She was pleased by the abundance of talent she found even in this remote, rural district. All school districts probably have their share of gifted leaders, but the system often prevents even the best from blossoming. Wallace would soon show her community just how talented its leaders could be when they parted ways with the bell curve.

Within her first six weeks in Vance County, Wallace had met with every one of her principals individually and in meetings with the central office curriculum and instruction staff. She wanted to be sure everyone knew where she was headed. Her aim was to remove her schools from the grips of the bell curve. That mission was not negotiable, but details of carrying it out were. Principals and teachers would be blazing the trail. Administrators needed to understand why they needed to steer this course. During a meeting in mid-August, Wallace urged her principals and central office staff to move forward as quickly as possible with her four-tiered plan to eliminate grade levels, grades, and destructive comparisons.

Most were skeptical but at the same time willing to accept that maybe, just maybe, schools could improve by parting with the bell curve. Wallace also suspected there were a few who thought she was naive or just plain crazy. Some principals had already seen five superintendents come and go. They were reluctant to go through the turmoil of change only to see Wallace up and leave too. "There are some who feel 'We'll just wait her out,' " said Rollins principal John Streb.

Teachers also had reservations. "We have gone through so many plans and you'd think, 'Oh, Lord, here we go again,' " recalled Diane Koontz, a primary teacher at Vance County who later became a firm believer in the changes.

Despite their doubts, the elementary principals agreed to eliminate grade levels and try some innovative teaching approaches. They were less comfortable banishing letter grades. They feared teachers would not be ready to construct mastery-based report cards soon enough to use them at the beginning of the year. That was a reasonable concern, and Wallace assured them they could take more time if they needed it. Yet she urged them all to press forward as quickly as they could.

Following a principals' meeting, Wallace returned to her office and already had a phone call waiting from Principal Nita Henderson at Clark Street Elementary School, a neighborhood bordering Pinkston Street. Henderson was calling from her own faculty meeting. Surrounded by teachers, she said she and her staff immediately wanted to carry out all of Wallace's proposals for change, including the development of mastery-based report cards. Wallace had not expected such enthusiasm. Perhaps Henderson's teachers sensed they were getting a rare chance to try something truly different. They also probably saw it as a fleeting chance, given the turnover in superintendents in recent years. In any case, Henderson's teachers had concluded they'd rather risk change than endure more stagnation. Wallace could hear them talking excitedly in the background as the principal described their plans for reorganizing into teams and departments. Nothing was more precious to Wallace than this enthusiasm. This was the engine that could send Vance County schools zooming down the fast track to change.

Days later, however, Wallace inadvertently curbed that exuberance by being overly blunt in a speech to the district's teachers on their opening day of work. She said that little science was taught in the county or in many other places in North Carolina, and test scores reflected that observation. Everybody had their desks in rows, she said. Her comments offended those who were teaching science and trying new instructional approaches. Other teachers asked, "How does she know these things? She's brand new," recalled William Mueller. The speech inadvertently alienated teachers, agreed Laura Joyner. "That really hurt what she tried to do in the beginning."

Wallace had wanted to make it clear to teachers that business as usual was over, that the district's status at the bottom of the state and nation was unacceptable. But she later conceded that she should have been more tactful. At a meeting with parents one evening later that month, her approach was less forthright.

Spreading the Word

On a steamy Monday night in late August, Wallace and three dozen parents stood on the dimly lit lawn outside the Vance County Courthouse talking about the education revolution. Lightning flashed in the distance, and an occasional blast of thunder ripped overhead. Up in the darkness loomed the shadowy form of a Confederate soldier high on his pedestal. The parents had hoped they could tell the board their concerns about Wallace's plan, but Board chairman Eugene Gupton said there was no room on the agenda for parents that evening. So after the parents filed out of the second-floor courtroom and gathered on the lawn, they approached Wallace as she too left the meeting. They asked her if she would talk to them, and so, for the next two hours, they talked.

The parents were skeptical of the school improvement plan Wallace had been pushing for the previous month in Rotary and country club meetings, church gatherings, school cafeterias, newspaper and radio interviews—anywhere she could find an audience. Most of the parents had children in E. M. Rollins Elementary School, the county's historically elite school. Though just over half of Rollins's students were black, not a single nonwhite face appeared among this group. The parents present saw no reason to change the status quo because it was serving their children well. Their children were the top achievers in the county, and now here came this flashy new superintendent with big plans to turn their children into guinea pigs. Wallace understood their anxiety and fielded their questions deftly.

What these parents didn't know was that even Rollins's test scores were low compared to the rest of North Carolina and the nation. If their children's test scores looked good, it was only because those of others in the county were so grim. Some parents refused to believe it. So Wallace reached into her armful of files and papers and pulled out test scores—she had begun carrying them with her everywhere because so many residents seemed satisfied with their children's achievement. As elsewhere in the nation, many Vance County parents, especially the more affluent, believed that other schools were having academic problems, but not their children's neighborhood school, thank God. Wallace showed the parents the school's test scores and high rates of absenteeism. She described to them the low countywide scores and the high dropout and teen pregnancy rates. The parents mulled over the sobering statistics and then began questioning her plan to change them.

The superintendent described how an ungraded system with clear learning objectives would allow students to move at their own pace and enjoy continuous success. Wouldn't disruptive students monopolize the teachers' time, shortchanging other students in need of guidance in this individualized system? asked one man.

"Students are discipline problems because they're in a situation where they don't have a snowball's chance in hell of succeeding," Wallace said. "I have never seen a student who feels successful, even slightly successful, who is a discipline problem."

What about the social problems created when a bright student advances swiftly and ends up in a classroom of eighteen-year-olds? asked another man.

"Right now, for every child we move along too fast, we hold back five thousand," Wallace replied.[1]

Two hours passed, and near midnight, a thundershower brought the meeting to a close. The bone-weary Wallace dragged herself home to her apartment, grabbed a few hours sleep, and rose to put in another eighteen hours spreading the word.

In this painstaking manner, fielding question by question at meeting after meeting, Wallace slowly built the foundation of community awareness and acceptance she needed to carry out her plan. For her first several months in Vance County, her time was not her own. She met with teachers, principals, and other staff members during the day and with community groups at night. Rarely did she do more than sleep in her apartment. During her first four months in Vance County, she and key members of her staff spent sixty-three nights meeting with various groups.

"She was in her evangelical phase: a combination of a Billy Graham crusade and a political campaign," recalled Mueller, who often joined her on the circuit. "She would speak to any group that asked her to come."

Wallace distributed thousands of copies of fliers, newsletters, and her tract: "Welcome to the Revolution: How We Can Break Out of the Bell-Curve Syndrome and Revitalize Vance County Schools with Outcome-Based Education." She carried these in her car and passed them out wherever she went, even the supermarket and laundry. She granted dozens of interviews to the *Henderson Daily Dispatch* and local radio stations. Wallace knew that before she could carry out changes to better educate Vance County's children, she had to educate their parents. Some clearly had misconceptions. On a local radio talk show, for example, Wallace fielded a question from an anonymous caller who had just been to an OB-GYN clinic and wondered if that had any connection to outcome-based education, or OBE.

"I want to know if OBE has anything to do with birth control," said the caller, "and if it does, I am against it."

Wallace was seeking what she called cultural permission to fight the bell curve. Without it, she was lost. Earning cultural permission meant more than convincing her staff and the community to accept change—they must grow to expect and, finally, demand change. Only when everyone refused to settle for anything less than the eradication of the bell curve could she be assured of success. Wallace had studied the politics of cultural permission for her doctoral thesis. Further, she had plenty of practical experience in politics, both in the state Department of Public Instruction and in the Democratic Party. In 1984, she and nine other Democrats ran for the U.S. Senate. She knew she would not win after former Gov. Terry Sanford entered the race, but she was not a quitter. She figured that by running she could get some recognition that might open doors for her in the future. And doors did open. In 1986 she was elected to a two-year term as secretary of the Democratic Party, and she later was reelected for a second term. She was not naive. By the time she became superintendent of the Vance County schools, she knew that to be successful, she must be not only an effective instructional leader, but also a strong and shrewd political leader.

Nowhere was political savvy more important than Vance County, where people clung so stubbornly to old ways that they were endangering their future—not that they had such a glorious past. The county did not even have a respectable birthright. Through history, it had been parts of eight other counties, and at one time it had belonged to Virginia. In 1881, two years after former North Carolina Governor Zebulon Baird Vance had been elected to the U.S. Senate, he carved Vance County out of three larger neighboring counties as a political favor to the state Democratic Party. Most blacks at the time voted solidly Republican and clearly dominated Warren County. But control in Granville and Franklin counties teetered between Republicans and Democrats. So Vance created the new county out of the areas dominated by Republicans, that is, blacks. While the Democrats would lose the new county to the Republicans, they would easily take control of what remained of Granville and Franklin counties. In short, the Democrats got two for one. Although the legislature named the county Vance created as a Republican throwaway after him, he called it "Zeb's black baby."[2]

Over the next century, Vance County became the wayward child of the region, an insecure teenager with a bellyful of bitterness. Too much of the county's cruel past, stretching from slavery to labor wars, weighed on the present. Shadows of a yeoman's aristocracy survived in the country club, modest old plantation houses, and all-white academies. Next to these thrived a deviant subculture dominated by poverty, drugs, violence, illiteracy, and teenage pregnancy. A mean streak ran through the county in a wall of distrust that separated haves and have-nots, blacks and whites, natives and newcomers. Residents viewed compromise and diplomacy, sometimes even civility, as expressions of weakness. So in their grim pretense of strength, residents remained divided and let their county languish. One week Wallace found herself speaking to a black congregation in a hot country church; the next she was addressing a predominantly white crowd of businesspeople in the air-conditioned Henderson County Club. Rarely were her audiences mixed.

She visited the country club at the invitation of the Rotary, which met there at 7:30 P.M. each Tuesday for dinner. The black congregation had more sympathy for Wallace's plan than these Rotarians, because most black children were struggling on the low end of the bell curve. The Rotarians leaned toward the status quo because their more advantaged children, like those of the parents Wallace had met on the courthouse lawn, tended to perform above average and draw accolades on the high end of the curve. Why change and risk spoiling their children's future? For some of them, this debate over change was all academic since they sent their children to either the private Kerr-Vance Academy or the Episcopal school across the Virginia line.

Before hearing Wallace, these businessmen and women in their expensive and comfortably outdated conservative suits gathered around good food spread among flowers on white linen tablecloths. Their handshakes were warm and calculatingly firm, and their interest in education genuine. During dinner they talked about the club's new chef and his cooking, the erratic stock market, the upcoming presidential election, economic development around Kerr Lake, the local cotton and tobacco markets, and the tragedy of Brazil using cheap labor to produce Italian loafers.

During dinner Wallace sat near Bennett Perry, a civic-minded lawyer who inherited one of the last surviving privately owned plantations in the county. Perry sat on boards of the library and other service groups. He was as committed to the community as the black church leaders who invited her to speak, Wallace thought. Though they lived worlds apart, citizens such as Perry and the church leaders all wanted the same things for the county's children. If they could set aside their differences, they could find common ground in something other than their inability to communicate.

When her time came to talk, Wallace stood at the polished oak podium and described how the bell curve was misused in schools. Her audience listened politely with perplexed but pleasant expressions. She shifted gears, she later recalled, and gave a less technical, more forthright speech about like this:

> I'm trying to get you to move away from striving for mediocrity. The rest of the world is going to bring change to Vance County. We can't stop it and should

not want to stop it. But we can reach out our arms and embrace it, and we can mold it, and we can even come to value it. The issue is whether we control it ourselves and whether we can make it the kind of change we want. And, you know, in the final analysis, a few years from now we might even come to like it.

Pretend this is a political campaign, though I am not asking you to support anything now, except perhaps a recognition of the problem. I want you to listen to what we have to say, to learn all you can about how we want to revolutionize our schools, and then, and only then, will we ask you to give a thumbs up or thumbs down.

Wallace wanted to give people a say in her plan. Given time to consider it, she believed they would warm to its commonsense logic. Some business leaders already had. Even before she came, they recognized the need for change in Vance County. They could see time running out. Too many junkyards and low-rent trailer parks dotted the landscapes where plantations once thrived. Too many children were moving elsewhere to raise their families.

By the early 1980s, major businesses in the area, such as Roses Stores and Harriet and Henderson Yarns, began to feel the sting of substandard education. They could not recruit the talented executives and managers they needed to keep competitive because the candidates did not want to send their children to Vance County schools. Doctors and other professional residents moved out of the county, even if they continued working in it, because of the substandard schools. Alarmed business leaders managed to pass an $18 million bond issue over the opposition of the county commissioners, who to this day continue to begrudge more spending on schools. Business leaders were so concerned, in fact, that they braved a rare alliance and joined forces with young black professionals to push for better schools. By the time Wallace arrived, this new and tentative partnership had made little progress. But its members were eager to back her plan.

One of these supporters was Marshall Y. Cooper, Jr., fifth-generation owner of Harriett and Henderson Yarns, son of the man who stubbornly resisted the union during labor battles of the 1950s. Cooper, Jr., kept the company strong and competitive by modernizing it with computer-controlled looms. As technology advanced, so did the educational demands on his workers.

"In the past we did not want educated mill workers," Cooper told Wallace one day. "We even called them mill hands, and we calculated how many hands we needed to staff the mills. We wanted them to check their brains at the door. Now times have changed."

Now the mills were so technologically advanced that Cooper needed brains, not hands—highly literate people with technical expertise to manage the computerized operations. Later Cooper would chair an advisory board that would help the district set standards for high school graduates.

In 1990 the Vance County Commission and local industries created the AdVance Strategic Planning Commission to revitalize the county's economy. The panel quickly recognized that improving public schools would have to be a major part of the plan.

"However goes the public school system, so goes the economic development of the county," said Sam M. Watkins, president of Rose Oil Company and one of the founders of AdVance. "And however goes the economic development, so goes the quality of lives of the citizens."

Watkins immediately embraced Wallace's plan for improving the schools, and his support never wavered. Two days before the forum at Rollins school, AdVance called a news conference to announce it was backing Wallace's plan. Among the leaders present was Abdul Rasheed, chairman of Vance Citizens for Educational Excellence. To critics who said Wallace was moving too fast, Rasheed said, "I don't know if we're moving fast enough considering the state of education in Vance County."[3]

Watkins introduced Wallace to key business leaders, including Lucious Harvin, Jr., chairman of Roses Stores, a chain of drugstores based in Henderson and one of the county's major employers. Wallace found another important ally in George Templeton Blackburn II, a young attorney with one of the county's oldest law firms and chief legal counsel to Roses Stores. Blackburn, also a local historian, had strong bonds with many of the progressive young black professionals in the county and important insights into local race relations.

Residents were understandably skeptical about Wallace's radical plan for their schools. But they were talking about it, just as they would if a major industry was moving into the county or a new freeway was being laid across it. The new superintendent had their attention. She was in the newspaper nearly every day, usually on page 1. This first stage of her campaign came to a climax on the evening of September 5. She organized a public forum, and more than 500 people showed up at E. M. Rollins Elementary School auditorium to grill her, her principals and administrators, and board members on the reform plan. The forum was broadcast live over local cable television and radio. Wallace told the group she would stay until every person with a question got a chance to ask it, even if it took all night. She believed the community needed this chance to respond to her hard-charging initiatives, maybe even to vent some steam. Parents and residents took turns at the microphone. Many worried Wallace was moving too fast, pushing too hard.

"I've been contacted numerous times over the past two weeks by educators," said Jean Thompson, an active, outspoken parent through whom teachers knew they could complain without revealing their identity. "They say, 'We don't have a how-to. We don't have a plan. We don't know what we're doing. We know we have the ability to do it; we just don't know how to do it.' "

On the last point, she was right. Many teachers did not know how to do it. No school of education had taught them to work in a system with uniformly high expectations for all students and no grades or grade levels. But Wallace figured the only way they were going to learn was by doing it, just as the only way to learn to ride a bicycle or to swim or to dance is to do it.

Other parents questioned how the district would handle teachers unwilling to change, whether Vance County graduates could meet college admission standards, and how teachers would individualize instruction within mixed-age groups. Wallace reassured the crowd that much of the first year would be devoted to planning. Schools would begin when they were ready. The state was threatening to take over the school district, and Wallace used the warning to add urgency to her cause.

"If we don't improve within two years, the state has the option of appointing outside administrators and will have the option of dismissing the school board, superintendent, and finance officer," she told the crowd. "We need to get in there and swim."

Despite the concerns, Wallace was impressed by how willingly most people seemed to consider a plan so radical and how readily some grasped the structural problems she was proposing to correct. Irving Henderson, a parent, described the problems with tracking.

"What tracking says is 'In every course, we're going to determine your level of achievement,' " he said. "The concerns being stated here are relevant. But let's get behind the program and see if we can make it work, and if it does work, we can all pat ourselves on the back."[4]

Shortly after midnight, with 200 people out of questions but still willing to listen, the board finally brought the forum to a close. Wallace had stood at the platform fielding questions for more than five hours. When she tried to walk out of the auditorium up the inclined aisle, her knees buckled. She had to hold on to the seat backs to make her way out, a frazzled survivor of her first public trial as Vance County superintendent.

Upon reaching her apartment that night, she put on a cotton gown and set her radio on the kitchen counter near the back door. She tuned into a country station in South Hill, Virginia, and turned the music low so it wouldn't disturb the neighbors. She poured a shot of Jack Daniels, sat on the back porch step, leaned against a garbage can, and massaged the cramps out of her calves. Slowly she melted into the soft sounds of Randy Travis and let her mind drift.

The Soothsayer

Early in September, Betty Wallace got an ominous telephone call from one of the more experienced principals, one whom she had already grown to admire for his grasp of the Bell-Curve Syndrome. He said he had been "elected" by the other "local boys" to issue a few cautions, much like the soothsayer warning Caesar of the Ides of March. Conspirators were afoot in Vance County, he warned.

The principals admired Wallace's courage, supported her plan, and would help her in every way, the caller said. The conversation, as Wallace later reconstructed it, went something like this:

"This is Vance County," he said, "a strange place that prides itself on being provincial and different. The 'locals' and 'outsiders' occupied distinct niches in Vance County."

"But I am an outsider, and always will be," Wallace said. "I'm missing the point, unless the point is that I might as well pack up my bags and leave."

"No, no," he said. "The point is that all the other outsiders—Howard Maniloff, Bob Gordon, and Kenneth England and the other former superintendents, five in just the last ten years—were forced out. They simply gave up and left. We have let Vance County become a cesspool, and we feel guilty. After burying our heads in the sand, we can't become aggressive all of a sudden, but we can help you change things if you will keep pushing ahead and let us help you."

Wallace asked, "Why didn't you try harder to change things earlier? What is different now?"

"The difference is that Vance County is now at a tipping point," he said. "Other counties to the east of us have tipped, poor and destitute and probably incapable of rebounding. Counties to the west and south of us have chosen progress, have chosen the future. Vance can go either way, but it is headed east if there are not some remarkable changes, and we all know that the school system will be the barometer, the thing that indicates change, progress or decline."

"Do you think we can pull this off?" asked Wallace.

"It's doubtful but worth a try, if you keep trying and do not cave in under the heat."

"What exactly do you mean about 'the heat'? Is it racial? Is it sexist? Will I have bullets through my windows?"

There was no simple answer, the man said. "It means power and control and resistance to change, especially by the whites," he said.

"Tell me about the blacks and other ethnic groups in this region," urged Wallace. "What is the connection?"

"Well, just discount the Hispanics, Asians, and Native Americans for now," he said. "They are so few that they have no impact at all on the county. This county is all black and white, with special-interest cliques operating within each race. And the intraracial battles can be just as vicious as the interracial battles. One does not talk about this in polite company, either black or white. But it is there, and we all talk about it among friends, in small groups, in strategizing for our own personal agendas."

As the principal saw it, Vance County's enduring racial tensions were remnants of slavery, the sins of the fathers visited upon their modern-day sons. Prior to the Civil War, what is today Vance County belonged to a swath of North Carolina bordered by Virginia and extending from the Central Piedmont east to the coast. This section had North Carolina's highest concentration of slaves, just as it today has its highest proportion of black residents. The region had antebellum plantations mansions with such names as Ashland, Burnside, Nine Oaks, and Belwood, many of which still stand in Vance County. These plantations spread over hundreds, even thousands of acres, but they were not nearly as vast as those owned by the Southern aristocracy of Virginia, South Carolina, and Georgia. Early accounts of plantation life in Vance County suggest, however, that it was exceptionally cruel. In his journal, a cleric who traveled a circuit through the area described slaves on these second-grade plantations as "poor, naked starving creatures." The principal told Wallace that the lingering shadows of that harshness, of tension between class and race, still cast a gloom over Vance County.

"The times have changed, but the mind-set has not" said the principal. "And that is the problem. You are caught in the middle of it all."

His words left Betty Wallace with a chill.

The Vote

The superintendent took her plan to the school board on September 9 for a vote of confidence. While the board had in effect adopted the plan when it hired Wallace, in the last two months, she and her radical proposals had become the county's top news. She needed to make sure the board would still support her when the friction of change began generating heat.

The only board member who seemed reluctant was Deborah Brown. She saw no need to eliminate grade levels or grading, worried about letting each school "do its own thing," and felt no urgency for swift change. Brown, one of the board's black members, wanted the district to take a year to plan before acting. Wallace countered that her changes could be phased in over the first year and up and fully running by the second.

"Progress has never been kind to idlers," she said, borrowing a line from *A Nation at Risk*, "and it never will be."

Wallace refused to compromise. She was not interested in any plan that would allow the bell curve to survive as a part of school practices. Either the bell curve would go, or she would.

"If you are not willing to accept the reform package as planned, then I do not want to be part of a reform with a less-than-good chance at succeeding," Wallace told the board. "If your intention is to water down the reform plan, then I will withdraw the entire proposal. I do not want to do it halfway."

Board member Margaret Ellis immediately moved that the board adopt the plan in its entirety. Jackie Jackson seconded it, and all but Brown approved. Wallace was reassured. The board, or at least six of its members, still stood behind her. Now she had the authority to press on.

The board's action captured headlines statewide.

"Vance County students will never get another F—or an A or a B for that matter," wrote Tim Simmons for *The News & Observer* in Raleigh. "There won't be any kindergarten through eighth grade either. Vance's children next year will be thrust into some of the furthest reaches of school reform."

The Herald Sun in Durham advised the state education community to keep its eyes on Vance County.

> Engineers often say they can learn more from their failures than from their success. The Vance experiment is an attempt by some innovative educators and county commissioners to learn from the worst kind of failure— human failure. If outcome-based education works in Vance County, it has a reasonable chance of working almost anywhere."

Schools Open

Vance County schools had already changed when they opened under their new superintendent in the fall of 1991. The elementary and middle schools had abandoned letter grades and, to varying degrees, grade levels—two giant steps away from their dependence on the bell curve. Northern and Southern Vance high schools mixed ages in homerooms, eliminated low-track classes, and began planning for a major overhaul but made no other substantive changes. It would be two years before they would be ready to tamper with their basic frameworks. Eaton-Johnson Middle School began mixing ages for select courses. Henderson Middle teachers designed a plan to reorganize into teams and eliminate grade levels by the following year.

Meanwhile, the team of teachers and administrators was scrambling to define student learning objectives geared to the state curriculum. It would be up to each school, though, to reorganize as it chose to ensure that all students met the learning goals. Each school would move at its own pace, just as its students would. Forcing fourteen schools all to change in lockstep would subject them all to the same bell-curve style comparisons they were trying to deliver their students from. Wallace instead wanted to foster a diversity of schools that would be judged solely on the proportion of students they could guide to mastering learning objectives. Someday, she believed, that proportion should near 100 percent. In a system free of the Bell-Curve Syndrome, there would be no reason to expect less.

As is typical elsewhere in the country, the elementary schools were the quickest to change. All began organizing their teachers into teams and shifting to some stage of a staircase structure that would group students by achievement levels rather than age.

Teachers at Clark Street created just two teams of teachers, one for the primary level and another for the intermediate. The four primary teachers divided their duties by subject. One would teach reading all day, another math, the third science, and the fourth social studies. Each teacher would teach his or her specialty at various levels geared to match the varying learning needs of students. Students were grouped according to what they knew and were able to do. When they learned more, they would advance to a higher group. Where there were conflicts in a child's schedule, reading, then math, took priority. In other words, a child might be forced to stay in a lower social studies class to work with the advanced reading group. In such cases, though, the social studies teacher tried to raise that child's lessons to a higher level.

Teachers were encouraged to allow students to pursue individual learning paths. So while the reading teacher might have a classroom of children who were all just beginning to read simple sentences, the children could choose from a variety of books. Students responded in individual ways to group lessons. Teachers also had the option of mixing children at various levels in larger groups for projects that could benefit children of all levels. All of the primary children, for example, could be grouped to see the high school kids put on a play or hear a teacher read an engaging story. Other teachers, then, would have time to plan.

E. M. Rollins Elementary organized children into teams named for animals, such as the Berenstein Bears, Eagles, Owls, and Toucans. These corresponded roughly to grade levels, but students were allowed to advance from one team to the next whenever they were ready. As at Clark, Rollins teachers specialized in specific subjects, and students were grouped by the level of academic needs within each subject.

Rollins teachers wanted to make teams flexible enough to accommodate the continuously changing educational needs of students. If, for example, a lower team worked itself out of students by promoting them all, it could dissolve, move up the staircase, and regroup either as a new step or as a reinforcement for an overcrowded existing step. That, at least, is what they hoped to someday see. The aim was to keep students moving and the stairwell from clogging. Teachers would be assigned and reassigned where students needed them, a departure from the old system where students were assigned to fit the needs of the organization.

Most of the other elementary schools—including Aycock, Clark Street, Dabney, Pinkston Street, Zeb Vance, and L. B. Yancey—settled on similar plans. New Hope, Carver, and E. O. Young Elementary schools took more tentative steps. New Hope kept its youngest students with one teacher, though it mixed five- and six-year-olds. Carver Elementary grouped children for reading based on their skills rather than age, resulting in mixed-age reading groups. Young allowed second and third graders to mix as they moved to different teachers for different subjects, but kept other students in a single classroom all day with one teacher.

Young may have been more reluctant to part with traditional practices because the Reverend David Jones, pastor of a local church, and Young's PTA president, Joyce Carpunky, were skeptical of the new plan and opposed a leap fully into it. Jones made wild claims (though he would later apologize to Wallace) probably based on national literature from the Christian Right, which was attacking outcomes-based education elsewhere in the nation. He charged that Wallace's new program had connections with secular humanism and the new world order and would promote liberal attitudes, corrupt the youth of Vance County, and cause promiscuity. As Wallace would learn, some residents would find ways to blame just about every problem in Vance County on outcomes-based education. Aycock Elementary School was forced to use bottled water because petroleum products had contaminated its well, and Wallace occasionally joked, "I categorically deny that OBE caused the contaminated water at Aycock."

Carpunky had more understandable worries about Wallace's plan. She insisted that neither teachers nor parents understood outcomes-based education well enough to do it. She was not entirely wrong.

Teaching the Teachers

No teachers had ever before taught in schools without grades and grade levels. The nation's schools of education do not teach Guided Learning.

"What Betty had was a vision of where she wanted us to be," said Laura Joyner, director of community relations. "The lack of specifics has been a thorn in her side. The teachers did not have any idea what to do."

The Vance County staff would have to learn by doing, a method that they would soon begin using with their students. Wallace was confident they could, and she tried to instill that same confidence in her professional employees by giving them broad authority to reorganize their schools.

"The framework for this place is a given, set in concrete," she would tell teachers. "But you have total freedom to set up learning environments within the framework. I'm not going to write a manual for you. You are the instructional professionals. I am the keeper of the organizational framework."

Each school staff was free to choose its own teaching materials and to use its resources, including time, as it saw fit. Wallace distributed to the control of the principals as much money and authority as the law would allow. She encouraged the principals to do the same, by pushing as much authority as they could onto teachers and students. She pushed so many decisions out to the principals that some of them suggested she take some back. Few were used to such freedom. In extending additional responsibilities to principals and teachers, Wallace conferred professional respect that she hoped eventually would be returned in hard work and loyalty.

At the same time, teachers needed all the help they could get. Wallace reshaped the central office's primary role from enforcer to servant. The central office would help teachers find their way in this new structure. Teachers and principals had to shift their mind-sets from teaching to learning, worrying less about what they covered and more about what students were learning. They needed to see themselves more as guides to than sources of knowledge.

Wallace hoped to see fewer lectures and textbook assignments and more small-group seminars, team projects, and independent study and research. As long as students were moving toward the benchmarks, their individual learning paths could be as varied as the school and teachers could imagine. Schools, traditionally teaching places, would become learning places.

The central office staff scoured the country for experts who could help teachers put these changes into practice. In October Wallace sent Ginger Miller, her director of elementary education, to Paint Branch Elementary School in Maryland to see the structure and fruits of Linda Dudley's innovative ungraded school. Miller had quickly become one of Wallace's chiefs of staff. She was bright, committed to Wallace's vision, and had worked in an ungraded school in Greensboro, North Carolina, during the 1970s. Based on Miller's report, Wallace invited Dudley to provide training sessions for her teachers. Dudley was a hit. She offered just the kind of practical information from the trenches that teachers were looking for. She was invited back repeatedly over the year to help teachers design and operate their overhauled schools. The central office also tapped the Raleigh Technical Assistance Center, a field office of the state Department of Public Instruction, which had a knowledgeable staff eager to help.

Wallace also began to look at ways technology could help teachers in a more individualized education system. Vance County Schools already had begun using a computer-managed evaluation system for primary children who had been in the traditional grades kindergarten through 2. Wallace asked her testing supervisor, Jodi Brame, to explore the possibilities of expanding that system or developing a new one to serve all children. She wanted a computer that could provide teachers with testing tools, including test item scanners and scorers, not to compare students but to measure whether they had mastered outcomes.

Slowly, through trial and glitch, Brame and Trudy Tidwell, program evaluator, began building the electronic system. They bought commercial test questions and combined them with questions developed specifically for the North Carolina curriculum by the state Department of Public Instruction. By refusing to settle for mediocre tests, Brame and Tidwell performed a critical service for Vance County schools. They brought in teachers to review and rewrite items, with a focus on designing provocative open-ended questions that would demand critical, complex thinking of students rather than the mere regurgitation of facts. They tossed hundreds of simple, fact-based items, the staple of traditional norm-referenced tests. Brame, Tidwell, and their teacher recruits worked diligently to ensure students would meet high standards. This would be critical to making the new nongraded structure work.

Vance County couldn't have picked a better time to shift to a system based on learning goals. After North Carolina's average scores on the Scholastic Aptitude Test slipped to dead last in 1989, state leaders formed a task force to help lead the state out of the nation's academic cellar. More than a half-dozen panels and groups studied the state's education system. They concluded that schools must offer a tougher core curriculum, set higher standards, and move toward learning goals or outcomes-based education. That meant the state would give extra money to school districts willing to try outcomes-based education. Wallace immediately stepped up to apply. She wanted the money to set up a more sophisticated computer system that would enable the district to track the progress of all students. But even if she won a grant, the money would still be a year away. And it would take even longer to refine the computer testing and student management system.

In the meantime, Vance County's administrators and teachers stumbled and scrambled to carry out the vision, learning even as they acted. Even with occasional training from an expert, by and large most teachers found themselves winging it.

So it was with GLOBE 2000 in Vance County. Wallace had reminded her staff the road is never smooth for the people who make it. Action, however clumsy, was preferable to stagnation. Though the transition would not be smooth, it would be brisk, and eventually they would be able to clear away the clutter and confusion, settle in new territory, and plant new roots in soil untainted by the Bell-Curve Syndrome.

Report Cards Without Grades

The first grading period ended in November, and Vance County teachers issued report cards without traditional letter grades. Instead, they listed the objectives the child was expected to master and an M, meaning "mastery," or an IP, meaning "in progress," next to each. This was the first take-home test on the new system, the first sign of significant change most parents would see. Wallace and her staff braced for a deafening public outcry.

But what came was more like a soft whimper. Most complaints came from parents of the top achievers and academically gifted children who were upset they no longer had an easy way to show their children were superior to others. To say one child had more Ms than another was too subtle; these parents wanted comparative grading. Though they did not realize it, they were asking that some children be branded low achievers or failures so that theirs would stand out as bright, successful winners by contrast. How could they say their children were smarter than others when everyone was expected to master every objective? Some parents also worried how the elimination of grades in the high schools would affect their children's ability to compete for college admission.

Most parents, though, were willing to tolerate new report cards and mixed-age grouping, at least for a while. Thus by November of Wallace's first year as superintendent, two of the most sacred cows in public education—grades and grade levels—had been cut down with little more than a sigh of public discontent.

That didn't mean parents were comfortable with the changes. Many clearly were not. If Wallace was eliminating conventions of the bell curve, she also was eliminating conventions that parents were familiar with. Nearly two years after Vance County schools eliminated grades, a number of parents still harbored reservations about report cards.

"It is a little difficult to get used to this 'M,' " said Charlene Sorrells of Henderson, whose daughter attended Zeb Vance Elementary. "It is a lot harder to read the report card and understand what the kids are doing in school."

Teachers found this common objection hard to fathom since the new cards actually told parents so much more about what their children learned. By the spring of 1993, most parents had accepted the elimination of grade levels, but many still wanted grades back. Laura Joyner of community relations said that if Wallace left, parents would be clamoring for the return of grades.

However, parents of academically gifted children relaxed after they realized their children would be allowed to move up through the system as fast as their bright minds could carry them. No longer would these gifted children be moored in special classes to kill time while waiting for their peers to catch up.

"If this works like it is supposed to," said Sam McCaskill, president of Parents for Academically Gifted Children, "there would be no need for students to be labeled AG."

Children seemed to adapt more effortlessly than adults to their gradeless schools. Some missed the old way, but most seemed to welcome the changes. Eventually they would realize that they no longer had to worry about failing and they would see more clearly what they needed to do to succeed. They would discover they could help their friends work toward more Ms without lowering their own grades, which was the case with the old bell-curve system. They also liked the freedom to advance at their own pace.

"I enjoy it because instead of As, Bs, and Cs, I've got Ms," said Leanne Anderson, a nine-year-old student at Zeb Vance with a bright red bow in her long dark hair. "I know what grade I'm getting."

Anthony Riggan, a freckled ten-year-old at Zeb Vance, said he liked being able to move ahead of others. He had advanced to prealgebra in mathematics and was already talking about going to North Carolina State University.

"In regular school, you finish something, and you have to wait until everybody else catches up," he said. "I'd rather have this than grade levels. In grade levels you have to stay in that grade and do the same thing over and over."

Vance County schools shifted so quickly into more individualized organizations geared to learning goals that they began drawing the attention of educators elsewhere almost immediately. With the school year hardly under way, Wallace began getting invitations to speak at conferences about her bold experiment. Educators were desperate for solutions to old, recalcitrant problems. In the fall of 1991, Wallace spoke at an economic development conference and a school boards association meeting in North Carolina and to superintendents' groups in Pennsylvania, Georgia, and Washington, D.C.

And educators began coming to see Vance County's radical changes. As is often the case in education, Vance County was winning accolades for a bold new plan it hadn't yet had a chance to put fully into place. But Wallace understood politics. She welcomed visitors; they would add credibility to her work. So when leaders of the national outcomes-based education movement came to Vance County, Wallace called a news conference to make sure they all said a few words to the local press. Among them was William Smith, the executive director of the National Network for Outcome-Based Schools; Robert Bingham, a state director of the National Academy for Local Boards of Education, based at Appalachian State University in Boone, North Carolina; Alexander Erwin, assistant dean of

Appalachian's college of education; and Roy Forbes, executive director of Southeastern Regional Vision for Education based in Greensboro. County leaders and state legislators showed up for the meeting.

"Be assured Vance County is moving in the direction the nation is going," Erwin said.[5]

Smith agreed, noting that in traditional schools, students are sorted on a bell curve. "The youngsters that fall on the wrong side—we don't just consider them slow kids; we consider them dumb kids."

Wallace found it heartening to hear her own words from the lips of other education leaders. She continued to draw favorable headlines. After weathering some initial public and staff skepticism, she now seemed to be slipping into a pleasant honeymoon with her new district.

After spending Christmas break at Skeenah Farm, Betty Wallace returned to her home in Henderson on New Year's Day, stopped at Byrd's Supermarket, and, as usual, picked up a copy of the *Henderson Daily Dispatch* on her way out. There she was grinning on the front page again under a headline that said OUTCOME-BASED EDUCATION 1991'S TOP STORY. In Vance County, the schools rated bigger news than the Persian Gulf War and Roses Stores' brush with near bankruptcy.

By month's end, however, events took a dark turn. For the third year in a row, Vance County slipped on the North Carolina Report Card; some residents did not understand that this report was based on the 1990–91 indicators gathered before Wallace arrived in Vance County. She did some fast explaining and used the downturn to add urgency to her quest for change. This drop put Vance County in the state's academic cellar and on the short list of three school systems destined for state takeover. What better evidence did residents need that Vance County had to try something new?

"Any way you cut it, these scores are abysmal," she told the newspaper. "It's a pattern of failure, a downward spiral that we have to break out of."[6]

Wallace expected a backlash, but she did not wait for it. Instead she pushed harder, and the backlash never came. She hammered on the need for change every chance she got. The people of Vance

County had to move to deeper stages of commitment. She wanted to see them evolve beyond only tolerating change—in itself a major feat in Vance County—to sharing her passion for change. She wanted them to *insist* on change. So, of course, her state-of-the-schools address on February 3, 1992, focused on change:

> It is time to stop blaming each other, blaming the teachers, blaming the students, blaming the economy. It is time to stop swatting at gnats while the vultures are circling overhead. It is time to change.
>
> . . . We must make a major shift in the way we think about the purpose of schools. We must shift our thinking from schools being teaching places to schools as learning places. Schools in Vance County must become learning laboratories where both students and teachers engage in activities that bring out new insights about the learning processes of the brain—new learning about how people learn and how teachers can arrange the learning places to bring about increased learning by students.
>
> . . . Vance County citizens must learn and internalize the need for change, the need to move the county forward economically and culturally in such a way that our children will be ready for the jobs of the future, for the lifestyles of the future, for the things that give quality and meaning to their lives. Vance County must decide to demand change and to become indignant if change does not happen fast enough.

More than anything else, Wallace needed teachers with this appetite for change. In late winter, she set out to measure just how deeply her teachers were committed to her restructuring plan. She needed their support in order to receive a share of the grant the state was offering to four districts willing to try outcomes-based education. Unless the new plan received strong teacher support, the state would not fund the effort. So teachers across the district cast secret ballots for or against GLOBE 2000. On the day of the vote, the curriculum staff fielded tallies. The results grew rosier as the day wore on. By afternoon, the central office was erupting in high-fives and cheers.

Every school voted in favor of the project, and in every case, votes were nearly unanimous. Wallace now believed she had the confidence of her teachers, a critical step in her battle to wipe out the Bell-Curve Syndrome. She felt secure enough to move out of her apartment into a large, two-story house in an affluent Henderson neighborhood near the golf course. As usual, she bought a neglected house ripe for remodeling.

By March, all of Vance County's elementary and middle schools had waded deep into change. They had abandoned grades and grade levels, even though technically they were still in a planning year. Bobby Etheridge, the tall, plain-talking state superintendent of public instruction, visited Zeb Vance Elementary School with Wallace. After they had strolled through the school, Etheridge told her, "This has the potential for bringing national attention to North Carolina." He praised the district for being at the forefront of the promising outcomes-based education movement.

"You didn't wait in this county," he said. "It's like being willing to not just walk on thin ice, but being almost willing to walk on water. . . . The best way to keep children in school is to have them engaged. And that's exactly what I saw this morning."[7]

Such words from the state education leader were reassuring for Wallace, especially when she was hoping to win a chunk of that generous state grant. Two months later her hopes were realized. Etheridge called and told her she would get $1.65 million over the next five years to make Vance County schools a model for outcomes-based education. Betty Wallace was tempted to jump up and dash through the central office proclaiming the good news, but she stayed at her desk and took a moment to savor it.

More important even than the money was the boost this grant gave to staff morale and the credibility of GLOBE 2000. In less than a year, Vance County's image was changing: Once one of North Carolina's most troubled districts, it was now a state model of how a system can break with its past and redefine its future. The grant capped Betty Wallace's sales campaign. She now had official backing from the business community, local press, school board, teachers, and the state Board of Education. This support, however, was about to be challenged in a nasty political firestorm.

As the school year drew to a close, Wallace's principals collectively decided that 289 students were not ready to advance to intermediate, middle, or high school stages in the reorganized system. Everyone knew this would be a painful step, but it had to happen. Student progression in this system would no longer be based on time but on knowledge. To advance, they had to learn. To parents whose children did not move on, it appeared that the students had flunked, a practice that had all but disappeared in the traditional system. Before Wallace had taken over, only twenty students districtwide had been retained in grades 3, 6, and 8—and those had all been special cases of children who were seriously ill or absent for large portions of the school year. For the last decade, the system's de facto policy had been that no one failed even when they failed to learn. This practice of social promotion, which prevails in traditional schools everywhere, combined with grade inflation, gives parents and the community a misleading picture of student achievement. Only when students reach high school still weak on basic skills and either quit or graduate functionally illiterate does the public really begin to see how little some students have learned.

Students would not fail in Vance County's new system. They also would not be promoted from one level to the next without meeting learning objectives, because that sets students up for even more serious failures in adult life. Principals and teachers explained to parents that the retentions were not the same as flunking. The children would be held back only as long as they needed to master whatever learning objectives they had not yet learned. Once they learned the objectives—whether it took them two months or a year—they could advance to the next stage. Hard as this was, the district had to stand firm or the whole system would become another charade.

This hard line paid off with an immediate, visible change in attitude among summer school students, principals said. In the past students just put in time, knowing they would be promoted to the next grade in August. During the summer of 1992, however, there would be consequences for what students did and did not do. Students were given individual achievement profiles and were shown the standards they must meet in order to be promoted by the end of the summer. Once they could see clearly what they needed to do, the children did it. Many produced good work for the first time.

"Those students were convinced that we meant business, and they came through," said Anna Hager, principal of Henderson Middle School.

Nevertheless, the retentions came as a shock to some black parents, who saw racial implications in them. And why wouldn't they? The system always had relegated their children to the academic slow track because they fell on the low end of the bell curve in comparisons with children from more affluent, better-educated families. Somehow Wallace had to convince these parents that, in the long run, her system would free their children from these negative comparisons, give them a chance to learn and truly succeed, and ultimately serve them as well as advantaged children.

But another Vance County official also took an interest in these parents and stepped in to champion their cause. This was what the anonymous principal had warned Wallace about. She was on the brink of battle with Vance County's most powerful black leader. Nothing could be worse for her war against the Bell-Curve Syndrome than this plunge into racial politics.

CHAPTER 6

▼

POLITICS OF CHANGE

Representative James P. Green—physician, legislator, landlord, and community activist—had a long history of organizing and fighting for the black residents of Vance County. He had fought to save cemeteries, stop developments, and transform Vance County into a Democratic Party stronghold. Now he was taking up the cause of black parents who felt their children were being hurt by a school system reorganized to help them. Friends and local officials warned Wallace that Green, whom she had never met, was politically adept and powerful enough to quash her reforms.

Green told reporters that he had received calls from a dozen parents complaining their children would not be permitted to advance to higher levels in Vance County's new four-tiered system, even though they had had no warnings that their children were having problems progressing. The fact was the parents had received plenty of warnings. Nevertheless, without consulting Wallace, Green called a public forum on Wallace's new education plan. "We need to get a report on this system before the whole system flunks out," he said.[1]

About 175 people showed for Green's meeting. They complained that teachers ill-prepared for the new system were letting students learn on their own without providing adequate guidance. Students need to be motivated, even pressured to learn, said Wallace Lewis, who had a child at Dabney Elementary School.

"Teachers seemingly are doing less teaching," he said.[2]

Green appointed a committee to explore these problems further with Wallace. Green's challenge of her work seemed to inspire W. L. "Bill" Fleming, chairman of the conservative and all-male

Vance County Board of Commissioners, to take a shot. On the day of Green's meeting, Fleming and his fellow commissioners voted to freeze the county's contribution to schools at the 1991–92 level of $4.2 million level—$600,000 less than Wallace had requested and $500,000 less than the county manager had outlined in his proposal. Fleming said the board denied the school system more money because "there is widespread concern about the state of schools."[3] Wallace also learned Fleming was trying to get backing from local businessmen to buy out her contract.

She suspected that Fleming was angry because the school system had stopped buying produce from his fruit and produce company. Wallace had instructed the finance officer to buy produce from the lowest bidder, and that eliminated Fleming. The finance officer warned Wallace to expect repercussions.

"Our job is to get the lowest price," she replied, "not to subsidize elected officials."

Wallace felt like a soldier lost behind enemy lines. Problems were getting worse. A week earlier Laura Joyner had stepped forward as the first of six women to bring sexual harassment allegations against the district's top-ranking black administrator, Ronald E. Gregory, an assistant superintendent. She charged that Gregory was harassing her with unwanted, unsettling sexual comments. After a preliminary review, Wallace concluded that she had no choice but to suspend Gregory pending an investigation, though she knew that meant trouble.

The first blow would come from the new board chairwoman, Deborah Brown, a friend of Green's and Gregory's. Brown and Wallace already had crossed swords over Gregory the previous fall after Wallace decided to shift the assistant superintendent's duties, putting him in charge of auxiliary services and community relations and removing the personnel office from his control. Brown protested the change during a closed-door executive session of the school board, accusing Wallace of taking the personnel office from Gregory because he was black. Wallace wanted to seize control of personnel, Brown charged. On the latter point, Wallace agreed.

"The personnel office is supposed to be under the careful administration of the superintendent, and yes, I do want to restore it to a good reputation for technical management of personnel functions," she said. "It is not a position of power, and it should not be perceived as a position of power."

Brown flattened her palms on the old, worn courtroom table, demanded fairness and reminded Wallace of the black pride in having a black man control the personnel office. Wallace held her ground. As the two women glared at each other, other uneasy board members led by Larry Beckham broke the standoff by backing Wallace. Gregory's new assignment would stand. And so would the battle lines.

Now Wallace knew a confrontation over Gregory's suspension was inevitable. She called the board chairwoman, as required by North Carolina law, immediately after Gregory was suspended on June 22. Wallace took notes and had the new personnel director in her office listening during the telephone conversation. It unfolded, according to her notes, as follows:

"When are you going to stop this foolishness?" asked Brown. "This is just foolishness, and you're not going to get away with it."

"This is serious business," replied Wallace, "a matter of investigating charges of something illegal—sexual harassment."

"You're just digging up this stuff because you're just out to get Ron," said Brown. "But you're not going to do it. I'll bring you down."

"Are you suggesting to me or telling me I cannot carry out this investigation?" asked Wallace.

"I'm saying for you to stop this stuff right now," Brown said. "You're not going to investigate Ron Gregory. If I can't stop you, I'll see that the board stops you."

"This is my job, and I have to do it," said Wallace. "I have to investigate any such charges that are brought to me. I cannot just ignore them."

"Well, I'll bring you down and everybody who helps you," Brown said, and then slammed down the phone.

Later that evening Brown also called Gloria Lunsford-Boone, the district's new director of personnel, and made similar threats. Lunsford-Boone, a black woman, was in tears when she recounted the conversation to Wallace the next morning.

At the next executive board session, Wallace described the threats. Brown did not deny she made them. Nor did the board respond, even though its attorney and Wallace had explained the board's legal responsibilities under state and federal law. No one was coming to Wallace's defense. Seeing her apparently abandoned, her enemies moved in for the attack.

Bill Fleming, the county commission chairman, called a radio talk show and said he was denying schools money because he disagreed with Wallace and outcomes-based education. He said the district should have two high schools, one academic and the other vocational, and the district otherwise should be left alone. Outcomes-based education was causing dissension, he said, and should be abandoned, even though the state had given Vance County schools a huge grant to become a model for the whole state.

Meanwhile, James Green and his new committee, the Vance Association of Concerned Citizens for Better Education, again publicly attacked Wallace, charging she was moving too fast without properly training teachers. Parents complained Wallace was an ineffective, uncooperative, and overly defensive superintendent, Green said, although he could not give names or examples. The media and business leaders had brainwashed the local school board, he added. Wallace countered that she had invested heavily in training with fifty-six workshops and seminars on GLOBE 2000 over the last year. Further, she had won a $1.65 million grant, much of which would be spent on training. As for her lack of cooperation and defensiveness, no one was producing any examples.

"I'm not known to be a shrinking violet," she said. "I won't be intimidated."[4]

Wallace talked to Green during the last weekend of June. She asked if his real aim was a black superintendent. He said he had always promoted blacks and would like to see a black superintendent, but in this case, his goal was simply to help parents who could not help themselves.

She agreed to meet with Green's newest committee on outcomes-based education during a closed-door session on July 1. This eight-member panel picked by Green included a teacher, parent, minister, and business leader Sam Watkins, representing AdVance Strategic Planning Commission, one of the first groups to back Wallace's plan. The superintendent brought some staff members and board member Margaret Ellis, but Green would not allow them to join her in the meeting. So Wallace faced Green's panel alone and politely answered its questions. She told the group she could move slower and provide as much training as school funds would allow. But to her, the meeting smacked of a political charade. She later told Watkins and Ellis that the meeting was a setup and never to expect her to sit through another like it. Hundreds of parents had met with her directly, and none of them needed Green to speak for them, she said.

"I'm not going to be the pawn for these silly little local battles again," she said.

After the meeting, Green told the *Henderson Daily Dispatch* that Wallace failed to address the committee's concerns and just "gave the same set of rhetoric she's given the past few months."[5]

The next day two members of the committee stepped forth and said they thought the meeting was positive and productive. One of them was Watkins. "I thought we were heard," he said.[6]

Wilbur Boyd, a county commissioner at the meeting, expressed similar sentiments in a letter to the editor.[7] In mid-July Green said he was disappointed that the newspaper had portrayed him at odds with Wallace when he was only trying to address some community concerns. He said the newspaper was trying to divide the board and community along racial lines.[8] Now it was Green who was becoming defensive.

But Wallace found little solace in this. Her battle with Green, the board's failure to support her and to censure Brown, the commission's withdrawal of financial support all left her feeling abandoned. As she saw it, the county had cowered before a small group of self-serving bullies, and if the county had no self-respect, who was she to bear the heat?

"It is like falling out of love," she told her friends. "The going looks better to me than staying, although I really don't want to leave."

Ginger Miller, whom Wallace had appointed to take over as principal of the new Zeb Vance Elementary School, would later observe, "Betty's eyes just lost their twinkle for a while there."

Wallace wanted to fight back, but even her friends advised against it, warning it would be a nasty battle. Community agitators were interconnected, they said, and used one another to further their own agendas. Take the high road, they advised her—take cover and hope you have something left after the bullies move on. That was not easy for a woman who'd been raised to stand her ground. It was not Betty Wallace's way. She felt dejected.

"Why is this happening?" she asked a friend, a local attorney who had lived in Vance County all his life. Why, she asked, were community agitators making her the lightning rod for their discontent rather than the mayor, sheriff, or other elected officials? His reply, Wallace later recalled, went about as follows:

"Because they're all local boys," he said. "They can't be run out of town. The school superintendent can."

He told her she should not take the attacks personally. If she could hold on long enough, perhaps she could remove herself from the local power struggles, improve the schools, and set the county on a course toward renewal.

Wallace had no interest in seeing how much abuse she could endure. She would rather leave than hunker down in the trenches. Yet leaving now would be like abandoning her child. Her teachers and administrators had worked so hard, changed so much. She wanted to see these reforms work, particularly for the disadvantaged children who were being ravaged by the Bell-Curve Syndrome. But that no longer seemed possible. So one morning in July 1992, Wallace began looking for a new job. She also paid $25 for a custom-made "For Sale" sign and pounded it into her front lawn with a big rock.

On July 30 the *Henderson Daily Dispatch* ran a front-page story saying that Wallace was one of four finalists for superintendent of Brunswick County Schools, another academically troubled rural school district trying to shift its focus to learning goals. The news stirred some self-reflection among residents of Vance County, the paper reported.

"It's the fault of the entire community," said Nancy Bobbitt, chairwoman of the AdVance Strategic Planning Commission. "Everybody seems to have their own agenda. No one seems willing to put aside the things they're personally interested in for the good of the whole."

Ann Jaeger, president of the Henderson-Vance Chamber of Commerce, said Wallace had too many bosses. "It's a shame she hasn't been given the opportunity to do what she says she can do," she said.

There was a note of fatalism in these and other voices, a resignation to Vance County's self-destructive pattern of rejecting those who tried to help it. Reporter Tammy Stanford used a biblical analogy to describe the situation in the *Henderson Daily Dispatch*:

> Betty C. Wallace may be remembered as the Moses of Vance County Schools. But as the biblical leader who dashed on the rocks the covenant he carried to the people of Israel, Wallace may believe that she cannot lead the people of Vance County to the promised land after all.[9]

Two days later, on the evening of August 13, Wallace took another double-barreled blast. After nine days of closed-door hearings involving testimony from more than twenty witnesses, she had recommended that the school board fire Ronald Gregory for sexual harassment and misconduct. Six women had testified that Gregory sexually harassed them. The U.S. Equal Employment Opportunity Commission (EEOC) would support their charges eight months later.[10]

In Wallace's mind, the evidence of misconduct was overwhelming. But the board voted 4 to 3 along racial lines that Wednesday evening to go against the recommendation and let Gregory keep his job. The same evening the Brunswick County School Board offered the superintendent's job to another candidate.

Once again Wallace had been deserted by her own board, almost at the same moment her escape hatch was sealed. But if she must stay, she decided, there would be no more rolling over. If she was going to stay, she was going to fight. Laura Joyner was doing the same. Joyner filed a complaint with the EEOC, inviting federal investigation of the board's improper handling of the Gregory sexual harassment case. That alone picked up Wallace's spirits.

She spent what remained of the summer pulling her central office staff together. Her administrators had strayed in different directions, and she wanted them to focus again on GLOBE 2000. She loosened up from all the tension by breaking away for a couple of weekends to do some honky-tonk dancing in South Hill, Virginia, and Raleigh. Then she plunged back into the revolution with renewed vigor.

Her plan to eliminate the Bell-Curve Syndrome through an ungraded system with high standards was about to unfold districtwide after a turbulent year of planning and trial and error. All of the elementary schools and the two middle schools would open without grades and grade levels. Only the high schools retained the old structure, though they too had reduced tracking; established mixed-age home rooms, where students met with teacher advisers; and were making plans for their move into a bell curve–free system in the 1993–94 school year.

Wallace gathered her teachers on August 22 for a pep talk. She reminded them they were facing a great opportunity to save students from despair and to win respect for themselves and their community. She reminded them of how far they had come in a year that had elevated discussion about education to perhaps its highest level in the county's history.

"I promised myself several years ago that I would never again work in a traditional school system," she said. "And I hope you are coming to feel the same way."[11]

Five days later Vance County's scores on the Scholastic Aptitude Test, a college entrance exam taken by seniors, were released. They had dropped 41 points in 1991–92 to a dismal 756 out of a possible 1,600 points. That put Vance way below the state average of 855, the second lowest statewide score in the nation. While the drop had nothing to do with Wallace's work since the high schools were still just planning for change, critics used the results to attack the district's reforms. This capped a bleak and gloomy summer for Wallace. But her fortune was about to turn.

Brown's Blunder

Less than two weeks into the new school year, Deborah Brown went to Wallace's office, demanding that Wallace sign a student transfer form allowing her to take her daughter out of Eaton Johnson Middle School. The chairwoman of Vance County's school board wanted to send her child to the neighboring Granville County School System.

"I did not feel my daughter was being academically challenged or motivated," Brown would later tell reporters. "People can draw their own conclusions about what that means for the schools."[12]

Wallace refused to sign the transfer request, reminding Brown that the full board had to approve any out-of-county transfers. So Brown called a special daytime board meeting. The board members all showed up and granted her request to transfer her daughter, but they were furious she'd called them away from their jobs to address her own personal agenda.

The board's reaction was mild, however, compared with that of the other county residents, who felt betrayed. Angry letters poured into the newspaper's and superintendent's offices, and the radio station talk show air waves sizzled with parents' fury. Wallace too had had enough. She was not about to take the high road this time.

"The reaction from parents is that they've been poked in the eye with a sharp stick," she told *The News & Observer*. "Educators feel they've been hit up side the head with a 2-by-4. Mrs. Brown's actions just aren't fair to the other 7,000 students and their parents who are trying to make school reform work in the county."[13]

Brown initially blamed her decision to move her child on Wallace's reform plan. But when that failed to carry any weight, she said she wanted to remove her child from an "immoral and unhealthy situation," though she never explained precisely what was immoral or unhealthy. Her credibility plummeted. Petitions calling for her resignation began circulating throughout the county. An editorial in *The News & Observer* advised residents to decide whether they wanted to "retain an education board member who thinks the schools she helps govern aren't good enough for her own child." At the regular September 14 board meeting, several parents presented petitions and demanded that Brown resign. One of them, Dana Jenkins, said Brown had "thoroughly demoralized an entire system of teachers."

Meanwhile, Wallace made headlines of her own at the meeting by confronting the full board with an impassioned ultimatum for support. After hiring her and supporting her plan, they'd abandoned her to be bludgeoned by self-serving critics. They'd taken an adversarial stand against school employees, arguing the board's job was to serve voters by holding the feet of teachers and administrators to the fire. The exception was Jackie Jackson.

"The only way I want to represent anybody is if they want me to help build a good school system," Jackson said, "and that's what I intend to do as long as I am on this board."

Wallace was grateful for Jackson, an occasional point of light on this disheartening board. But she'd lost all patience with the board's flaccid support of GLOBE 2000, its seeming indifference to seriously deteriorating school facilities, and its rare mention of children. Why, she wondered, do residents elect these people?

Her disgust with the board welled up as she outlined her Ten-Point Plan for 1992–93 on overhead transparencies projected on the wall above the judge's bench in the Vance County Courthouse. This was not to be confused with GLOBE 2000, the district's broader school restructuring plan, she told the board. The Ten-Point Plan outlined the district's specific goals for the immediate school year. The plan, for example, called for more training; installation of a computer system to track student academic progress; expansion of social services; more decentralization; increased citizen and parent involvement; construction of two new schools; and improved relationships among employees, residents, school board members, and other government leaders.

Wallace proceeded with a sense of futility. There she was outlining ambitious ideals before a board that did not even have its own place to meet. As at most board meetings in the last year, the bolted-down theater-style seats were full in the hot, steamy courtroom this evening. School board meetings had become a popular form of local theater. Hollywood could shoot a remake of *To Kill A Mockingbird* in this courtroom with its high windows, gray banisters, and tawdry tan carpeting laid over creaky wood floors.

As she described the plan to her smug overseers, Wallace suddenly concluded it was pointless to proceed without their firm commitment. Once again it was time to confront the board and force it to take a stand, one way or the other. She did so, spontaneously and passionately.

"You know about everything in this plan. There is nothing new here. Its content is not the problem. The problem is the board does not support anything. You have not supported what you hired me to do, and it is difficult for all of us in the school system to carry out changes in this school system without the support of the board.

"It is the obligation of the board to set the direction of the school system and then support it. In the final analysis, it's up to the board. Either you help or you don't, and right now you are not."

She told the board she expected them to be cheerleaders for Vance County schools and to give her at least a year of solid support to allow the reform plan to work.

"I don't want to be evaluated on whether [County Commissioner] Terry Garrison likes me or not," she said. "I can't do a whole lot about that. But I can do something about the curriculum and the assessment and raising the professionalism and dignity of teachers in this school system."

She asked the board to review seriously the ten goals and decide by its next meeting what, if anything, it wanted to change or eliminate.

"Whatever the ten points come out to be, let us all agree on them," she said. "If you're not willing to support a plan, let me know. I'm tired of fighting battles for change alone. If there is any piece of this you don't want me to be doing, I sure as hell am not having fun beating my head against the wall."

Wallace paused and sensed a tense stillness in the big room, now so quiet it could be empty.

"I came to Vance County with a missionary's zeal," she said with a tired smile. "I still have that, even though I feel a little bloody around the edges sometimes."

She told the board there would always be a small pocket of resistance to change, but Vance County leaders must not be intimidated by a few rabble-rousers. Instead, they must honor the majority of citizens who want change.

After the speech, Chairwoman Brown called for a recess. Wallace stepped down and was hugged by two principals, John Streb and Wayne Adcock. Bob Fuller, director of maintenance, stepped up to her and whispered, "If I ever get in a barroom brawl, I want you on my side."

That sentiment prevailed among the crowd and in the community. Wallace soon learned that she had won widespread respect with her strong and courageous stand. Immediately following the board meeting, several civic organizations and a parent-teacher group asked if they could publicly support the Ten-Point Plan. Other county residents called Wallace's office, asking how they could help support the annual goals. Wallace had not attempted to solicit public support for this phase of her program, but if the community wanted to show its support, she certainly wasn't going to get in the way. Such support could help convince the board that the majority of residents wanted change. So she and Laura Joyner sent copies of the plan to major organizations throughout the county, asking for suggested changes and endorsements. Everyone knew that the board would respond to the community and that its vote would reflect the community's confidence in Wallace.

The response was explosive. Within the week, the Kiwanis Club of Henderson paid for a quarter-page advertisement in the *Dispatch*. It stated:

> The Kiwanis Club of Henderson endorses and supports 100 percent the Ten-Point Plan for Reforming Vance County Schools, and we support Dr. Betty Wallace 100 percent. We appreciate and welcome the vision and leadership Dr. Wallace has brought to Vance County, and we encourage the School Board, the County Commissioners, and the entire county to rally around her efforts to reform our school system. With her leadership and our support, we can build a world-class school system right here in Vance County. Making the world a better place for young children is the number one goal of Kiwanis International, and we believe that our work for children begins in our own community.[14]

The *Henderson Daily Dispatch* printed the plan and a response form along with an editorial that encouraged people to support the goals and Wallace. The newspaper and the district office received 212 responses, 93 percent of which supported the plan. Another 6 percent backed it with suggested changes, and 1 percent opposed it. Many of the respondents asked the board to leave Wallace alone. There also were a few critics. Queen Mason said she hated the plan and outcomes-based education. J. Henry Banks, Gregory's attorney, said the survey was flawed and designed to produce an endorsement of Wallace. But the overwhelming support heartened Wallace, her staff, and hundreds of teachers.

Perhaps the surest signal of Wallace's growing grass-roots support surfaced in an invitation from Kittrell Grocery Store, the unofficial community center of a town too small for a stop light in southern Vance County. Farmers and fox hunters gathered daily at the country store along U.S. Highway 1 to talk about hounds, sports, and politics. Mike Faulkner, the store's young owner, commanded respect in this close-knit community for his common sense and willingness to get involved. He and the local residents had been following Wallace's battles with Green and Brown and had decided to act. They'd have the superintendent over to share a morning ham biscuit and let her know they were behind her.

Before long, the event had expanded into a lunch. So many people wanted to come that Faulkner had to move the gathering out back to a white warehouse with a metal roof and DOG FOOD printed in big blue letters on its plywood siding. Growing up in the Blue Ridge Mountains had taught Wallace enough about country politics to understand the political power of a country grocery store. And she knew that Vance County political leaders understood this too. So her appearance at the Kittrell store would earn her respect not only in Kittrell but also among her political enemies. Besides that, though, she wanted to meet these people. They and their children were the reason she was in Vance County.

The Kittrell lunch was served on a beautiful, clear mid-October day. Dressed smartly in a white blouse, plaid jacket, and long dark skirt, Wallace crossed the lawn to the warehouse and began introducing herself to the Kittrell community. Several residents said they were surprised a woman of such stature in the county stood only five feet three inches tall. "Somehow I thought you'd be taller," they said.

About thirty people gathered inside the warehouse. Fifty-pound sacks of dried Red Dot Chunks dog food were stacked along the walls to make room. Among the group was John Floyd, a candidate for the school board; Ginger Miller, principal of Zeb Vance; W. A. West, a tobacco farmer wearing a baseball cap emblazoned with

Dismal Swamp Fox Hunters Association; Sarah Wente, a *Henderson Daily Dispatch* reporter; Janey Brown, member of the Zeb Vance PTA; a man dressed in U.S. Army camouflage fatigues; and Danny Stanton, a beer distributor who grew up in Kittrell and figured Wallace's plan deserved a chance.

"The positive side is it doesn't keep the kids who want to learn, who want to advance, back," Stanton told a reporter. "This community is behind her more than a lot of other communities."

Faulkner had set up some folding tables and chairs and brought in some big metal pots full of Kittrell Fried Chicken, potato salad, coleslaw, and rolls. He described his motives to Wente.

> I just wanted to show some support for Dr. Wallace. Maybe if people can come together and talk, some of this bickering will stop. Dr. Wallace is a tough lady. She's trying to move Vance County forward. It seems like everybody's fussing and fighting and going off in different directions. Now, I don't know a lot about education, but all this pulling apart and bickering can't be good. If we all really care about the children and the schools, we've got to work together. Driving off the past school superintendents has gotten us into this mess. This is my effort to get everyone together to work it out.[15]

The folks talked plenty, about cotton, cows, 'coon hunting, football, and schools. After everyone had eaten, they invited Wallace to say a few words. She stood, smiled, and spoke from the heart.

"I'm from Macon County. My daddy hangs around a store up where they live called Stamey's Grocery that's very much like Kittrell Grocery. All the fox hunters and farmers hang out at Stamey's and discuss things. And folks who just appear to be hanging around can get things done. A bunch of men at Stamey's decided things in Macon County weren't going the way they thought it should. So they decided to run the president of the fox hunters association for county commissioner.

"Word spread from one little country store to the next, and believe it or not, he was elected. That just goes to show what can happen when a community works together."

Wallace then told a Southern yarn about her encounter as a young girl with a mountain encampment of fox hunters who "were sitting on lawn chairs, drinking Jack Daniels and listening to the dogs running." When her tale was done, she gazed over her small, attentive audience with an affectionate and grateful smile, reluctant to bring this special meeting to an end.

"I understand this," she said quietly.

And they nodded, as if to say "We know."

Kittrell marked a turning point. Betty Wallace knew her battles weren't over, but she also now knew she was no longer fighting them alone. A few days later she pulled out the FOR SALE sign stuck in her lawn.

Turning Point

In November the school board voted 5 to 2 in support of the Ten-Point Plan, with Brown and Roosevelt Alston, a newly elected board member, casting the dissenting votes. The board's support still rang hollow, but at least Wallace had the official authority she needed to press forward without compromise. Another important victory came two weeks later when Vance County learned its drop-out rate had plummeted from 5 percent to 3 percent, the lowest level in ten years, during Wallace's first year at the helm. The state reported the dropout rate as a percentage of all students in grades kindergarten through 12. But since nearly all students quit in high school, a more meaningful way of looking at the county's losses was to consider the proportion of students a class of entering high school freshmen would lose by the time it graduated four years later. Viewed that way, the number had previously been about one in three. During Wallace's first year, however, it fell to the national average of about one in four. That translated into 126 students, a figure Wallace still considered appalling. Nevertheless, in previous years the county had seen as many as twice that number become so discouraged they up and quit.

Again, Wallace could hardly attribute the improvement to GLOBE 2000 since that was still in the planning stages at the high schools. But she did think internal changes contributed to the reduction in dropouts by shifting the system's focus away from groups to individuals and raising the community consciousness about the importance of education. Public schools were gaining stature and value in Vance County. People were talking and thinking more about their schools. The turmoil that had made education front-page news proved residents believed better schools were worth fighting for.

Even this victory, however, was not enough to silence the critics. James Green and his supporters showed up at the November school board meeting to put more pressure on Wallace. She was not about to be intimidated. She had put her support to the test with the referendum on the Ten-Point Plan and had clearly passed, and she had a political base that Green could not undermine. Green urged the board to put a hold on outcomes-based education, possibly by restricting it to one or two schools. The Reverend Clyde B. Walton, pastor of a local church and longtime friend of Green, said "the plan needs to be cut back, cut down, or even cut out."

A week later Green took a step as desperate and ill-conceived as Brown's decision to pull her child out of Vance County schools. He and Walton wrote a letter to Weaver Rogers, executive director of the state Board of Education, on behalf of Green's group, the Vance Association of Concerned Citizens for Better Education, asking for the ouster of Wallace and outcomes-based education. The letter claimed Wallace and the school board bypassed required training and proceeded to revolutionize the entire school system. It also cited inaccurate SAT scores for Vance County and the state as evidence the plan was a mistake.

Rogers's response was not sympathetic. He said the state board was optimistic that the state's four outcomes-based education pilot projects "will bring significant improvements to the public schools in North Carolina." State educators also said pioneering districts were free to move from planning to action whenever they wanted. The state flatly rejected Green's complaint, and the *Henderson Daily Dispatch* reported the details on its front page, including the superintendent's response. Wallace took full advantage of this low attack by Green to deliver him a powerful counterblow.

"Representative Green just pops up here and there like the Energizer bunny, beating his drum and disrupting other people's business," she told the newspaper. "And he just keeps on going and going, spreading his negative energy in the most unexpected places.

"I don't know how to respond to something so irrational. I don't know why an elected official would try to cut $1.65 million and a chance for us to become a model school system. All the other legislators I know are trying to bring opportunities into their districts, not cut them out. I've never seen anything like this before, except maybe in Harlan County, Ky., or Dothan, Ala."[16]

With a few sharp words, Betty Wallace made Green look like a trivial figure in Vance County, a meddlesome toy who was not to be taken seriously—at least not in her arena. But Green didn't give up. He called a public meeting for the Vance Association of Concerned Citizens for Better Education. This time Wallace and some supporters, including lawyer George Templeton Blackburn II and Laura Joyner, showed up at New Bethel Baptist Church to attend. When they arrived, though, Green asked them all to leave. He said announcements about the meeting being public were a mistake. It was Wallace's ouster, not Green's complaints, that won headlines in Monday's paper. Wallace told the newspaper only about thirty or forty people showed for the meeting, and there was great division among them.

"Green kept sending us out because he did not want us to see the hostile division among the troops," she said.[17]

Wallace had Green on a rout. Every time he took a shot at her, she turned it into a missile that roared right back at him. She was destroying his credibility while increasing her own. The more he attacked, the stronger she became. This final skirmish apparently was enough to convince Green it was time to lie low.

In an interview nearly a year later, Green said he had never intended to try to derail Wallace's plan. He just wanted to slow down the change, he said, because many teachers and parents were complaining they were under pressure to move too fast.

"I thought it had good potential," he said of the plan.

After her final skirmish with Green, Wallace took action to protect herself from Deborah Brown and her political foes on the school board. On December 17, 1992, two days before the six-month filing period expired, she filed charges with the U.S. Equal Employment Opportunity Commission. She claimed she had become the target of retaliatory discrimination because she investigated employee complaints of sexual harassment by Ronald Gregory. In the complaint, Wallace mentioned Brown's threats aimed at her and Gloria Lunsford-Boone.

During the Christmas break Wallace got a chance to think about how far she'd come in the last eighteen months. I must be crazy, she thought. There she was, an outsider in her first county superintendency post in one of the worst school systems in the United States, battling her own school board and the leader of the black community while carrying out one of the most revolutionary changes in public education ever tried anywhere in the country. She smiled at the thought of her daddy's words: "Remember, when you're dealing with son-of-a-bitches, you just haf'ta figure out some way to out-son-of-a-bitch 'em."

He would be proud of her now, she thought with a chuckle.

Victories

News over the next few weeks made the entire county proud. On December 18 the state Department of Public Instruction announced that it was going to recommend Vance County be removed from the state's takeover list because of the dramatic progress it had made in reducing its dropout rate. This was the first good news Vance County had had about its schools in years. The *Henderson Daily Dispatch* praised Wallace and her staff in an editorial that said "the results are encouraging not only for them but also for Vance County's future."[18] A week later it again named the school district and its struggle to change the top news story of the year in its circulation area of Vance, Warren, and Granville counties.

Wallace's big victory came a week later, however, when the state issued its annual report card and showed Vance County among the most improved. During its first year under Wallace's leadership, the district nearly doubled the proportion of state standards it met, climbing from 39 percent in 1991 to 68 percent in 1992. The county met standards in twenty-three of thirty-four areas, falling just three shy of meeting state accreditation. In the previous year, the system had met only eleven of twenty-eight standards. The most dramatic improvements were in primary and intermediate mathematics, primary and middle school science, primary social studies, and high school chemistry and geometry. In most of these cases, Betty Wallace believed at least part of the gains could be attributed to internal changes that had discouraged instructional practices based on uses of the bell curve and that had increased focus on learning goals. The district was moving from group-oriented instruction that served only some students to a more individualized approach that served them all. And it was working.

This was the first time the county had rated at par for school systems of similar economic and social makeup. The *Henderson Daily Dispatch* called it a "dramatic turnaround."[19] Wallace was ecstatic when she talked to the newspaper:

> All the outcome-based education skeptics kept saying they would wait for the test results. Well, the test results are in and they show that our students are winners big time. We raised our expectations and pushed our students to learn more and to learn in different ways, and they did. Our teachers believed that all students could learn at much higher levels and the students came through.[20]

Wallace's critics could not dismiss this kind of success. She had turned the county around after a ten-year decline. Betty Wallace assumed this was just the beginning. Student achievement would continue to climb because the disease that had been hurting so many children was weakening.

Two weeks later, as President Bill Clinton took his oath of office and promised change for the nation, Vance County allowed more than one hundred students to advance to higher levels and new campuses either at the middle or high schools. This midyear shift symbolized Vance County's commitment to change and its parting with tradition, mediocrity, and the Bell-Curve Syndrome.

Rough Edges

By 1993 political problems abated and Vance County's restructured school system settled into a relatively quiet routine for the remainder of its second year. The new structure, however, still was crude, like a framed but unfinished house. Conventions from the old system hung on like cobwebs.

Schools and teachers clung to their old habits. There continued to be far too much whole-group instruction, too much age-based grouping, too many references to the grade levels of students who were not supposed to be in grades anymore. Even the structure of some schools retained traditional age-based features. At E. M. Rollins Elementary, for example, students still were grouped largely by age within each team. Apparently the animal names now used for teams pretty much represented its earlier grade levels. This produced far less flexibility than some teachers had envisioned.

"We're not the graded structure we used to be, but we're not totally ungraded either," acknowledged Principal John Streb. "We've chosen a path of transition."

That caution would later cause Rollins, once the district's top-performing school, to lose ground to other schools that were carrying out change more aggressively.

Teachers also were tending to track students within their teams. While it makes sense to group students, say in reading, by achievement levels, this needs to be done with expectations that students in the low group eventually will advance to the highest group before moving on to the next team. Groups within teams should then function like steps on a staircase leading from one level to the next. But at least some schools, including Rollins, were letting students at the bottom steps jump to the next team's bottom steps. These schools, in effect, were resorting to the old practice of sorting expectations for students.

In addition, teachers were still pulling students out of class for special categories of learning. Martha Anderson at Zeb Vance Elementary School, for example, said her team referred eight to ten students out of a class of twenty-six to a learning disabled class because they weren't making sufficient progress. Other schools still were sending students out of class for federal math and reading remedial services or isolating them in gifted and talented classes.

Some teachers were confusing Vance County's new focus on learning objectives with a practice called mastery learning, which shares some similarities. Mastery learning, however, is group-oriented, requiring all students in a group to master one skill or objective before the group moves on to the next. This means the fastest students are forced to kill time doing special activities while they wait for slower classmates to master a lesson. Only then can they all advance to higher study levels.

Teachers also stumbled over just when to allow a student to advance from one level to the next. The standards spelled out what students needed to be able to do in the areas of reading, writing, and mathematics, and what they must know in core subjects such as science and social studies. In some cases, however, students were able to do what was required to advance to a higher level, but they still didn't know enough. An intermediate student, for example, might be able to read and do math at the middle-school level, yet still have a few holes in knowledge, say about electricity and magnetism or economic relationships in the Western hemisphere. Teachers questioned whether sometimes it wasn't wiser to allow students with all the required skills to move forward and fill the gaps in knowledge at the higher level. After mulling the issue over, Wallace and her curriculum staff agreed.

"After all," Wallace told her curriculum leaders, "there is no such thing as an intermediate-level amoeba, a middle-school Civil War, or a primary-level Eskimo."

The computer management system that was to be a tool in both assessing and tracking student progress became more complex than the curriculum and instruction staff could handle. It would not be ready for evaluating students' mastery of learning goals until the 1993–94 school year, and then only in mathematics.

"We were enormously naive about how difficult it would be," said Bill Mueller, the testing director.

State grade-level testing posed another problem for the district. Since Vance County had no grades, it was not clear whom to give the tests to. The district, for example, could give the annual spring tests, which were based on the state curriculum, to students who had reached its primary-, intermediate-, and middle-school exit-team levels, the closest thing it had to grades 3, 6, and 8. But what about the students who were advancing from those levels at earlier quarters in the year? Some teachers were inclined to hold students back rather than let them advance early because those students were likely to score higher on the tests. Allowing them to advance

early and miss the test could make the school's test scores drop—
not the kind of incentive the district needed. Fortunately, it was
able to win state permission to give the test to advancing exit-level
students four times a year, thus removing the incentive for teachers
to hold students back.

There were other concerns. Coaches worried that children moving into the middle and high schools early would be physically un-
derdeveloped for athletic competition, as if that should be reason to
hold back their academic advances. And two board members
agreed with them. Then there was college. Betty Wallace assured
parents that the high schools would not drop course credits until
they were sure students could compete for college by meeting high
standards, producing portfolios, and taking entrance exams. Most
colleges already had alternative admission procedures, and some
were establishing formal portfolio admission options. Still, parents
worried their children would not be able to compete for college
without grades or honor roll memberships on their transcripts.

Many teachers, parents, and students remained confused about
progress in the new system, which was supposed to be flexible
enough to allow students to move continuously at their own pace.
This meant some students would move slower than most for a variety of reasons. Students would have the option, for example, of
slowing down at some stages in their learning to savor and explore
knowledge they found particularly intriguing. Yet some parents,
teachers, and students were still in the habit of judging how smart
students were on the basis of how they compared to others the same
age. This posed problems for children who were not advancing as
fast as their peers.

"They feel like they are being retained," said Gail Washington, a
teacher at Rollins.

That feeling would persist as long as adults focused on comparisons rather than standards and continued to expect students of the
same age to advance en masse on specific dates. The stigma that
came with slipping behind the pack would diminish only when the
pack began to dissipate in a mixed-age stream. And for this, the
system needed to become more fluid so that students moved continuously from level to level, team to team, school to school, like
hikers following different paths to the same mountain lake.

Despite these many obstacles, Wallace and her staff pressed forward. And for all their troubles, they began to get glimpses of the new territory they were all seeking. Vance County schools were changing in more ways than most residents realized.

CHAPTER 7

▼

FIRST FRUITS

Robert Pirie fairly disappeared among the hive of students humming about him in his airy classroom at Zeb Vance Elementary School. Students clattered away at an assortment of computer keyboards fringing the room. Some students worked in pairs. Others worked on paper at their desks. Everyone was busy, and no one seemed to stay in one place long. Pirie usually had a few students hovering about his desk, which served as his command center. There, like an air traffic controller, he monitored the progress of students working at various levels and paces in their common quest to master mathematics.

Anthony Riggan, ten, reviewed percentages on one computer. Lee Toya Jones, twelve, learned fractions on another. Nicole Faucette, eleven, studied line segments on a third.

"I like it better than just doing math in the book all the time," Nicole said, on this sunny morning of April 19, 1993. "I like computers a lot."

Pirie, his blond hair askew, sat calmly at his command center with a puckish grin, providing a running commentary as he orchestrated his learning traffic.

"Weelllll," he said, giving the word a good Southern stretch, "Raymond just mastered multiplying fractions at the intermediate level, and he's now ready to go on to the advanced level."

Heads turned and gave Raymond a smile and nod. Pirie kept a keen eye on his charges, swift to praise and quick to send help when someone got off track or bogged down. If another student couldn't help, he would. He had even wired his machines to single out students for recognition. Pirie set up select computers for more difficult programs in geometry and story problems involving decimals, fractions, and percentages. Only when students mastered those concepts did the printers spill out their names and scores. So the noisy clatter of a computer printer signaled that someone had just solved a set of difficult problems.

"When one of those printers starts printing, the student just beams, and the students around him stop to listen to it too, and their responses add to the good feeling," Pirie said.

Next door, Wanda Dawson's students were similarly engaged in diverse activities. Some worked on reports related to a book they all read, *Where the Red Fern Grows*. One boy composed a report on the black gum tree. Others read novels. Dawson used the same individualized approach in reading that Pirie used in math. She and other language arts teachers in the school had opted to dump reading textbooks for a rich selection of literature. Dawson still would have her classes all read the same book on occasion, but her students also are expected to read at least sixteen books on their own. Many read far more. A few had read more than one hundred books. Reluctant readers usually changed their attitudes after they'd spent some time with Dawson. Sometimes she'd send them in pairs into a courtyard outside to read to one another.

"I find them easy things to read that they like, and they feel so good because they can read them," she said. "Then they want to move into harder books. They start with a favorite like *Give Us a Great Big Smile, Rosie Cole* and then move into *The Bridge to Terabitha* and *The Borrowers*. Once they get a taste of success, there is no holding them back. They want more success, and they learn that reading truly good books is fun."

One reluctant reader, Telitha Holden, discovered the joy of reading in Dawson's class during the 1992–93 school year. Before the year was out, she had read more than fifty books. Students left Dawson's class independent learners.

"They are critical thinkers," Dawson said. "They can function with little assistance. They can all write a paper with a beginning, middle, and end."

Here in the classrooms of Pirie and Dawson and other teachers at Zeb Vance Elementary School, Wallace's vision was becoming reality. Teachers were combining individualized instruction with high standards and largely ignoring the bell curve. Comparing and sorting disappeared with grades and grade levels. Students were taking more control over their own learning, working for knowledge and skills rather than grades. Teachers were lecturing less, guiding more.

Pirie and Dawson were part of what Zeb Vance calls its exit team, the final team of four teachers that students must work under before they can leave the school. Laura Tigsbee, who taught science, and Valerie Hawkins, who specialized in social studies, made up the second half of the team. The lower teams—known as early primary, upper primary, and transition—were similarly organized. Students were placed in each team and grouped and continually regrouped within teams based on what they knew and could primarily in reading and mathematics. Therefore, students of many ages might have been in the same group because they shared similar education needs. A beginning reader was grouped with other beginning readers, and an independent reader was placed with other independent readers. Even with these more academically homogeneous groups, however, teachers still tried to avoid group instruction in favor of more individualized approaches that let students take control of their learning. Students advanced from team to team based on what they learned rather than their age.

To leave the exit team, they had to meet the intermediate-level standards established by the district the previous year. That meant they had to understand fractions, decimals, basic properties of geometry and principles of algebra, and applications of measurement, graphing, probability, and statistics. They had to know how to read independently, write well, and understand grammar and punctuation. They needed to know the major systems of the body, the general relationship between matter and energy, features of the solar system, ecosystems, weather, oceans, electricity, and magnetism. They required to understand the difference in life cycles between seed plants and conifers. They had to know about the culture, economies, and histories of North Carolina in particular and countries in the Western Hemisphere in general. They had to know a lot.

The Zeb Vance staff launched its new plan in August 1992, when it moved into a beautiful new building designed in an art deco style with pink and turquoise pastel tiles and bullnose-brick patterns.

Classrooms of varying shapes and sizes wrapped around a central courtyard designed with multilevel brick platforms. The new school symbolized Vance County's new start, and Wallace put Ginger Miller, a strong advocate for change, at the helm. Miller had taught in a nongraded school. Further, as the district's elementary education director, she had visited other schools, such as Paint Branch, that were also doing away with grades and grading. She understood the Bell-Curve Syndrome and was committed to crushing it. The school opened with that mission.

As the school year unfolded, the school became more flexible. Initially, the teams roughly mirrored grade levels. But slowly, teachers began letting students move from one group to another, and from one team to another, when they proved they were ready. Young students advanced into groups with older students. In some cases, students were allowed to advance to higher teams in single subjects, such as reading. In January the exit team sent a dozen students on to middle school. The system quickly became more fluid and more focused on individuals rather than groups.

"One of the strengths of this system is these teachers know these children better than in any school I've been in," Miller said in April. "I've had a number of parents tell me this is the best year their children have had."

This new school and structure emerged as paradise for Pirie and Dawson. Both had been setting high expectations for students and allowing them to find individual ways of meeting them for years. Long before Betty Wallace came to Vance County, they had both been team-teaching fifth graders. Pirie taught science and math; Dawson, reading and social studies. They were forced, though, to comply with the bell-curve conventions of a group-based system. They were forced, for example, to compare students with grades and standardized tests. They also flunked the district's standardized evaluation system for teachers, they reported with a chuckle. The system was geared to judging a teacher on the basis of whole-group instruction, something neither engaged in often. Their method of letting students take charge of their learning was viewed more as a practice reserved for gifted and talented children. Pirie and Dawson treated all of their students as if they were gifted.

"The evaluators always gave me lower marks than other teachers, but my students always scored higher on the state tests," Pirie said. "If I taught like everybody else, my students' scores would be like everybody else's—low."

Pirie, a Henderson native, had always done things differently from most teachers. He even got into the education business in an unusual way. After college and a tour in Vietnam compliments of the U.S. Marines, he returned to Henderson. Shortly thereafter the school board chairman stopped him on the street and asked if he wanted to be a teacher. Pirie was soon in the classroom under a state provision that allowed him to teach with probationary status while he worked summers for his teaching certificate.

Pirie knew nothing about teaching other than what he could remember from his own days in school. So he did what made sense. He gave different students different learning plans because they had varying needs. He rarely taught lessons to the whole class. Students learned best, he observed, through hands-on experience that gave them instant feedback. Students lost interest in math, for example, when they had to wait a day or two to see if the problems they solved were correct. So Pirie started looking for ways to provide students more responsive learning experiences. There were no computers then, but he built pegboards with lights that glowed when students got problems correct. His students were intrigued by these, just as they are with computers today, because they gave them instant feedback. He built boards with blinking lights to study the human body and the solar system. He set up inviting learning centers around his room where students could study various subjects in small groups. When computers came on the scene, Pirie began scouring garage and rummage sales and wiring together more sophisticated learning machines for his students. Slowly his collection grew, turning his classroom into an increasingly sophisticated learning laboratory.

With his wry grin, wild hair, and eyes that flash like his lights, Pirie looks like an eccentric scientist. He has an uncommon belief in the ability of all children to meet high academic standards. He sees his role as helping children discover their own competence. Some have lost confidence in their ability to learn because they come from

low-income families or the poor side of the railroad tracks, which
literally divide Henderson by class. That usually means they also
end up on the low end of the bell curve.

"Some of them are so street smart and have so much experience
in figuring the angles, the probabilities of the situation, that they
can grasp mathematics better than some of the rich kids who have
just had everything handed to them," Pirie said. "But at first they
don't realize they can do it. . . . You just can't accept failure. That's
just crap, and a waste of time. Then you 'hurray' them to death
when they come through. And then you all feel good."

As these students begin having small successes, he says, they can't
get their fill of the sweet taste. "Not even the worst bunch wants to
move backward to a lower level. It's just common sense. . . . Once
they do it, 99.9 percent of them will begin to realize that if they
work even harder, they are just as good as anybody else."

Dawson became a disciple of Pirie's at age eleven, when she was
in his fifth-grade class.

"I went home and told my mother that I wanted to be a teacher
just like Pirie," said Dawson, a trim, soft-spoken young teacher
with an ever-present soft smile. "He expected everybody to learn
everything."

His lessons worked so well for her that after finishing college, she
went right back to teach just like him—in the room next door.
They've been together ever since. Both have long had a reputation
for producing the top-achieving students in the district. Still, they
were viewed as mavericks, and other teachers were not inclined to
follow them—until Wallace came. With the advent of GLOBE
2000 in Vance County, Pirie's and Dawson's status shifted from
oddballs to innovative leaders.

A stroll through the school revealed that their way was becoming
everyone's. In Martha Anderson's class children ages eight to ten
worked in groups, searched for compound words in *Charlotte's
Web*. A chart on the wall showed that every child in this class, part
of the transition team, had met Anderson's goal of reading fifteen
books. Many have read far more, so many that there was no room
on the chart to record them all. Emily Hudson, a ten-year-old with
freckles, gold-rimmed glasses, and long brown hair, had read 110

books, and appreciated the chance to reach as high academically as she can stretch.

"I needed a challenge," she said. "I used to get bored."

Anderson said she was slowly finding the courage to give her students more control over their learning. She could see the wisdom and benefits of doing so, even in the progress of her own daughter, who has quickly advanced in the more flexible school.

"It is still very hard for me to let go," Anderson said. "I'm not sure children of this age can take responsibility for their own education and move at their own pace."

Diane Koontz, a reading teacher on a primary team, was as skeptical as anyone of the nongraded structure. But she soon became a convert after she watched how quickly some of her students, unbridled by standardized lessons and a group pace, surged ahead. She was impressed with the school's new flexibility. She watched one boy skip upper primary and go right on into the transition team. Some upper primary children would go up to the transition team for math, and some transition children would slip down to a primary group for reading. This flexibility allowed teachers always to place children where they fit.

"In this, no one gets shortchanged," Koontz said. "The kids who need more assistance and time do not feel bad because there is not anybody in their class that is that much higher. We had kids who hated school. Now they like coming to school. Even parents are coming in a little more."

Like most teachers at Zeb Vance, Koontz was not interested in turning back to traditional practices. "I like it [the change]," she said. "I think it really needs to be here. It has helped the kids."

Most students, particularly those who struggled on the low end of the bell curve in traditional schools, also seem to like it.

"I learn here easier," said Jerome Williams, a twelve-year-old who transferred to Zeb Vance from a neighboring county shortly after the school year began. At his old school, Williams was having behavioral problems. He failed to do homework and put in long hours at the principal's office. At Zeb Vance, however, he fit in and swiftly became productive.

"At the other school I could hardly understand anything, they were going so fast," he said. "But here I can."

The new nongraded structure dramatically changed school for Heather Jones, a robust ten-year-old girl with long brown hair. Almost from the day she entered, it seemed, Heather languished in the traditional school. Her parents, Sarah and Jesse Jones, were concerned. They had to push and prod her to do homework, and even then, she just got by with mediocre grades and an occasional D. There was just no fire in those bright blue eyes.

"She could do it, but she just did not apply herself," said her mother. "Heather couldn't get what she needed to do in order from kindergarten all the way up. She didn't want to do it. She did not want to do homework. She was frustrated. We made her do it, but she did not apply herself."

When Zeb Vance abolished grades, it put Heather at the lower level in the transition team. Heather was uneasy with her placement. She felt she could handle more challenging work. Her parents and teachers said she would have to prove it. So she did.

"She did a complete about-face," said her father. "She started off this year in the lower level. She's already in the top-level class now."

Heather also for the first time was happy with school, her parents said. She said she initially was driven to work harder so she could be with friends who had already advanced to higher levels. But soon success became its own reward, as it always does.

"I like this way better," Heather said. "When we had As and Bs and Cs, some kids were faster than me, some were slower than me. Most of the time I was behind or ahead of the class. Now I can go at my own pace and be where I want to be. Now I can go as fast as I can or as slow as I need to."

Like her classmates, Heather was discovering that it was not intelligence but effort that helped her so swiftly reach the high levels of the exit team.

"We're not smarter," she says. "We work harder."

Heather's experience convinced the Joneses that Vance was wise to part with the bell curve. "I'm impressed with this system," said Sarah Jones. "For Heather it has worked."

Patricia Tabourn, a teacher's assistant at Zeb Vance, was not so impressed. But she had to admit it seemed to suit her daughter.

Charity Tabourn was among fifteen Zeb Vance Elementary students who advanced to Henderson Middle School in January. Her mother had reservations about the move, just as she did about report cards without grades and school without textbooks. None of these changes seemed right to her. Still, she said, her daughter thrived on an accelerated learning path.

"She was ready for the challenge," her mother said. "It seems like she is more motivated over there than she was over here."

The exit team saw the early promotion of children such as Charity as the first fruits of their labor.

"The mark of success is to get rid of your students, to bring out the best in them, and then send them on to greater heights," said Pirie. "It's kind of sad to see them go, but at the same time, pushing them out of the nest and expecting them to fly off into the future is what's fun about doing this."

The midyear promotions of more than one hundred students to higher programs—from primary to intermediate, intermediate to middle school, or middle school to high school—reflected the growing pliability of the system. While the schools were all in various stages of transition, none was what it used to be.

E. M. Rollins Elementary School

The brick corridors of E. M. Rollins school stretched out near downtown Henderson in traditional factory style. But traditions were crumbling like old mills inside. Grade levels and textbooks were disappeared and traditional group-based instruction faded fast.

In April of 1993, Teri Grissom's science class provided a window on the emerging new system. Her classroom bloomed like an exotic garden. The room was fringed with plants, aquariums, cages, and life. Duffy the lovebird perched in the back of the room, grooming his feathers. Two big fish fetched from a nearby lake swayed lazily in a tank nearby. Barney the rabbit hopped freely on the floor among students working in small groups on a variety of environmental science projects. Four students ages ten and eleven, for example, charted the results of their recycling efforts with a bar graph on poster board. These children belonged to the Toucans, the exit team at Rollins. All were busy, engaged, learning science by doing it. None was bored. Grissom, a young teacher who grew up in Henderson, was convinced this was the way to teach. Her students took some control over their learning. Her job was to give them an inviting place full of choices to learn and then to guide them in their explorations. This was Guided Learning, which cannot occur in classrooms organized the way they were when Grissom was a student in Vance County's traditional schools.

"All the way through school, I realized I didn't have all the hands-on content and the critical thinking skills I wished I had had," she said.

Grissom wanted to make learning more relevant, tangible, and individualized, and Vance County's new structure, with its focus on learning rather than teaching, gives her the freedom to do so.

"The children needed to be doing the learning, and teachers need to be facilitators," she said.

> I used to do more lecturing than I do now. That was just spitting out my knowledge and students were memorizing it. I don't spit something out and expect them to spit it back at me. They learn it by building things, through analysis and research, through recording results. It is really science. They understand more because they have experienced it themselves. I've found active learning and cooperative learning are strategies that work for me.

Down the hall, veteran teacher Rebecca Kita was trying her hand at similar strategies with her students, most ages six and seven. They were part of a primary team known as the Berenstain Bears. She sat at the center of a semicircular table with nine students before her. On the chalkboard behind her were the letters WHALE, which the children knew stood for Water, Habitat, Air, Life, and Energy. It was Earth Week, and Kita was integrating several lessons under that broad theme. She spread about one hundred plastic cubes before her students.

"This is how much water is on Earth," she told them.

Then she picked up one cube and said, "This is how much water we can drink."

She talked about acid rain, pollution, nuclear radiation, and some of the other hazards afflicting the earth's environment. Then she gave each child a card, according to his or her interests, that gave a simple two- or three-sentence explanation of an environmental problem. One child got a card describing the greenhouse effect; another got a card on the endangered elephant. The children were to write sentences based on the cards in their writing notebooks.

"I don't want you writing something you can't read to me," she warned.

Each child picked a topic and left the semicircle. When there were only three children left at the table, Kita gave each two plastic cubes. Each cube represented a tanker truck full of water, she said, and each human on average drinks two tanker trucks a year.

"How many tanker trucks of water do you all drink at this table?" she asked.

"Six trucks," they said, without hesitation.

Kita wrapped lessons in science, math, and writing into her morning session. She introduced small groups of students to a variety of environmental issues and used cubes to convey the mathematical relationships between the volume of water they drink and that covering the Earth. She allowed them to explore their interests in more depth through writing. While the group was studying the environment, individual students were given the freedom to explore their own interests within that broad area in as much depth as they chose. This was a clear departure from traditional group-oriented instruction geared to average needs in common lessons, usually pulled from textbooks. Kita liked the departure. She was lecturing less and using hands-on, small-group activities more. The only thing she didn't like, she said, was having to switch students with other teachers in her team. She'd rather have kept the same children all day.

"It is good to get away from the structured things," she said. "It is working in every way except having my kids all day."

Working in teams after years of classroom isolation poses a major adjustment for most veteran teachers, said John Streb, the tall principal with white hair and a neatly pressed white shirt.

"We are asking teachers to commit an unnatural act, and that is working together," he said. Still, he added, it was a change worth making.

Like the teachers at Zeb Vance, the Rollins faculty organized into teams that shared a group of students. Each teacher on the team specialized in a subject, and the team then rotated its students throughout the day until every teacher had taught every student. The team met at least twice a week to coordinate lessons, share ideas, and discuss children's progress. The teachers might, for example, all focus on the mountains of North Carolina. Students could research different aspects of mountain culture in social studies; explore mountain plants, animals, and geology in science; figure distances and mountain heights or chart health statistics of the region in math, and read mountain literature in English.

But on this morning, five teachers were planning a school show on recycling that would star their primary team, the Koala Bears. They debated which boy and girl should read a poem about recycling in this "throw-away world."

"I tell you, LeJean can do this," said teacher Lisa Baker. "I would love for him to do it. He needs to feel like he's not a throw-away boy."

The teams allowed teachers to share views on a common group of students they all know. The drawback is that they see more students for less time. To compensate, the teachers each served as an advocate for one-fifth of the team. As advocates, they were responsible for giving daily personal attention to the children in their group and ensuring every child made healthy academic progress. With experience, the teams would become more innovative and find more ways to utilize each teacher's strengths. One teacher, for example, might enthrall two-thirds of the children with a good story while the other three divide up the remaining third of students for more personal attention in small groups. On balance, a properly organized team of teachers could become more powerful than the sum of its parts.

"The teams tend to motivate everyone," said Streb. "It makes the good teachers better, and it makes the weak teachers stronger."

Rollins still retained qualities of its traditional structure, but it loosened up. Students advanced from team to team during the course of the year. Teachers lectured less and guided more. Instead of learning in isolation from group-based lessons, students worked more in small groups on individualized lessons. The school was subtly changing in profound ways.

"I'm seeing a rebirth," said Streb. "You return here next year, and I think you will see a much different school."

Pinkston Street

Principal Oddis Smith looked like a modern-day Pied Piper, ambling down the hallway of Pinkston Street School with children hanging onto his hands and coattail. He was easy to spot in his characteristic blue jeans, sports jacket, and boots, and he seemed to be everywhere and accessible to everyone. He was reading to children, calling their parents, imitating the Drifters' version of "Spanish Harlem" in an assembly program, coaxing more food out of the cafeteria workers, or hugging a restless student who lived with a drug-addicted mother. In one year his upbeat energy transformed the staff and climate at Pinkston Street School, which serves the largest concentration of poor children in Vance County. A school that had seemed silently resigned to failure suddenly came to life. Smith invigorated teachers and parents with a renewed faith in the ability of all children to achieve academically. The school simply needed to change its ways.

Smith was selected by a committee of teachers and parents at Pinkston Street as one of three final candidates to take the school's helm. He struck Wallace as a handsome grandfather, looking confident and young for his age. He spoke with the deft tongue of a resident from Vance County's affluent neighbor, Chapel Hill—home to the University of North Carolina and to one of the highest concentrations of doctorate degree holders in the nation.

After interviews with the candidates, Wallace concluded that Smith was what Pinkston Street needed. She joked to her personnel director, Gloria Lunsford-Boone, that Smith must be an imposter since he was missing his Chapel Hill tweed coat with suede elbow patches. Lunsford-Boone agreed he appeared to be his own man and a good choice.

"I never met Oddis Smith before today, but I know him," she said. "I understand him. I think he was a street-smart kid with a phenomenal brain who grew up to fit in anywhere he wants to go. I think that right now at this time in his life, he has a need to be where he is needed. And he and Pinkston Street need each other right now."

The administrators' instincts and insights proved true. Smith showed up for his first day of work July 1, 1992, with a bucket of paint for the faded, peeling Pinkston Street School sign. He planted shrubbery, put up goals on barren basketball courts, installed a playground for the four-year-olds, and put up an engraved bronze plaque recognizing the Parent-Teacher Organization and the federal Chapter I program for their contributions. He garnered copiers and more instructional materials and equipment for teachers. He brought overstuffed furniture into the school lobby and brightened the hallways with colorful posters. He treated the school with dignity.

And he did the same to teachers, parents, and children. He went into homes, churches, and businesses, boosting spirits and inviting involvement. Wherever people gathered and were willing to have him, he spoke. He built bridges between the school and community, convincing people the school was theirs and, with hard work by everyone, could be worthy of great pride. He turned a rock into a jewel.

Smith called his teachers together even before summer ended and set their seasoned spirits afire. He embraced GLOBE 2000 and had no patience for slow transitions. He wanted swift change and had a way of making teachers want it too. Ada Miller, a willowy veteran preschool teacher who could double as a fashion model, said Smith convinced the staff that all children can succeed in school. He gave teachers and children confidence in their ability to improve their school and have fun at the same time, she said.

The staff reorganized into teams of two to four teachers. As in the other schools, students of mixed ages were grouped according to their needs. They were allowed to advance at their own pace from one team to the next as if climbing steps until they reached the top level and moved on to middle school. Teachers specialized by subject and regularly met with team members to develop thematic units of study, such as ecology, to connect their lessons. The school began using its federally funded remedial teachers in the classroom instead of pulling children out to go to a remedial laboratory. This allowed the school to reduce class sizes in reading and mathematics.

Smith encouraged the staff to create a variety of learning environments suited to small-group and individualized instruction. And he was quick to show them how. He began bringing more books to the school and learned he could use federal reading money to buy books for more than half of the students who did not have them at home. These were books students could write their names in and keep.

The principal also brought eggs that hatched into fluffy baby chicks; snakes and insects and butterflies; ethnic food from around the world; and an endless stream of other intriguing creatures and creations of the world. He and the teachers plowed under a section of the school lawn for a vegetable garden, and children living in projects planted their first seeds. Soon more plots appeared as a gardening fervor spread through the school. By spring, five gardens were producing fresh salads daily, and sixteen more plots were on the drawing board for fall. Teachers and students began growing trees, bushes, and plants too, and soon the boundaries separating the school's landscaping and learning projects disappeared. The whole campus became a learning laboratory, as will the whole community in time.

Smith emphasized reading in the school, partly by setting up a "Rip Roaring Reading Club" that any child could join. Just about every child did. Each day the school set aside a time for DEAR—drop everything and read. Everyone in the school, including cooks and custodians, stopped what they were doing and picked up a magazine or book. Local businesses provided the school with tutors and more books. Through its nationwide "Book It" program, Pizza Hut gave students free pizza if they read a set number of books. Smith pushed a bookcase stocked with an assortment of inviting books into the cafeteria, and students began reading during lunch break.

By spring of 1993, Pinkston Street was a different school. The climate was upbeat. Teachers were more enthusiastic; students were more engaged. Teachers were working together more than they ever had before. Discipline problems diminished; attendance improved. Everyone was more at ease. Teachers felt they were being treated with professional respect, and parents felt welcomed in the school, which all worked for the good of students, said teacher Valerie Rider.

"Students are taking pride in themselves and their abilities," she said. "They are more willing to be taught and more willing to do their best."

Smith helped pull the staff together in a shared vision, teacher Valerie Jackson said. A teacher assistant, Piccola Hicks, described changes at Pinkston in another way. "The iron gates have been removed," she said.

When the year ended, Smith had no doubts about his mission. He was leading a battle against the Bell-Curve Syndrome in one of the toughest schools in the state—and he was winning.

"Here I can see that I can make a difference," he said. "I need this place. I feel married to Pinkston Street, and the marriage is good."

Henderson Middle School

At first glance, a visit to Sylvia Lowery's class suggests the same old bell-curve sorting practices were at work at Henderson Middle School. And to some degree they were. Here eight students, pulled from other classes, sat before Lowery for special help. This was a remedial class, which should have disappeared in a nontracked, individualized system. Lowery, however, made a change that would eventually convert this class from a remedial room to a learning center of use to all students in the whole school. Instead of giving her students low-level, group-oriented basic work, she challenged them with individualized, high-order thinking skills. After a brief meeting, her students fanned out to take their places at personal computers, where each embarked on his or her own computerized journey along the Oregon Trail.

The computer game gave students a supply of food, bullets, clothing, miscellaneous supplies, and money. They had to use their assets wisely enough to sustain themselves on the long journey west. Along the route, the computer arranges for complications such as wagon breakdowns, lost horses, bad weather.

"You are going to have to have enough to make it to Oregon, but you also have to have enough to hole up in Oregon while you come up with a house and the things you need," Lowery said.

Students kept journals documenting their individual journeys. When they got to Oregon, they designed their homes and, in some cases, the towns they would live in. Some did make it and ended up in a plot on Boot Hill. Instead of creating a house plan, they designed a headstone and wrote themselves an epitaph.

This project fully engaged students while it forced them to think lest they made rash decisions. It also gave them an interesting way to sharpen basic skills in reading, writing, and arithmetic. So in their own way and at their own pace, these students found their trail to Oregon just as they found their own paths to the academic standards they all must reach to go on to high school. The school no longer expected less of them than of other students. They were all expected to reach the same high academic destination.

"If you aim for the top," said Lowery, "you have to leave the bottom."

As higher expectations became the standard at Henderson, the structure became more flexible so all students had enough freedom to find the path and pace that would allow them to meet those expectations. The sprawling, fifty-eight-year-old, factory-style brick school traditionally served grades seven and eight. Grades vanished, and the students who once belonged to them were mixed up with a few midyear transfers from the elementary schools. In the humanities class taught by John Sadler, Jr., small mixed-age groups of students prepared presentations on the Civil War. Sadler, a twenty-year veteran in the classroom, in earlier years might have taught these children out of a textbook with daily assignments and worksheets, weekly exams, and quarter and semester finals that would force the ambitious students to put in some late nights cramming. But like many of his colleagues at Henderson Middle School, Sadler was changing his ways.

Now he had his students digging up information even he didn't know about history, art, and science and various other subjects, which they were free to explore in his interdisciplinary two-hour class. His students had already read about the Civil War and watched Ken Burns's powerful television documentary on the conflict. Now their job was to find out more on their own. Each group was free to explore its own topic. One searched to learn whether children were ever kidnapped and held hostage during the war. Another group explored what was on soldiers' minds during those grim years on and off the battlefields. One member might have read Stephen Crane's *The Red Badge of Courage,* and another might have read some soldiers' diaries. Another group explored what scientific discoveries and advances emerged from the creative forces of war. Each group was responsible for a class presentation on its findings, including pictures and a narrative. In other words, it would have to look something like Burns's documentary.

Sadler became convinced that this approach to teaching was deeper and more meaningful for children than the traditional practices. "I'm introducing them to more than I ever have," he said.

Some of the students, particularly those who used to earn As and Bs, weren't so sure. Jason Grissom, thirteen, always used to be on the honor roll with straight As. Now all he had to do was master learning standards, which seemed easier.

"I've kind of slacked off on my homework because I can pass the test without problem," he said.

School was coming easy for Grissom because he was not pushing to advance. He'd been with the same students for a long time in the graded system and didn't want to move ahead of them. Even so, Sadler believed students like Grissom were learning more than they thought they were. They are getting involved in projects out of pure curiosity rather than a desire for high grades. This was to become even more the case as time passed, memories of grades faded, and the school evolved.

"This [approach] could deemphasize grades in exchange for an emphasis on the acquisition of knowledge," Sadler said.

Teachers had begun making some preliminary structural changes at Henderson even before Wallace arrived. They had decided to divide the school's 670 students into five groups, each of which stayed with the same team of teachers for their duration at Henderson. The five groups were named after colors: the Golden Eagles, Green Dragons, Red Bulls, Blue Thunderballs, and Purple Pirates. Each team of teachers met daily to coordinate their lessons.

When Wallace came, the teams replaced their two grade levels with two academic levels. While there was initially little difference, the aim was to put students at the level that best suited them, regardless of their age. This would mean that some of the former seventh graders might belong in the upper level and be moving on to high school in one instead of two years. By spring of 1993, teachers were cautiously mixing ages, integrating subjects, and moving away from their old lecture styles toward more small-group and individualized instruction like Sadler's Civil War project.

The old bell-curve rigidity had not disappeared, but it was beginning to crack. The district's new structure was forcing the school to become more flexible. When the elementary schools sent a group of students on to Henderson midyear, the school had a place for them. Most of them ended up with the Purple Pirates.

"I felt kind of special," said Elliott Peace, a husky twelve-year-old who was among the group. "It's harder, but it is not so hard that I give up and quit. . . . I like being able to move at my own pace and being promoted and stuff. But I liked As and Bs, too."

Sadler said teachers, parents, and students all were uneasy giving up grades and other traditional, group-based conventions.

"We're not there yet," he said. "It's going to take a lot of work. I believe it has to come. I believe it has to be this way. . . . It is going to help us tighten up our act. There now is a method to the madness of education."

The Same, Yet Different

After a full year in a gradeless system with learning goals, Vance County schools still looked much the same as they always had. Teachers still spent their days with groups of students in classrooms. Students were still grouped in teams that looked a lot like grade levels. And, here and there, children were still being sorted into advanced and remedial classes.

Yet nothing was really the same. Students in those classrooms were not all the same age anymore. They could move from one level to the next whenever they were ready. And even those sorted out for special classes now faced the same high expectations as all students.

The incentives had changed, too. Students no longer worried about failing. Now they could fail only if they failed to move. Any movement marked success. And movement was based on knowledge and skills, not grades. The more students knew, the farther they went. So they saw knowledge. And they were discovering that getting knowledge and skills has more to do with work than intelligence. Students who were led to believe they lacked smarts in an old system preoccupied with comparing were rediscovering their competence. Vance County students no longer distinguished themselves with grade point averages and honor roll memberships, but with what they knew and could do. So we see students working to set Pirie's computer printer a-clattering and students reading more than one hundred books in their English classes.

Incentives changed for teachers, too. They no longer worried so much about covering a particular curriculum, regardless of what children learned. Instead, they had to be concerned that students gained the knowledge needed to advance toward learning objectives. They had to focus less on their teaching and more on student learning. That shift persuaded teachers to concentrate more on individuals than groups. And when teachers focus on individuals, they begin looking for learning opportunities that give children choices.

So Vance County teachers sent children beyond textbooks into novels and the diaries of Civil War soldiers, down the Oregon Trail on personal computers, and beyond classroom walls to plant gardens and read to one another in an outside courtyard.

As the incentives changed, so also did the roles of teachers and students. Vance County teachers left their classroom cocoons to work in teams, which naturally inspired them to perform well, share ideas, and improve. And as they met more, they were drawing more connections among their lessons, weaving the curriculum into a web of knowledge that carried more depth and meaning. Teachers were less often in front of children giving lectures and more often at their sides, giving them guidance. Meanwhile, students were taking more control over their learning. They were busy solving problems at computers, researching books, or working on projects in small groups. Instead of sitting passively in rows and listening to teachers drone, they were active, charting graphs of recycling projects, writing about environmental threats, and researching the trees growing in *Where the Red Fern Grows*. Vance County schools may have looked the same, but they were far different from what they had ever been before.

Making the Grade

In July of 1993, Vance County learned that its students had reached the traditional threshold of success in American public schools— they performed at state average on math and reading tests.

No one could deny that this marked extraordinary progress. In two years Vance County students had climbed from the bottom into the state mainstream of achievement. Under a banner headline reading VANCE STUDENTS' SCORES RISE TO STATE AVERAGE, the July 26 edition of the *Henderson Daily Dispatch* ran a front-page story that said the scores marked "a major turnaround for the county's school system."

What's more significant, these were not national norm-referenced tests, but state end-of-grade tests for grades 3, 4, 5, 6, 7, and 8. They were written to fit North Carolina's curriculum. The state tests were more difficult than national exams in that they required more analysis and problem solving. Since Vance County didn't have grades, it had to make special arrangements to group children by age for purposes of the exam. On a 100- to 200-point scale, Vance County scored one to four points below the state average at every grade level in both subjects. Fourth graders actually scored slightly above state average on math. Differences between Vance County and state averages were marginal.

While the state used these tests to compare districts and schools in an effort to make them more accountable, it also provided some general definitions of scores and proficiency levels. On average, Vance County students at every age scored at what the state called achievement level III in math and reading. The state explained, "Students performing at this level consistently demonstrate mastery of grade level subject matter and skills and are well prepared for the next grade level."

These measures were not ideal, but neither were they meaningless. They clearly revealed that Vance County's collective academic performance was climbing swiftly after a decade of decline. By every measure, from dropout rates to academic achievement, the county's schools were improving. Even at the high school, where the new structure had not yet been put in place, Scholastic Aptitude Test scores of seniors in the class of '93 climbed five points. And the proportion of seniors taking the college entrance exam climbed from 40 percent to 61 percent.

While heartened by these results, Betty Wallace knew that averages never told the whole story and that performing at average was not a sufficiently high standard. Further, these tests still evaluated students on the basis of bell-curve assumptions that Wallace and Vance County had rejected. The state was still judging students against the average performance of their peers. Yet Vance County no longer assumed that all students should be at the same achievement level just because they were the same age.

The new measure of success was whether all students were making reasonable progress up the staircases of achievement in Vance County's new system. After two years of transition, it was still difficult to gauge how well the county was meeting that standard. All students seemed to be advancing, but standards were still too murky, inconsistent, and mediocre. Wallace hoped to have a computer tracking system in place for the 1993–94 school year to keep tabs on student progress and get a truer gauge of their success in the new system. She would consider the district fully successful only when its benchmarks and standards were refined to high levels and every child in the system was meeting them. The ultimate measure would be whether all students reached the top exit standards. Vance County was shooting higher than the state.

Its gains and the wide interest they were attracting, however, seemed to make no impression on Vance County's self-absorbed school board. The National School Boards Association invited Vance County to give a presentation on its remarkable achievements during the association's annual convention in New Orleans in the spring of 1994. Wallace recommended that board members give the presentation, since they would be there anyway. It would cost the district nothing. The board voted five to two against doing so, apparently as a snub against Wallace. As mentioned, she had angered the board by complaining to the U.S. Equal Employment Opportunity Commission that the board had retaliated against her after she investigated sexual harassment charges against Ronald

Gregory. By the summer of 1993, Wallace's relation with the board had become strained, and her position had become precarious.

She still could count on broad public support, however, after her success in reorganizing the schools and boosting test scores. No one—not Representative James P. Green or the school board or the board of county commissioners—dared attack her publicly. She was even exploring ways she might invite Green to join her as an ally rather than adversary. Green later acknowledged they had found promising common ground. Wallace had brought more black administrators and teachers into the district and was establishing good political relations with the black community, he said.

"I really think she was sincere," he said. "We were talking the same language; we wanted to make progress. I didn't have any animosity toward that lady."

Wallace also had some reason to believe the changes she carried out would survive in Vance County, at least in some schools, even if she didn't. Many of the district's administrators and teachers had invested heavily in her plan. By 1993 they were more confident now that they had more than a year of solid practice running the new system, some encouraging results, and heavy training over the summer.

As they entered their third year under Wallace's leadership, Vance educators were prepared to let students advance to higher levels, say from primary to intermediate, every quarter instead of semester. This marked another step toward the ultimate goal of allowing students to advance at any time. The district also revised its evaluation reports with a system that would be more complete and meaningful to parents. For each objective students could get one of four marks: AM, advanced mastery, giving credit to ambitious students who surpass proficiency levels; M, for acceptable mastery; W, indicating a student is working on but has not yet mastered the objective; and NW, a red flag indicating a student has been introduced to a new objective but for some reason is not working on it.

Veteran educators said the district's opening in late August was the smoothest they had ever seen. Wallace saw at least two explanations for this. With more autonomy and responsibility, schools were working closer with their parent-and-teacher school improvement committees and planning more carefully. So they were better prepared for opening day. More important, students were no longer having to worry about being placed at uncomfortable academic levels that they could not handle. They all came back to school relaxed, knowing they could pick up where they left off. The Bell-Curve Syndrome was in remission.

Wallace's changes, though, were young. The new organization was soft, like moist clay. It would need time to firm in the heat of transition. If Vance County politics would allow Wallace a chance to see the district through this critical period, the new system would take hold and prevail over the old.

Once the Bell-Curve Syndrome is wiped out, schools will thrive without the need for a groundbreaking leader. Memories of the old system, of grades, grade levels, textbooks, tracking, and norm-referenced tests will fade. New incentives will give rise to a dynamic, ever-evolving, ever-improving collection of increasingly diverse schools. These schools will become less and less traditional, yet less alien to American culture, as classroom walls topple and learning spills out into communities in ways no one has yet fully dreamed.

Vance County was not the only place where these changes were unfolding. Similar patterns of change were emerging across the country. With the right leadership, these patterns could be brought into harmony and deliver millions of children from the Bell-Curve Syndrome.

CHAPTER 8

▼

BREAKING FREE FROM THE BELL CURVE NATIONWIDE

U.S. public education must change in two ways to become a truly American system that honors diversity, prizes individuality, and gives all children an equal chance to learn. The system must set high academic expectations, and it must destroy the Bell-Curve Syndrome so all children can meet them.

These are enormous and fundamental changes. Betty Wallace's adventure in Vance County shows how difficult they are to carry out and why most school leaders are reluctant even to try. National leaders, however, are taking action that will make it easier, even create incentives, for school administrators and boards to transform their schools. Further, local leaders, teachers, and parents all can take steps to foster changes that will separate schools from their bell-curve habits. Before embarking on change, though, everyone should heed the lessons of those who went before.

Successful Strategies

Wallace navigated her stormy course almost instinctively. An analysis of her strategies, however, shows she profoundly changed the framework of Vance County schools by clearly defining her mission, relentlessly selling it, and inviting the public and staff to help shape and carry it out so they could all share credit in its success. She bought herself a window of opportunity and acted quickly and without compromise before the window closed. She was able to deliver reassuring results before critics such as Deborah Brown and

James Green could build public doubt and impatience into an impassable wall of resistance. The critics lost hope of building that wall once Wallace began delivering results: a $1.65 million state grant, a reduction in dropout rates, dramatic improvement on test scores, deliverance from the state's takeover list, and early promotion of students. The public becomes comfortable with change only when it sees that it is for the better. And once people see change bringing improvement, they not only accept it, they demand it.

Betty Wallace's progress in carrying out swift and striking change caught the attention of those who study leadership. One of them was Karen McNeil-Miller, who works for the Center for Creative Leadership in Greensboro, North Carolina, and wrote her doctoral thesis on Wallace's leadership in Vance County. In her thesis, Miller concluded that Wallace's success stemmed from her clear vision; her ability to be direct and convincing in articulating it; and her push to carry it out swiftly on a districtwide scale—what Miller called frame-breaking change.

"She had to go in and do it full blast," Miller said in an interview. "Her whole notion of 'Here it is, and we are going to implement it all at once' was right on."

This made particular sense in the hostile political arena of Vance County. Wallace told Miller that her options were to "sort of outrun the people throwing rocks at you, or you can try to come back and pacify them—and let them just stone you to death."

But in her dash to avoid rocks, Wallace wasn't as successful as she thought she was in gaining the support of teachers, Miller concluded. Teachers understood and accepted the broad goals outlined in her plan, but they wanted a step-by-step blueprint to follow.

"Betty felt the vision itself was enough to motivate and inspire people," Miller said. "She was driven by it; she expected other people would be similarly driven. . . . She spent her time publicly and didn't spend as much time internally dealing with the motives and frustrations."

Wallace probably would have given more attention to the uncertainty frustrating her staff if she had not had to battle her board over the sexual harassment charges against Ronald Gregory.

"Betty hadn't planned for such a huge distraction," said Miller, "and when it happened, it took all of her energy. Then she wasn't able to put all the energy she wanted into her implementation plan."

Linton Deck, head of education applications at the Center for Creative Leadership, also followed Wallace's battles in Vance County. One reason she was convincing, he said, was because she could draw on her rich background in curriculum and instruction, expertise many superintendents lacked. She also was politically astute, he observed. She knew how to read the public and had good instincts for how far and hard she could push change. She skillfully used the newspaper as a forum by being open and providing lively quotes that helped publicize her plan. With her tart-tongued quips, she captured wide interest in the community, even from those who resisted change.

Wallace's adventures translate into tips for administrators trying to carry out change. They must:

- Keep their mission simple and plainly defined.

- Sell their plan for change in every corner of the community.

- Give residents and staff opportunities to participate in shaping and carrying out change.

- Teach their staff how to carry out the mission.

- Move swiftly before public doubt and impatience— or rock throwers—scuttle the mission.

Other public school efforts to rebuild school organizations based on learning goals or outcomes have become mired in turmoil because leaders failed to heed one or more of these principles. Leaders must not underestimate the scope of a shift to learning goals. It is fundamental. Students are judged on the basis of whether they meet academic performance standards rather than on how they compare to others the same age on a bell curve. What's more, standards shift the focus of the educational system away from processes—concerns with resources, course requirements, and time—to results, namely what students know and are able to do. In other words, school emphasis shifts from teaching to learning. This is the first fundamental structural change to be attempted widely by public schools this century. It is bound to make people nervous.

And it has. In 1992, Pennsylvania's state Board of Education adopted a well-meaning education plan based on learning goals. A year later the plan was all but dead. Among other things, the plan fell to opposition because it was made too slowly and too complicated without sufficient public involvement. Vague learning goals posed the biggest problem. After a year of haggling, the board adopted a numbing 575 goals to replace traditional graduation requirements. These included goals such as the following:

- All students develop an understanding of their personal characteristics (e.g., interests, needs, attitudes and temperament).

- All students understand and appreciate their worth as unique and capable individuals and exhibit self-esteem.

- All students explore and articulate the similarities and differences among various cultures and the history and contributions of diverse cultural groups, including groups to which they belong.

Many of the thirty other states shifting to outcome-based systems developed similar learning goals. Ohio said high school graduates must "establish priorities to balance multiple life roles." Minnesota would require its graduates to "understand the integration of physical, emotional and spiritual wellness."

These expectations were too vague, value-laden, and politically tinged to be practical for a public education system. "Are schools going to deny diplomas to students who don't exhibit proper attitudes or self-esteem?" asked critics. "And how does the state propose to measure prescribed attitudes and self images?"

A powerful backlash swept through many states, often involving but not limited to Christian conservative groups. Iowa state education director William Lepley called a cease-fire by shelving his state plan for a year. Minnesota governor Arne Carlson told the state Board of Education to drop its "soft social" goals. Governor L.

Douglas Wilder scrapped Virginia's learning goals, agreeing with critics that they emphasized vaguely defined values at the expense of academics. Even Albert Shanker, president of the American Federation of Teachers (AFT), attacked the fuzzy learning goals in one of his weekly columns titled "Outrageous Outcomes."

> But whereas the education standards in other industrialized countries call for things like solving algebraically and by graph simultaneous linear equations or analyzing the causes of the Cold War, outcomes-based education standards are vague and fluffy.[1]

Pennsylvania's long list of outcomes invited an assessment nightmare and predictable political attacks. How could the state ever hope to come up with new performance standards for 575 broad goals without going bankrupt? Vance County was nearly overwhelmed trying to define measures in just four academic areas: communication skills, mathematics, social studies, and science. Pennsylvania's list of goals was long enough to offend a broad spectrum of parents, not just those of the religious right. Further, the need to make a wholesale shift to learning goals was not clear to residents, including members of the state House, which voted overwhelmingly in February 1993 to nullify the state board's goals.

"Those making a radical change have the burden of proof to show how it works," said Bill Sloan, an aide to state Representative Ron Gamble, the sponsor of the bill. "If they want to experiment in a couple of places, that's one thing. But don't mandate an experiment statewide in 501 school districts."[2]

Pennsylvania Governor Robert P. Casey and the state Board of Education eventually settled on a revised plan that included fifty-three learning goals and an assurance that "achieving the outcomes shall not require students to hold or express particular attitudes, values or beliefs." By early 1994 it appeared that the revised plan would hold up against renewed attacks expected in the state legislature, educators said.

For learning goals to be effective, they must be clear, simple, and measurable. They should focus tightly on basic knowledge and skills Americans have always wanted for their children: the ability to read and write well and to understand math, science, history, and probably a foreign language. These should be strictly academic and noncontroversial. Including goals with overtones of politics or values—such as those addressing issues of character, sex, free enterprise, or multiculturalism—invite conflict and are not vital to the school's central mission. It is fine to list these and scores of other objectives as electives or even local requirements, much as the Boy Scouts do with merit badges, but not as statewide core requirements for graduation.

During the summer of 1992, when Betty Wallace was despairing over her battle with critics in Vance County, educators were celebrating in Gaston County, a similarly poor, blue-collar, textile region near Charlotte. A proposal by Gaston County Schools had been among eleven selected for generous funding by the New American School Development Corporation. President Bush had pushed for the creation of the private corporation to sponsor experimental break-the-mold schools that could become models for change nationwide. Over a five-year period, Gaston County would get $20 million to carry out a restructuring plan similar to Wallace's in three of the district's fifty-four schools. The plan, called the Odyssey Project, would abandon grade levels and shift to an outcomes-based system. It also would introduce older students to weekly seminars on multiculturalism and current events, require community service of all students, and increase parental and student involvement.

But by March of 1993, as Wallace was seeing the first fruits of her districtwide plan, Gaston County's project was in deep jeopardy. The Christian right had become so alarmed by the Pennsylvania plan that at least one of its national organizations, Citizens for Excellence in Education, based in Costa Mesa, California, was mounting well-planned attacks against outcome-based education across the country.

So when the Gaston County school board approved three schools for the Odyssey Project on February 15, the Christian community responded with a crusade. Hundreds of residents saw hellfire. They suspected the Odyssey Project was part of a larger, sinister movement to introduce secular humanism and New Age thinking into the schools. One letter to the editor of the local newspaper linked the project to the work of the Antichrist. Angry parents called one project planner a Nazi, Satanist, and Communist. Critics claimed the project would encourage children to try homosexual relationships and have them lie in caskets so they would know what it felt like to be dead, said Sandra Frye, executive assistant to district superintendent Edwin West. "You could not dream the fears they expressed," she said.

Opposition leaders warned that if the district did not abandon the project, they would demand West's ouster and work to unseat school board members in the next election. To make matters worse, Joseph F. Miller, an assistant superintendent and director of the project, was found dead in his garage four days after the board voted for the project, stirring unfortunate speculation. He died of accidental carbon-monoxide poisoning after starting his truck on a cold morning with the garage doors closed.

The Reverend Gregory Dry, a local Baptist pastor, led the war against the Odyssey Project. He told more than 400 members of Catawba Heights Baptist Church that outcome-based education requires students to accept specific morals and values and would cause student achievement to fall. He did not object to the academic aspects of the project, he said, but felt it also promoted values in opposition to Christianity.

Dry and his flock clearly were alienated from the schools. Such gaps result when school leaders introduce change without making sure everyone understands it. Christian activists in Gaston County were drawing outlandish conclusions about the Odyssey Project because they did not have a clear picture of it. They were relying on wild generalizations and distortions provided by distant conservative national groups. If school leaders had reached these parents before the Citizens for Excellence in Education did, they could have enlisted the parents' help rather than their wrath.

District leaders attempted to inform the community about the program through weekly columns in local newspapers and presentations to local leaders and civic groups. But they failed to reach parents, to go into the churches and spend time on the courthouse lawn, as Wallace had done. The board selected the schools before asking parents if they wanted the program, arousing suspicion among many parents that the board was being sneaky and manipulative. Administrators subsequently met with parents at each school in efforts to renew trust.³ By then, however, it was too late. In June of 1993, the New American Schools Development Corporation dropped the project.

A National System

Education leaders in North Carolina will remember Gaston County's nightmare and Vance County's turmoil when they consider making similar changes. Most will conclude the risk is too high. They would be reluctant to imitate Vance County, even if its schools were to keep the bell curve at bay and produce the top-achieving students in the state. Schools generally do not imitate exemplary models, even when the models are next door. Paint Branch Elementary School in Maryland produces students, many from poor families, whose academic performance rivals their peers in special gifted and talented schools, said Principal Linda Dudley. Yet the school remains an anomaly in a traditional system.

National leaders must make educational change less daunting if all American schools are to eliminate the Bell-Curve Syndrome and thrive. Otherwise, the nation's schools will continue to graduate more than 1 million frustrated students a year who are ill-prepared for adult life. Any school improvement efforts, including huge increases in spending, will not change these results significantly unless they deliver schools from the enormous weight of the Bell-Curve Syndrome. It is too much of a burden for even the best traditional schools to overcome. Yet determined people can eradicate bell-curve practices in schools just as they nearly wiped out smallpox from the face of the Earth.

Such determination grows out of a clear and shared vision. National leaders need to describe this vision, just as Wallace did in Vance County. Then they must offer simple, broad incentives that encourage local school districts to carry it out. The national vision should focus on eradicating the Bell-Curve Syndrome. This will foster national incentives aimed at the two critical changes schools need: high standards and a more flexible, individual-oriented system that allows all children to meet those standards.

Most advanced industrialized countries in the world made the first change long ago. The Commission on the Skills of the American Workforce, a group sponsored by the National Center on Education and the Economy, discovered this when it went abroad to study work training in other countries, said Marc Tucker, president of the center. He explained:

> We discovered there was not a country in the world that had high achievement that didn't have explicit standards. They went together like peanut butter and jelly. Sometimes they were curriculum standards. The ministry of education said, "you will teach this in detail, and we will come to see whether you do that." In other cases they said, "we won't do that. What we will do is have national exams." In some countries they do both. But in no country that had high achievement did they do neither. We do neither, but we don't have high achievement, so we don't break the rule.[4]

National and state standards are what set European schools apart from American ones. In most other ways, European schools remain crippled by bell-curve practices. Their students are rigidly tracked. As in the United States, these tracks tend to reflect class and race, with poor and minority students being steered into the lower vocational tracks. Even their lowest schools, however, have high expectations by U.S. standards.

In the vocational schools of The Netherlands, for example, students must pass a challenging English test. One part of the test requires them to read an essay from a London newspaper, *The Observer*, that describes Margaret Mead's contrast of the "permissive puberty of Samoan girls" with "the stresses and alienation of adolescents in Western society." The fifteen-year-olds in Ton Vendel's English class at Louise de Coligny, a general secondary school, read J. D. Salinger's *The Catcher in the Rye*. About half these students are bound for vocational school. High standards measured by national exams are the secret to the consistent high quality of Dutch education, says Principal Fred de Zoete.

"If there were no national exams here," he said, "there would be huge differences among schools."

Recognizing the mistake of expecting more of some students than of others, the Dutch Education Ministry is attempting to eliminate tracking and to develop new standards that all students must meet. Beginning in 1995, all students will be required to spend days taking the national exam that will determine whether they meet the new standards. They will be required to read, listen, and speak in two languages other than their own. In math, they will be expected to know geometry, algebra, and statistics.

National leaders should not expect less of American students. They should set high standards at four levels similar to the four-tiered system Betty Wallace established in Vance County or the ascending ranks in the Boy Scouts of America. As these standards become firmly established, they would tend to take precedence over letter grades in American schools because they mean more. They would not eliminate grade levels, but they would make them less important. Public education's focus would shift from keeping all students moving through the grades at an average pace to making sure all students reached the destination marked by benchmarks leading to final, clear performance standards. The secret to making this all work is, first, to keep standards plain and simple so students can clearly see what is expected of them and, second, to design a fair and reliable way of measuring whether students meet the standards.

Setting national standards would have been a social pipe dream even a decade ago. Perhaps the biggest change in education in the last decade, however, has involved the American attitude about the federal government's role, said Ernest L. Boyer, president of the Carnegie Foundation for the Advancement of Teaching. He told education writers gathered in Boston in April 1993:

> Education during the past 10 years has gone national. For more than 300 years, local school control was almost a sacred priority in this country. Education was grass roots. As recently as 1970, when I was U.S. Commissioner of Education, the words national and education simply could not be put together. During that period, if I had even whispered the words national standards, I'd have been driven out of town. Suddenly

this caution has been thrown to the wind with virtually little notice and hardly any national debate. People talk almost daily about national goals, and national standards and national assessments. According to George Gallup, more than half the people in this country support a national curriculum. Again, that is a position I think would have been unthinkable just 10 years ago. I really do believe that when future historians review this period, they will emphasize, I think above all else, that the decade of the '80s was a time when Americans became more concerned about national outcomes than local school control—an absolute, historic watershed in the history of American education.[5]

The shift toward national outcomes began in 1989, when President Bush and the nation's fifty governors, including Arkansas governor Bill Clinton, convened for an education summit in Charlottesville, Virginia, to set six national goals. They state that by the year 2000:

- All American children will start school ready to learn.

- At least 90 percent of our students will graduate from high school.

- Our students will demonstrate competency in science, history, the arts, civics, geography, and English and will learn to use their minds well, so they may be prepared for responsible citizenship, further learning, and productive employment.

- American students will be first in the world in science and mathematics achievement.

- Every adult will be literate and have the knowledge and skills necessary to compete in a world economy and exercise the rights and responsibilities of citizenship.

- Every school will be safe and drug-free and offer a disciplined environment conducive to learning.

Two years later, in April 1991, Bush announced his America 2000 strategy for reaching the goals. Part of this strategy advocated the development of high national standards and a national system of examinations. In June Congress established the National Council on Education Standards and Testing, to study the merits of establishing national standards and assessments. In a report released January 24, 1992, the council recommended that the nation proceed in establishing two kinds of standards for students: content standards that spell out what they should know and be able to do and performance standards that define the proficiency level at which students would be expected to demonstrate their knowledge and skills. It is not enough to say that students must write well; a standard also should specify how well. It could, for example, demand students write at level 4 on a five-point scale that clearly defines the criteria for each point. Currently such standards are used for advanced placement exams that high school students take to get college credit. Students cannot earn college credit simply by passing an advanced placement course. They also must earn a score of 3 or better on the exam.

In his first major education initiative in April 1993, President Clinton tried to build on Bush's earlier work. He proposed legislation, called Goals 2000, to establish a National Education Standards and Improvement Council that would promote and certify national and state performance-based exams and standards. The bill included a second element, called School-to-Work, that would set up a Skill Standards Board to identify standards for broad job clusters and help schools establish apprenticeship networks. Clinton requested money to provide school-reform grants, including $15 million for the skills board and $12 million for the other standards and assessment projects.

Nearly a year later, on March 26, 1994, the bill was passed in Congress, and Clinton signed it into law five days later. The bill authorized $647 million for school reforms nationwide, including $400 million in grants to states and local agencies willing to overhaul their schools so children could meet national standards. The bill marked a radical new role in education for the federal government, which previously had restricted its services to helping poor and disabled students.

U.S. Education Secretary Richard W. Riley said the Congress's support of Clinton's plan "will quickly help move our nation toward greater educational and economic progress and away from the low expectations which have too often held our children hostage and restrained our nation from achieving its full potential."[6]

Albert Shanker, president of the AFT, also applauded the legislation, noting it finally gives America a rational system of education.

"All else follows from standards—assessments based on standards and clear consequences for achievement," he said in a prepared statement. "Standards give states and local communities a sound framework for systematically overhauling their public schools for one purpose: improving student achievement."[7]

As Clinton's bill moved through Congress, a variety of other efforts to design national standards already were under way. During the Bush administration, the U.S. Department of Education made grants to professional and scholarly organizations to develop national standards for what students should know and be able to do in ten subject areas. Clinton's legislation keeps alive this effort. The National Council of Teachers of Mathematics already has prepared its standards, and the National Council for Geographic Education and four national art associations have developed the first draft of their standards. All subject groups were expected to have standards ready for classrooms by the 1995–96 school year. The math council expected to have performance examinations based on the standards by 1995.

Meanwhile, the National Center on Education and the Economy in Rochester and the Learning Research and Development Center in Pittsburgh are jointly developing standards at the elementary, middle school, and high school levels that will rival those anywhere in the world. In what is called the New Standards Project, these researchers are working with a consortium of fourteen states, including Oregon, and some selected school districts in creating a flexible national examination system. They want to give states a variety of ways to evaluate whether students meet standards held to the same high level nationwide. The project is working on three-part assessments that would combine performance examinations, projects, and portfolios of student work. Project leaders began field testing mathematics and language arts assessments in 1994.[8] For the first time in its history, the United States is building a national education system, and it will be based on learning goals and standards.

National leaders are rightly focusing first on the core subjects for which we should set high standards for all students—reading, writing, history, mathematics, science, and foreign language. They also are looking for standards that require students to understand connections among subjects and that should, therefore, encourage teachers to do the same. Students solidly grounded in these basics are well equipped to explore all other fields of learning. Educators may want to add subjects and skills to these core standards, but they all should be optional. For example, schools might set standards in all sciences, but require students to meet them in two of their choice. Additionally, they could require students to meet standards in one or more electives of their choice, ranging from agriculture to music, similar to the range of merit badges Boy Scouts can choose from in their quest to reach Life, Heart, and Eagle ranks. The Clinton education initiative and the New Standards Project also are trying to establish a higher set of occupational standards that students can pursue after they've mastered academic ones.

The national standards under design are voluntary, but if they are understood and accepted by teachers and the public, schools will not be able to ignore them. Textbook and testing companies also will feel pressure to revamp their products to reflect the standards. What parents wouldn't want their child to meet national standards, especially if they know other children are meeting them? It will be of little consolation to parents to learn their child is scoring above average on a norm-referenced exam, if the student still can't meet national standards. Schools also will be judged on whether their students are meeting the standards. Since these standards pose high expectations for all students, the standards will put pressure on schools to abandon tracking so all children have a shot at success. The standards will be high, but not too much to expect even of the nation's disadvantaged children, as the parents of those children said themselves in focus groups for the New Standards Project.

"The strongest support came from low-income and minority parents who wanted their children to be judged by the same criteria as other children, and who saw in standards a chance to improve the educational chances for their children," writes Lauren B. Resnick, director of the Learning Research and Development Center.[9]

The nation's colleges and universities could play a powerful role in reinforcing national standards by linking them to their admission standards and abandoning outmoded course requirements. Fortunately, such moves are already under way. In February 1993, for example, the Oregon State Board of Higher Education voted to make foreign language a requirement for admission to the state's eight colleges and universities. There is nothing unusual in that; most colleges and universities across the country already require that. What was unusual, however, was that in order to meet the second language requirement, which takes effect in 1996, students must show they can *communicate* in a second tongue. They must meet a performance standard. The university system is recognizing that just because students take two years of Spanish doesn't mean they can speak it. So instead of basing admission on how much time students spent studying a language, the system will judge how well they can read and speak it. The way in which students learned it will not concern admission officers.

A year after adopting its language requirement, the Oregon State Board of Higher Education voted to abandon its old way of judging students for admission altogether. Beginning in fall 1999, Oregon's eight colleges and universities will admit students on the basis of what they know rather than on grades, class standing, and course credits. The new standards will require students to prove through essays, tests, presentations, and science and math projects that they have the skills and knowledge needed to survive in college.

"It is one of the most exciting and dramatic moves we've made in education in a number of years," said Janice Wilson, president of the board of higher education. "Our work will end up being a model for systems of education throughout the United States."

Where possible, the higher education system will mesh its admission standards with exit standards being developed for Oregon public high schools. In meeting the standards for graduation, then, students also will meet standards for admission to the state's colleges and universities. The more than forty proposed college admission standards are explicit, academic, and rigorous. They would require students to show, for example, that they could solve problems using principles of geometry and calculus, understand reactions of matter and energy changes in chemistry, identify major world and national geographic features, and appreciate the themes and figurative language of classical literature. Following are three examples of what proposed standards say students must be able to do:

- Understand the conceptual foundations and applications of calculus and trigonometry and their relationship to other areas of mathematics and other disciplines.

- Demonstrate an understanding of unifying concepts of the life and physical sciences, including, but not limited to, cell theory, geological evolution, organic evolution, atomic structure, chemical bonding, ecological relations, biodiversity, and transformation of energy.

- Understand the historical evolution and philosophical basis of the United States government, its current configuration and operation; the relationship of the states to the federal establishment; patterns of democratic participation in the American political scene; the structure of power, authority, and governance; the role and responsibilities of citizenship; the Bill of Rights and the notion of conflicting rights as evidenced in modern American political scene.[10]

These standards promise to influence high school education in Oregon powerfully. They immediately caught the attention of William Korach, superintendent of the school district in the affluent Lake Oswego suburb of Portland, where 85 percent of the students go to college. If his students must meet those standards to get into college, he said, "We'll do it."

College admission policies always have a heavy influence on public schools. In the late 1980s, for example, the University of Colorado at Boulder added a course in geography to its stiff admission requirements. High schools swiftly responded.

"It is amazing how courses in geography appeared almost overnight," said Carol Ruckel, a consultant for the Colorado Department of Education. "Those entrance requirements drive high school graduation requirements."[11]

If universities across the country shifted to performance standards like Oregon's, high schools would be forced to do the same, even without national standards. Simply collecting credits would no longer open college gates; students instead would have to demonstrate a defined level of knowledge and skills. Schools would have to become more flexible and more focused on individual needs to prepare students for college. A student who could meet standards in reading and history, for example, might want to spend his or her high school days concentrating on foreign language, math, and science. Unlike ever before in American education, knowledge would replace time as the constant.

Properly established, high national standards alone will improve public education in the United States. But their power will be limited unless educators also abandon their bell-curve assumptions. If teachers continue to group children by age, march them en masse through the system by age, sort them by presumed abilities, and rely on textbook-based group instruction, large numbers of children will not reach the standards. All children will make it only if they are given the time and latitude they need to succeed. They must be allowed to pursue standards at their own pace and, as much as possible, in their own way. This means local leaders must pull educators away from the bell curve. Doing so is like prying abalone from rocks—difficult but rewarding.

Launching Change at the Local Level

National leaders can produce incentives for change, but local ones must make it happen. Superintendents and school board members have to lead teachers away from bell-curve practices and toward high standards if they want to crush the Bell-Curve Syndrome. They need to articulate that mission clearly and repeatedly for their teachers and communities. They must do as Betty Wallace did and preach in the churches, address Rotary Clubs, and talk late into the night at community meetings. They must talk until Americans are demanding these changes.

Leaders do not have much room for compromise in establishing this top-down structure. They must insist on high standards and reject instructional practices based on bell-curve assumptions about achievement or mediocre improvements in their schools. Grades, grade levels, group-oriented instruction, and norm-based testing all must go.

Within this new structure, however, administrators can and should give individual schools autonomy and freedom in how they meet administrative objectives for change. Just as students need the freedom to follow various paths to knowledge, so schools need the flexibility to chart their own courses to the new territory administrators want them to reach. That means teachers and parents should be given authority to decide how they will organize instruction in their schools—a practice commonly called school- or site-based management.

Since the late 1980s, leaders across the country have been giving more authority to local schools with the hope that empowered teachers and parents would take ownership of their schools and try innovations to improve them. The popularity of school-based management continues to grow in the United States. Large school districts such as Chicago, Denver, and Rochester, New York, have established school-based management teams. Many states are encouraging their schools to do the same, and at least nine states, including North Carolina, California, Texas, Florida, and Oregon, are requiring every school to establish a school-based management team.

The results of this decentralization, however, have been disappointing because administrators have given schools freedom without also giving them direction. Frustrated teachers find themselves working harder without knowing quite where to go with their new authority. Two years after North Carolina passed a law giving schools more autonomy to try new things, most still had made no changes at all, said a dismayed John Dornan, director of the Public School Forum, a private education policy institute in Raleigh.

"The level of enthusiasm was so high that many people had this notion of a race horse waiting to bolt from the starting gate," he said. "Instead, it has been more like a bird that isn't sure it wants to fly."[12]

Surveys show school-based management has boosted teacher morale and status, but there is little evidence it has had much influence on student learning. Studies in Dade County, Los Angeles, and San Diego showed no significant increase in standardized test scores. Further, school-based management has not given students any more power over their own learning.[13]

In 1986 the Dade County school district in Miami, Florida, became one of the first large systems in the country to decentralize. Administrators offered faculties more control over their schools' curriculum, spending, scheduling, and hiring. Within three years, teachers in more than half of the district's 260 schools accepted the challenge and the extra work that came with it. Some schools made intriguing changes, but they were shallow and did not alter the flawed deep structure of schools. The Palmetto Elementary School hired a local Berlitz language school to teach its students Spanish. Charles Drew Elementary School became the first public school in the nation to adopt voluntary uniforms: blue pants, ties, and white shirts for boys and white blouses and blue skirts for girls. The management team at Charles Hedley Elementary became concerned that children were spending too much time doing rote exercises and filling in worksheets and not enough time writing. So it limited teachers to a dozen worksheets per month. A district report on results for the first three years concluded that decentralization had improved teacher morale, reduced high school dropout rates, and improved the overall climate. Still, students in the school-based management schools did no better than others on tests in reading and mathematics.[14]

These local teams needed top-down direction that would have forced them to strive for more ambitious changes. If school-based management can be tied to high standards and flexible, more personal instruction, it can become a powerful force in wiping out the Bell-Curve Syndrome.

At Lassiter Middle School in Jefferson County, Kentucky, for example, thirty teachers used their school-based management authority to form six interdisciplinary teams. Five teams each took a group of students for three years. The sixth team took 150 students from all three grades at once and eliminated failing grades—two departures from bell-curve practices. Students who turned in unacceptable work simply repeated the assignment until it was acceptable. By the end of the first year, all but two students passed all of their classes.[15]

Perhaps the most successful examples of school-based management can be found in Germany, where some schools experiment with a plan called the team/small-group model.

A tour through the graffiti-splashed halls of Fritz-Karsen school in Berlin revealed teachers experimenting with this new model in the fall of 1992. In the science laboratory, four eighth graders lean over a beaker and study the effects of heat on gas. Hours later, they sit around a table cutting pieces of cardboard to build a pyramid for a geometry exercise. The same four students would work together the next day and every day in most classes for years, drawing on one another's academic strengths to learn. Rene Glorius, a tall teen with a glittering stud in one ear, says he learns more in this small group than he did as an anonymous member of repeatedly changing large classes. This is more personal. "There is more opportunity to ask for help," he says.

His group is part of a class that, in turn, is part of a larger group of 140 students who will be taught by the same twelve teachers for four or five years. This group functions like a school within a school of 1,200 students, and the teachers have full control over scheduling, textbook selection, and instruction. This concentric organization is becoming increasingly popular across Germany.

Germans began experimenting with the team approach in the early 1970s to see if it would work for a growing number of rudderless students, said Reinhold Fess, who trains teachers at an institute in the southwestern German state of Saarland on how to use the model.

"Since there is no stability outside of the school, the school has to provide more stability," said Fess.

The team approach fosters more cooperation among teachers and students and new roles for both that are well suited to a more individualized, outcomes-based system. Teachers spend less time lecturing and more time guiding the children. Students take charge of their own learning, often through hands-on activities and group projects. Teachers get to know their students well and are able to individualize instruction more. All, not just some, children are expected to meet high standards.

Deanna Woods, an English teacher at Wilson High School in Portland, Oregon, spent three weeks studying the model in Germany. She became so impressed by the approach that she worked to make sure it was advocated in Oregon's broad 1991 Educational Act for the Twenty-First Century. She considers the model the most promising strategy for reshaping education in the world. The team/small-group approach demands more energy and innovation, she said, but it also yields bigger payoffs by reaching "a far more sophisticated level of education than most American schools are promising now."

The dropout rate in Saarland, where all comprehensive schools now use the model, is steadily declining, from the German average of about 18 percent to less than 12 percent. Fess said schools are sending a larger proportion of their students to universities.[16] The most famous German school using the team/small-group model is Koln-Holweide in Cologne, which serves about 2,000 students in grades 5 through 13. About one in four of its students have unemployed parents, many have single parents, and one in three are foreign, mostly Turkish. The school divides students into groups of about ninety. Each group of fifth graders is placed with six teachers who take full responsibility for educating them over the following six years. Teachers eat with their students, counsel them, talk with their parents, and make all instructional decisions. The school gets remarkable results. It has only a 1 percent dropout rate, and about 60 percent of its students, compared to about 33 percent nationally, score high enough on the Abitur, the difficult entrance exam, to enter German universities.

This German model for school-based management works because it gives teachers a framework in which to exercise their autonomy and authority. More important, that framework encourages teachers to individualize instruction and rely less on textbooks, comparative grading, and other bell-curve practices. It does not simply turn them loose to invent new schools, as many districts and states have done to their teachers in the United States.

More Choices

The beauty of decentralization is that it fosters diversity among schools. Since American students are becoming increasingly diverse, it makes sense to offer them variety in schools and in programs within schools. An education system that focuses on individuals rather than groups seeks and thrives on diversity. Children succeed in schools that fit their learning styles. The wider the variety, the better a child's chances of finding the right fit. But a diversity of schools is of value only when students have the freedom to choose the one they want to attend.

Most advocates see market competition as the primary virtue of school choice, but in an individualized system, choice is most important as a vehicle for accommodating the varying interests of diverse students. By specializing, schools can focus on offering less in more depth. One school can emphasize art, another math and science, and a third foreign language, while all still ensure that students master districtwide, state, or national standards.

Cambridge School District in Massachusetts has created a diversity of schools with some success. Each of its thirteen schools has specialized, and every student has the freedom to choose which he or she wants to attend. Robert F. Kennedy Elementary emphasizes the arts, Haggerty offers conversational Spanish, and Fitzgerald focuses heavily on creative writing. Parents list their top three choices for their children. As the district must be careful to control racial balance in the schools, everyone does not always receive his or her first choice, but most get their second choice, and the 15 percent who don't get their third choice are put on a waiting list. Since the system was launched in 1981, student performance has generally climbed. Minority students score just as high, and in some cases higher, on tests as their white peers.[17] An achievement gap, however, continues to separate poor children from their more affluent peers, as one would expect in a district that still has rigid grading, grade levels, and other bell-curve conventions.

Few other districts in the country have developed school choice options as rich as Cambridge's, partly because doing so is expensive. In 1992–93 Cambridge spent $8,742 per student compared to a nationwide average of $5,425. At least fifteen states have loosened regulations to allow students to cross district boundaries, and hundreds of school districts offer varying degrees of choice among at least some of their schools, often for desegregation purposes. Minnesota led the nation in 1987 with statewide open enrollment. By the 1991–92 school year, however, only about 13,000 of the state's 749,000 students chose to go to schools outside their district. Further, many participants chose different schools for their location, special sports programs, and other qualities that had nothing to do with academics. In this case and others, only a fraction of students take advantage of the broader choices. This is partly because of transportation complications. But it also is probably because, in a uniform system, one school does not differ much from another. With some exceptions, the differences in American schools generally have more to do with their disparities in funding and in the students they serve than in the instructional programs they offer.

"In other words, 'choice' exists but there are few distinctive choices," writes the Carnegie Foundation for the Advancement of Teaching in a special 1992 report. "The public school in the next town doesn't offer anything remarkably different from the one just around the corner."[18]

Another problem with limiting choice to public schools is that it is almost always unfair. Even Cambridge cannot offer every student his or her first choice. More often, districts offer choice only among select specialized schools, sometimes called magnet schools because they are used to attract white students to schools dominated by racial or ethnic minority students for desegregation purposes. Districts must pour extra resources into these schools to make them special. They might build an art studio and hire dance instructors for a performing arts speciality, or build a computer laboratory for a math and science school. This is all great for the students who make it into the magnet schools, but they win at the expense of the rest of the students who must attend schools with fewer resources. Since magnet schools offer choices for some, but not all, students, they foster a dangerous elitism. More affluent and well-educated parents know how to work the system and lobby aggressively for a place for their child in special schools, whereas poor parents do not. So magnet schools draw the top students from other schools, leaving larger concentrations of poor students trapped in schools with even fewer resources. In his book *Savage Inequalities,* Jonathan Kozol, an adamant foe of school choice, points out that the magnet schools in Chicago are like a private school system within the district. As a result, Chicago's poorest children "have been forever, as it seems, consigned to places nobody would choose if he had any choice at all." For children who begin their education in the city's Mickinly School, for example, the high school dropout rate is 81 percent. Of the 6,700 children who enter ninth grade in Chicago's 18 poorest high schools, only about 300 graduate and read at or above the national average.[19]

Because the public schools of Washington, D.C., fail children on a similar scale, no one could begrudge President Clinton's choice to send his daughter, Chelsea, to the exclusive Sidwell Friends School, a private Quaker school with an annual tuition of $10,400. But poor children living in the shadow of the White House don't have that choice. They must attend second-rate schools. Who can say that is fair?

Government could give all children many more options by making its educational finance system student-based rather than district-based. Government could give parents choices in where they spend their children's share of school money. If, for example, federal, state, and local funds averaged $5,000 per child in Oregon, then every Oregon child should have the choice of spending that money at a public or private school, community college, business school, tutor service, or any other place that can help the child meet national standards. The government's primary concern should rest on what children learn rather than how or where they learn it. In many cases government already purchases private education services for children. Portland School District hires a private bus company to transport its students, and it contracts with a variety of private schools and consultants to provide specialized services that it cannot offer. Similarly, the federal government now gives loans and grants to students who attend private colleges and universities, including religious ones. Government could better serve itself and students by exploiting the private sector for a broader menu of educational service.

This could work in at least two ways: Government could give money directly to a child's parents in the form of a voucher and let them spend it where they choose, or it could give money to the school, institution, or service that the parents choose for their child. Presidents Reagan and Bush and many other conservative leaders advocated vouchers as a way to bring positive forces of free-market competition to bear on schools. Public schools would improve in order to keep students and the money that comes with them, they said. The United Kingdom is moving toward a system like this at the high school level by offering training credits to students ages sixteen through eighteen who choose to leave high school. All of these students are given between $1,500 and $5,000 to spend wherever they choose to get further training—college, business school, private tutor, even an employer.

A more politically palatable way to support a broad and meaningful school choice system is to allow the money to flow with the children to the institution they attend. John E. Chubb and Terry M. Moe advocate this in their influential book, *Politics, Markets & America's Schools*. The authors concluded that substantial choice could change the deep structure of schools and foster dramatic improvements in education. This is true, they added, only if schools have near total autonomy. Chubb and Moe feel that, as far as possible, all higher authority, including school boards, would need to be eliminated. Then teachers and other school professionals could concentrate on responding directly to their clients—parents and students—without worrying about the interests and peculiar agendas of local and state authorities.[20] Imagine how swiftly Betty Wallace could have moved, for example, if she did not have to contend with the opposing forces of Deborah Brown, Representative James Green, a reluctant school board, and hostile board of county commissioners.[21] While Chubb and Moe's proposal would not have as wide-ranging effects as they predict, particularly if it did not also address the Bell-Curve Syndrome, it would foster a system of more responsive and diverse schools.

Choice in The Netherlands

The education system in The Netherlands offers one example of a national school choice plan with many of the features Chubb and Moe advocate. The government offers a system of public schools. But in addition, any group can approach the education ministry and propose opening any kind of school, whether it is Montessori, Waldorf, Latin grammar, Roman Catholic, or Muslim. The government will pay for the school, its teachers, and its operations, provided that the teachers are certified and the school agrees to meet government standards. The government gives every school the same amount of money per student to operate. Because parents can send their children to any school in the country, schools must sustain high quality to attract and retain students and stay in business. Most schools produce colorful marketing brochures describing their specialities and qualities.

"If you have competition, it is better for the schools," said Fred de Zoete, the principal of the public Louise de Coligny in Leiden. "You think about your product."

De Zoete's school, for example, is in a fierce battle for students with a nearby Catholic school. About 60 percent of the nation's schools were established by churches or interests other than government and are called private, though they receive all or most of their money from government. These private schools may levy tuition, though few charge much because it makes it more difficult for them to attract students.

The Netherlands' nationwide open enrollment system has yielded a complex assortment of schools, but they all have many similarities because they all must follow detailed government curriculum outlines. The heavy government involvement limits the scope of diversity the system can promote. At the same time, high national standards and competition help protect the quality of all schools. The country has no inner-city schools plagued by massive academic failure such as those we see in most of America's largest cities.

In the heart of Amsterdam's Bylmer section, where poor immigrant children live in an expanse of high-rise projects, stands the Augustinus School, a private, ecumenical religious school that would rival America's finest suburban high schools. About 85 percent of Augustinus's students come from Morocco, Nigeria, Surinam, and other countries. Most are black.

Augustinus School is clean, orderly, and modern with brick hallways decorated with ceramic tiles. It has qualified, well-paid teachers and high academic expectations. The instruction seems rigorous by American standards. One morning in the computer room, for example, fourteen-year-old Marja Terlage and her classmates write to Danish pen pals in German. Down in the science room, their peers are busy using wires and meters to figure the electrical differences between alternating and direct current. The school depends on its academic quality to keep students.

Unfortunately, Augustinus is battling another force that even its quality is failing to overcome—racism. White Dutch parents assume that a school dominated by poor minority students cannot be as good as a predominantly white school, so they take their children elsewhere, said a frustrated Nicholette Schulman, assistant headmistress. In three years white flight has cut Augustinus's enrollment from 1,200 to 760.

"We think the standard of education here is not lower than other schools," Schulman said, "but white Dutch parents assume it is."

While the Dutch school choice system has features U.S. schools would want to avoid, such as tolerance for segregation, it generally offers a good model.[22] By funding private schools, the government in effect absorbs them into the public system, creating diversity that opens up more learning paths for students.

Minnesota, California, and other states have begun taking small steps in this direction by experimenting with charter schools. In these programs, the state gives teachers and parents the chance to create their own schools with state funds, allocated on the basis of the number of students they enroll. The state will give charter schools great autonomy from state controls, but they also are given three years to meet achievement goals or risk losing their charter.

City Academy opened in September 1992 in St. Paul, Minnesota, as the nation's first charter school. Operated by a team of parents and teachers, the school serves students who have been kicked out of other high schools. Along with traditional studies, the school's students work on community projects such as the Christian-based Habitat for Humanity. In the spring of 1993, the school issued diplomas to its first ten graduates. One of them, Jack Garcia, previously had been drifting from one dropout program to another between bouts with the law. Through City Academy, he and his nine classmates all found places in trade schools, technical colleges, and universities.

"Now I've got all kinds of opportunities I didn't expect," said Garcia.[23]

Ted Kolderie, a St. Paul policy activist who pushed for charter schools in Minnesota, said the government's chief objective in chartering schools is "to create some dynamics that will cause the mainline system to move." As charter schools propose innovations, mainstream schools will feel pressure to do the same. This happened in Forest Lake, Minnesota. A group of parents wanted an elementary Montessori school in their district. Administrators said they could not find the space, teachers, or transportation to meet the request, so the parents asked for a charter from the school board. When the board agreed, the administration swiftly found ways to provide a Montessori school. The charter option gave parents leverage to broaden the public school choices for their children.

Kolderie believes charter schools also can serve to elevate the professionalism of teachers. Teams of teachers could operate a charter school much as partners run medical, legal, and accounting firms. They would work for themselves, setting their own salaries out of the money they have available to run their schools. They'd hire their support staff and buy their own supplies. As it is, to be a teacher in the United States, one must be an employee of someone else. Charter schools offer teachers a way to work for themselves.

California authorized up to one hundred charter schools, and the state Board of Education approved the first nine on February 11, 1993. Nearly fifty more were expected to open in the 1994–95 school year. As one would expect, these schools reflect some departures from tradition. In Sonomo County, one school was chartered to serve children in grades 6 through 12. Another opened to provide an elementary school of resource teachers for parents who teach their children at home. A third school chartered in El Dorado County focused on serving students in all grades countywide who are in danger of failing in traditional schools.

The charter school concept began catching fire in 1993. New Mexico, Georgia, Colorado, Massachusetts, Wisconsin, Kansas, Arizona, and Michigan adopted charter school legislation. New Jersey, Pennsylvania, Illinois, and at least six other states were weighing whether to do the same in 1995.

Charter schools offer government an avenue to absorb model private schools into the public education system. This may enable a variety of private initiatives to build new and improved schools. The ten projects sponsored by the New American Schools Development Corporation, for example, may produce schools that become worthy of government support and replication. Some already involve public schools, but others do not. Through a charter system, government can make these schools available to all children, not just those who can afford them.

Most of the new school designs emerging from private groups and consortiums appear to be moving toward individualized learning geared to high standards. James A. Mecklenburger, president of an education consultant's consortium based in Alexandria, Virginia, observed these qualities in the New American Schools Development Corporation projects. He writes:

> Virtually all tend to school readiness, changing relationships between community and school, increased use of technology (although the published summaries of most of these projects don't yet reflect much sophistication about technology), altered school schedules and calendars, site-based management, various spins on performance assessments, teachers acting as "guides," and "coaches," and curriculum ideas that favor the integration of subject matter.[24]

A project in Bensenville, a town of 17,000 outside Chicago, will make the community the classroom with flexible, cross-disciplinary, year-round scheduling and heavy use of technology. The

Modern Red Schoolhouse project will attempt to transform schools in seven districts—Columbus, Beech Grove, Greentown, Indianapolis, and Lawrence Township in Indiana; Charlotte-Mecklenburg in North Carolina; and Kayenta Unified in Arizona. The project will blend a classical curriculum with self-paced learning, a heavy use of technology, and high standards for all students. The Community Learning Centers of Minnesota project proposes to exploit the state's charter school law by creating learning centers in districts throughout the state, beginning in St. Cloud, North Branch, and Rothsay. These centers will offer programs with high performance-based standards characterized by active and experiential learning, projects, community service, and an interdisciplinary curriculum.[25]

The Edison Project, a private, for-profit venture launched by Chris Whittle of Knoxville, Tennessee, also could produce schools that the government might want to replicate. In the late 1980s, Whittle Communications successfully created a broadcasting network that delivers daily programs by satellite to 10,000 schools in forty-seven states. Whittle offered these schools free televisions in every classroom if they would agree to show their students a twelve-minute television news program for teenagers called Channel One. The company profits by selling two minutes of advertising for each news show.

Then in 1991, Whittle set out to build a national network of schools through the Edison Project. The project, led by Benno C. Schmidt, Jr., former president of Yale University, initially set out to build 1,000 schools serving 2 million students by the turn of the century. These schools were to cost no more than public schools to operate, yet would be expected to give all students educations that rival any in the world. Three years into the project, Whittle realized he could not raise the billions he needed for such a huge venture and reduced the project's scope. Edison would contract with communities to manage existing schools, probably beginning with ten to forty schools in 1995.

The project appears to be moving in the same direction as schools commissioned by the New American Schools Development Corporation, combining a flexible, more individualized instructional plan with high standards. The project is using a $60 million research and development budget to explore ways to provide a broad, deep, accelerated, and integrated curriculum with an instructional plan that allows students to spend more time alone and in small groups, learning by doing and by using technology. A computer network will link schools, classrooms, and homes. All students will study a second language from the time they enter school. Fine arts, social sciences, and physical education will be part of the standard curriculum. The school day will be two hours longer, and schools will stay open into the evenings for extracurricular activities. The school year will be extended to 210 days, about 30 days longer than most states require.

There will be no ability tracking. The thirteen-year schooling cycle will be divided into five sequential academies, or blocks of two or three grades. Teams of teachers will work with the same group of students over several years. The school will keep a cumulative portfolio of writing assignments, presentations, projects, and other student work. Portfolios also may be stored in computers. Every student will be expected to meet rigorous standards to advance up the staircase of achievement from one academy to the next. Students will be taught to read from literature, such as *Aesop's Fables,* rather than textbooks. By the time they reach about the equivalent of grade 3, according to one planning document, they will be reading classics such as *Treasure Island* and *Little Women.* By the time students leave the top academy, according to the plan, they will be prepared for first-rank colleges. All, for example, will have completed either college-level calculus or introductory probability and statistics.[26]

If it succeeds, the Edison Project will put a healthy pressure on public schools to improve. The first sign of that pressure appeared in February 1994, when the project applied and won approval to run five charter schools in Massachusetts—one-fifth of the total allowed under state law. The Edison Project, the New American Schools Development Corporation, charter schools, and other initiatives are adding diversity and choices to the nation's education system, and for that reason they should be encouraged. Eventually they could contribute to a national education system that gives children what adults already have in a diverse higher education system that remains the envy of the world. Adults can choose scores of ways to learn. In North Carolina, for example, they can attend small, liberal arts colleges, such as Davidson College or Guilford College in Greensboro; the prestigious Southern cousin of the Ivy League schools, Duke University in Durham; the historically black Shaw University in Raleigh; the Baptist-affiliated Campbell University in Bules Creek; the all-women Meredith College in Raleigh; and a public, top-notch technical and engineering institution, such as North Carolina State University. American adults can choose among hundreds of public and private institutions that specialize in business, agriculture, medicine, and every other discipline. They also can go to a variety of community colleges, technical institutes, and business schools. Adults can take courses for credit on television or by satellite or by following individualized programs on computers. Some learn on the job in company training programs.

Children would benefit from a similar array of learning options. They should be free to learn from tutors, on the job, in community colleges, in trade schools, or at home, which will be easier soon through emerging video and computer information networks. Schools could evolve into learning centers, where students would register and chart their individual learning paths. They could spend part of their day at the center, using its computers, libraries, seminars, and courses, and go elsewhere for the remainder of their educational needs. Ultimately, walls separating schools and communities should disappear as the nation's youth and their adult guides learn to capitalize on the wealth of knowledge that awaits them in every human endeavor. Then children will be scattered everywhere in their quest for knowledge. They will visit courtrooms, attend city council meetings, shadow professionals, join survey teams, interview police officers, feed the homeless, and engage in countless other activities to learn through experience what they must know to master world-class standards.

The New Teacher

Until this learning society emerges, however, children still must spend their days in schools. If children are going to be given the range of choices they need to succeed in those schools, teachers must give up some control and help students take charge of their own learning.

As a growing number of American schools embark on change, schools of education in the nation's universities and colleges will begin training more teachers for the demands of flexible schools where students advance at their own individual pace. These new teachers will learn how to help students learn in groups, projects, and independent research. They will learn how to use computers and community resources to create relevant learning options for students. They will learn how to integrate subjects and work in teams rather than in isolation and how to guide students to knowledge.

The bigger challenge facing schools seeking high standards and more flexible structures is training the teachers they already have. A growing number of teachers recognize they cannot continue to rely on traditional practices and expect all students to meet the high national standards under development. The teachers want to change. A recent survey by the American Association of School Administrators showed that experienced teachers were more willing than administrators to change their ways. More than two-thirds of the experienced teachers surveyed said they favored restructuring education and making it more individualized.[27]

One of the nation's most adamant advocates for a change from the traditional teaching model has been Albert Shanker. He has said repeatedly that of all methods of instruction, lectures are the worst and guided experience the best. "We have to think about what structures and approaches will actively involve students in their own learning," he wrote in his weekly column.[28]

Yet most teachers in the country continue to follow the traditional model of lecturing and dishing out assignments from a textbook. They teach the way they and virtually all Americans learned to teach because no one has showed them any other way. As school-based management experiments have demonstrated, teachers need direction. They must be trained.

Administrators also can help teachers improve by giving them time to work together and by preventing them from isolating themselves in classrooms. German educators have discovered this in their team/small-group schools. So have teacher teams in Vance County. Teachers feel both inspiration and professional peer pressure to keep learning when they work in teams. They also are able to give students more options for learning through flexible grouping. Investing in training teachers to work together and individualize instruction eventually will pay off in improved student performance and lower operating costs.

An intriguing national project may help foster a new generation of professional, exceptionally skilled teachers suited for schools parting with the bell curve and embracing national standards. In 1987 the Carnegie Corporation of New York helped create an independent, nonprofit organization called the National Board for Professional Teaching Standards. The organization has a sixty-three member board of directors, most of whom are teachers, and was led initially by Jim Hunt between his terms as governor of North Carolina.

The board wants to develop a national certificate for teachers who meet high and rigorous standards. It is creating high national performance teaching standards, similar to the kind of national standards being designed for students, and a variety of tests to measure whether teachers meet those standards. These will define what teachers should know and be able to do in thirty certificate fields. The certificates will be based on subjects and student achievement levels. Teachers will be certified in four overlapping developmental levels that would mesh well with a four-tiered, outcomes-based system such as Vance County's. The four levels are early childhood (ages three to eight), middle childhood (ages seven to twelve), early adolescence (ages eleven to fifteen), and adolescence and young adulthood (ages fourteen to eighteen).

The board rejects the traditional model of teaching and will not certify those who fail to go far beyond it. Following are some of the expectations the board is setting for the teachers it aims to certify.

Teachers worthy of national certification know and care about their students and believe all are capable of reaching high levels of achievement. They know theories of cognition, intelligence, and human development. They watch their students, know what interests them, and know whom their students go home to at night. They are models of educated persons who exude a contagious passion for the subjects they teach. They have a firm and broad knowledge of all subjects and the capacity to integrate and draw connections among them. The history teacher describing the Civil War can also, for example, draw on the poetry of Walt Whitman.

Nationally certified teachers make students feel important and eager to know more. They have skills, wisdom, and judgment and exemplify the virtues of honesty, curiosity, and fairness they try to inspire in their students. They do not pretend to know everything and subject students to lectures. Instead, they are like trail masters, adept at helping students find knowledge for themselves. Here they give students the greatest gift of all—the means to teach themselves. Board-certified teachers know there are many kinds of intelligence—linguistic, musical, mathematical, spatial, personal—and that children learn in different ways.

The National Board for Professional Teaching Standards aims to spend about $50 million—$30 million from the federal government—to design its standards and assessments. It planned to certify its first 2,000 teachers in 1994–95 in early adolescence/English language arts and to be certifying teachers in all other areas by 1997.

The organization hopes to raise the status of teaching by setting standards so high that the national board becomes akin to other professional screening bodies such as state bars and medical licensing boards. It expects schools will compete for nationally certified teachers and use them as mentors for other teachers who are preparing for national certification. As the professional status and rewards grow for nationally certified teachers, more teachers will strive to increase their skills and knowledge.

Another project sponsored by the Council of Chief State School Officers, an organization of the state commissioners and superintendents, is developing a model set of standards for beginning teachers that will define the common core of knowledge and skills they all should possess. The council is sponsoring the Interstate New Teacher Assessment and Support Consortium, which is borrowing heavily from the work of the National Board for Professional Teaching Standards. Like the National Board's standards, those of the consortium will be outcomes-based, judging teachers on what they know and can do rather than on the courses they've passed. The consortium hopes its standards will become the model for all states, many of which are revising their teacher certification standards. Forty states already are involved in the consortium.

Thus, a national certification system for teachers appears to be emerging. What's more encouraging is that the National Board and consortium are defining standards that will produce teachers well equipped to work in flexible schools without grades and the other rigid conventions of the bell curve. These standards call for teachers who focus on individuals rather than groups. They are teachers who will understand national standards and ways to ensure all students meet them. They are just the kind of teachers the nation needs to stamp out the Bell-Curve Syndrome.

What Parents Can Do

Parents can become powerful partners in transforming the nation's schools. As Gaston County discovered, they also can stop change dead in its tracks. The better they understand how a system shaped by the bell curve gives rise to dull textbooks, to bored, frustrated, and misplaced children, and to widespread student failure, the more apt they will be to support change.

Parents have tremendous power to affect their schools. Minority parents proved that in the Portland School District on one February day in the winter of 1991. Upset with the low academic achievement of all students in general and minority and poor students in particular, parents boycotted the schools for a day. After the boycott, led by the Black United Front of Portland, the school board launched a series of planning sessions that led to the creation of school-based management teams composed of teachers and parents.

The spread of school-based management across the country gives parents a perfect place to get involved and push for changes that move schools away from the bell curve toward high standards. On or off such councils, however, parents must begin refusing to tolerate school practices that use the bell curve to hurt their children—or anyone else's. These practices violate their children's rights to a good education, which, more and more, means access to a decent living.

Parents, for example, should not tolerate tracked classes that expect less of their children than of others. These are blatantly unfair. They should insist that their children be expected to aspire to high standards.

Parents should protest group-based teaching practices that bore their children by going too slow or frustrate them by going too fast. They should encourage schools to eliminate grade levels and standardized teaching methods in favor of more flexible organizations that allow their children to progress at their own pace toward clearly defined standards.

Parents should object to schools that hurt their children's self-esteem by using negative comparisons—whether grades or test scores—with other children the same age. They should protest when schools label their children below average, slow, or underachievers. They should urge schools to compare their children against benchmarks and standards. Parents should ask teachers to give them more meaningful evidence of what their children know and can do than abstract grades. They should demand to see examples of essays their children wrote and math problems they solved.

Parents also can help transform schools by actively supporting nationwide efforts to establish high standards for students and teachers, promote more diversity and choice in schools, and foster more flexible, student-oriented schools. Parents should support national standards, the elimination of grades and grade levels, and more school choice because all of those changes will make schools better places for their children.

Polls repeatedly show that parents and the general public remain too complacent about traditional schools, even as schools continue to doom millions of children who fall on the low end of the bell curve. A 1994 Gallup poll commissioned by *Phi Delta Kappan* magazine showed that 44 percent of Americans would give their community schools A or B grades, and another 30 percent would give them a C.[29] Most Americans are satisfied with their schools. As long as this acceptance of the status quo continues, improving schools will be difficult to do. Schools will improve only when parents not only tolerate change but demand it.

Prescription for Change

All levels of government should change their way of looking at schools. Instead of worrying about institutions and the collective average performance of masses of students, the government should shift its focus to the academic welfare of each child. Its primary responsibility is to ensure that all children meet high academic expectations and do not wander off their personal learning paths into some dead-end swamp. Government, probably at a county or district level, could do this by assigning an adviser to keep tabs on every child, preferably for many years. Ideally, the same adviser, or advocate, would work with a student and parents throughout the child's educational journey. A portfolio of the child's work—which might include samples of writing, projects, problem solving, test scores, and even a videotape of presentations—could follow the child. Portions of this portfolio along with a record of the child's progress toward benchmarks and standards could be stored in a computer file. The computer could be programmed to flash lights automatically when the student started wandering off course.

A choice system similar to that of The Netherlands could be organized, probably on a state level, in the United States. But it should be combined with other initiatives, namely decentralization and school autonomy, national standards and the elimination of educational practices that use the bell curve. These changes would establish the framework for a powerful national education system capable of thrusting American students to the top of the world in academic performance.

Seven steps are required for American schools to build this new structure. The schools must:

1. Eliminate uses of the bell curve by ending age-based grouping and evaluation.

2. Establish national standards in core subjects, defining high proficiency in reading, writing, mathematics, science, and history for all students. Establish similar standards for a broad assortment of electives in arts, crafts, and humanities. Students would need

to meet the core standards plus three to five electives to graduate.

3. Encourage colleges and universities to mesh their admission standards with the national proficiency standards.

4. Establish a staircase of benchmark standards at primary, elementary, and intermediate levels to guide students toward the final national standards they must meet to graduate. Allow all students to progress from one level to the next whenever they meet the benchmark standards. They should be allowed to advance not only at their own pace, but also, as much as possible, along their own learning path.

5. Allow students to learn wherever they choose as long as they meet national benchmarks and standards. Establish a student-based financial system for schools and let the money follow the student to any school, public or private, that adopts national standards and eliminates bell-curve practices.

6. Assign a government-employed adviser to every child at each of the four levels of schooling to ensure the student charts a fitting individual learning path and properly advances toward benchmarks and standards.

7. Reduce and strive to eliminate the authority of school boards and central office administrators, giving every school as much authority as possible within the broad national framework. Central offices should become service centers for local schools. School boards should be retained at the state level. If not done away with at the local level, at least they should be limited to no more than four meetings a year. Administrators should be licensed by state boards, and local boards should be advisory only, unless they have tax-levying authority.

Given proper leadership at three levels—national, local, and state—this improvement plan could evolve within six years. National leaders must establish volunteer national standards and benchmarks in core and elective subject areas (step 2). They also should urge universities and colleges to align their admission requirements with the national standards (step 3). Once those steps are taken, parents will begin pressuring state and local leaders to make sure their children are meeting national standards. Parents will be less interested in the abstract results of national, norm-referenced tests. The importance of averages will decrease as the importance of seeing that every child meets standards increases. In short, a national system based on high standards will give educators incentives to abandon instructional practices based on the bell curve.

State leaders could accelerate these important changes by adopting national standards and giving more freedom and autonomy to local schools committed to helping their students reach standards (step 7).

Local school district leaders must sell these changes, as Betty Wallace did in Vance County. They must convince their boards, teachers, and parents to part with the bell curve and hold children to high standards. Local leaders, for example, have the responsibility of eliminating grade levels and grading. For their part, parents should embrace rather than resist these changes.

Finally, teachers need to take more control over the instructional practices in their schools while at the same time they surrender their control over the classroom. They need the freedom to reorganize their schools so children can take responsibility for their own learning. Teachers must become expert guides who help children learn through independent inquiry, hands-on experimentation, and small-team projects that reveal connections between art, history, science, math, and other disciplines.

Leaders, parents, and teachers can build an education network with high national standards and a diversity of schools, and paths within schools, leading to those standards. This system will have no use for the bell curve. Schools will blossom as the Bell-Curve Syndrome dies. Pioneers of this new generation of schools already are emerging like spring shoots, not only in Vance County, but across the country.

CHAPTER 9

▼

NEW PIONEERS FOR
SCHOOL CHANGE

Judy Darby's class looked about like any other on this May morning in 1993. Twenty-seven students sat cross-legged at her feet on the blue-carpeted floor of her spacious classroom in Boeckman Creek Primary School of Wilsonville, a suburb of Portland, Oregon. Darby used a felt pen to write words with "shun" sounds on a white plastic panel that had replaced the traditional chalkboard. The children supplied the words: information, transportation, direction, constipation, and so forth. They were big words for such small children, a mix of first and second graders.

At first glance, it seemed Darby was giving a traditional group-oriented lesson narrowly focused on the "shun" sound. She was not, however, seeking a group response. Instead, she asked her students to respond in individual ways by drawing on their imaginations and all of their verbal skills to create sentences out of words that they, not she, supplied. The children returned in groups of three or four to their tables to write sentences using the words. The children did not have individual desks. Some children asked others at their tables for help in spelling.

After about ten minutes, Darby had the children sit in a big circle on the carpet at the opposite end of her classroom. Two parakeets twittered in a cage nearby. Each child was invited to read his or her favorite sentence.

Derek, a first grader, read the sentence he wrote: "I went on vacation and brout my imagination and made an illustration."

"Excellent," said Mrs. Darby. "Derek, you always bring your imagination."

Wassim Fakih, a seven-year-old from Lebanon who often is up late working in his parents' bakery, read his: "I whet to the ocean for a vacatin."

No damaging comparison goes on during this exercise. The less advanced children, generally the younger ones, look to the more advanced writers as models. They may not be able to write as well yet, but they know they will be expected to eventually. Then they will become leaders for the children looking up to them as models. The children know that the more they learn, the more their teacher expects of them.

Boeckman Creek, like a growing number of American schools, is beginning to part with the bell curve. These bold schools are changing not because they recognize the dangers of the bell curve so much as because they see that more individualized instruction is the only way they can hope to teach an increasingly diverse population successfully.

At the same time, schools also are raising their standards for all students instead of expecting more of some than of others. These moves away from the bell curve and toward higher standards reflect the same two patterns of change at the grass-roots level that are being promoted at the state and national level through national standards, national teacher certification, charter schools, the Edison Project, and other efforts to improve education. In a variety of ways, pioneering schools such as Boeckman Creek are emerging like beacons across the country, lighting the way for the rest of the nation's schools to follow.

Vestiges of the old ways—group instruction, age-based grouping, and comparing—still survive at Boeckman Creek, as in most schools in transition. Teachers, though, are striving to move away from those practices in favor of a more personal system that allows children to take more responsibility for their learning. Boeckman Creek's strategy for individualizing differs from that adopted by Vance County schools, where students were grouped according to their achievement levels and educational needs rather than age and were allowed to step up a staircase of increasingly more advanced groups at their individual paces. Boeckman Creek's approach is based on the research of Lilian G. Katz, a child development psychologist who advocates mixed-age grouping.

At Boeckman Creek, teachers do not try to sort students by achievement levels; instead they design open-ended lessons that allow students at various stages of academic progress to respond at individual levels. So instead of passing out a worksheet that requires all students to circle the same "shun" sound in the same words, Darby asked her children to make a collective list of words with the sound and then write their own sentences using those words. Advanced students composed more complex sentences that inspired beginners to strive for higher goals.

Most Boeckman Creek teachers have a mix of two grade levels of diverse children. Like the historic one-room schoolhouse, this structure discourages large-group instruction and encourages teachers to design lessons that allow students to work alone or in small groups at learning activities that suit their varying educational needs and interests. "The one-room schoolhouse had a lot going for it," said Principal Nancy Hays. Rather than forcing children to remain silent, teachers allow and even encourage them to talk to one another about their work and to help one another, just as adults do in the workplace.

In traditional schools, teachers loathe combination classes because they are impossible to teach from a single textbook. But in Boeckman Creek's individual-oriented system, grade levels are becoming increasingly irrelevant.

Sarah Stafford loves her combined second- and third-grade class. "One of the real pluses is I get to keep half of my class the second year, and they become teachers and role models for the incoming class," she said.

This structure also encourages teachers to extend the classroom beyond the four walls with computers and rich learning environments that can accommodate student diversity. Darby does this with her daily writing workshop.

The children had been studying Africa and were doing a variety of projects connected with animals. Again, they had the freedom to respond to the general assignment according to their individual interests. Some worked with partners or in small groups; others choose to work alone. The children fanned out over the classroom.

"Who needs help?" asked Darby.

No one raised a hand.

"No one needs help?" she asked with a note of disappointment. With that plea, a couple children volunteered to be helped. But most were too busy.

Amber Lawrence, eight, and Jessica Knox and Meghan Thomas, each seven, gathered at one round table to write about how the chimpanzee got its tail. Meghan and Amber each wrote similar beginnings, so Meghan agreed to trim part of hers and to add the rest to Amber's. Nearby at a square table, Mickey Clark and Harry Achilles, both eight, were each writing a story about how the flap-necked chameleon got its skin designs.

"We're going to write them and see which story we like the best," said Mickey.

At another table David Schroeder wrote about how he feels about the cheetah: "A cheetah makes me want to sprint." Next to him Ian George drew a chameleon; he struggled with the legs. Chris Fogg was over at the magazine table, sifting through animal magazines for a picture of a rhinoceros.

Meanwhile, Leah Clark, who was only six, read her story on how the lion lost its teeth to Darby, who was typing it into an Apple computer. Darby was troubled by the pronouns in the following sentence: He was so hungry that he took eighteen sticks and put them in his mouth. The "his" could refer to an animal mentioned in the previous sentence instead of the lion. To clear up the confusion, Darby proposed starting the sentence with "The lion" instead of "he." Leah agreed. To be sure it is clear, Darby tried the sentence out on Chris Fogg, who was standing nearby.

"Who put eighteen sticks in his mouth?" asked Darby.

"The lion," said Chris.

"See, he understands it," Darby told a smiling Leah.

As the morning stretched on, the children spread out, led by their curiosity to different corners of the room and, in some cases, out of it. Two girls dashed to the library to type their stories on one of the computers. Rachel Megan slipped out into a commons area, called the pod, opening off this and two other classrooms for second and third graders. The pod had several learning centers, one with reference books, another with computers, and a third loaded with literature books. Rachel had finished her story on how the lion lost its paws and had found a quiet corner among the computers to read her book, *No Monster in the Closet*.

"It's quiet out here," she said.

Nearby, at a table by the reference books, Becky Jahns, a teaching assistant, listened to Rachel Spence, a first grader, and Mark Cummings, a third grader, read stories.

Soon Darby would gather her children together again and then move into reading workshop, during which they would drift apart again to read to one another or to themselves in books of their own choosing or on computers.

A stroll through the school revealed scene after scene of children working alone or in small groups on a variety of projects. In one pod, a young girl sat in a couch, reading to a child with Down's Syndrome. In another a teaching assistant worked math problems with a small group of fourth and fifth graders. Inside a classroom off the pod, Christopher Jorgens was at an overhead projector, telling classmates how he solved a fraction problem. A group of first graders drew posters while others read to one another, and still others read to themselves. The school hummed with the purposeful soft conversations of children engaged in the work of learning.

In this school, the roles of teacher and children differ from traditional ones. Teachers spend less time lecturing and more time setting up inviting learning environments where children take charge of their own learning. Classrooms spill out into pods and the library and mix.

"There is a lot of activity," said Mary Loveland, a primary teacher. "If you teach this way, it allows you to meet their needs where they are."

At Boeckman Creek, children are not judged by how they compare to others of the same age. Instead, teachers focus on telling parents precisely what their children know and can do. They do this with a portfolio of each child's work. You can tell a lot about a second grader named Monique, for example, by the picture she's colored on the cover of her portfolio. The picture depicts a smiling girl in a pink dress with a pink bow in her hair. She stands proudly in front of a big house with matching pink curtains and a glorious yellow sun blazing above it. Inside is a short biography of Monique and her view of what she is accomplishing in school: "I'm proud of the way I read and how I tell time," she writes. "My goals are how electricity works and how to speak a different language."

The portfolio includes a sample of how Monique spelled select words and sentences early and later in the year. In the fall, for example, she wrote, "Marry had a little lam its flise was as white as snow and avery were that marry went the lam was shir to go." By February, that had changed to "Mary had a little lam its fleece was as white as snow and every where that Mary went, the lam was sure to go."

The portfolio lists books Monique has read and math problems she has solved along with an explanation of the strategy she used to solve them. There are samples of problems in multiplication and fractions that she has mastered, as well as samples of her writing, including first drafts, and poems. The teacher adds her own comments, describing Monique as an independent reader and learner. Sometimes teachers send home videotapes of children presenting a project or giving a speech. Darby, for example, videotaped a first-grade boy reciting from memory Robert Frost's "Stopping by the Woods on a Snowy Evening." Children work hard to build impressive portfolios so they can show them off to their parents. None has to worry about failing.

Boeckman Creek offers a glimpse of what a school begins to look like when the Bell-Curve Syndrome has less of a presence. Children seem engaged, happy, and learning. They are not bored by a lack of challenge or frustrated by work they cannot handle. More often they appear to be learning because they want to than because they have to. There are no bells, no textbooks, no desks in rows. In fact, there are no desks at all, only tables. Grade levels have become less important, instruction less standardized. The children have more room, though not complete freedom, to pursue their own interests at their own pace. They are mixed rather than sorted and tracked. Even special education students are included in the mainstream. One of Darby's students was blind.

Boeckman Creek's teachers said they would never go back to the traditional classroom. Even Diane Pinkney, who taught the traditional way for twenty-eight years, prefers the new approach. Her students are more responsive and involved, she said.

"Because children are more engaged, there are fewer discipline problems," said Donna Dennison, the school's instructional coordinator.

That deeper engagement also is reflected in student performance. All of Boeckman Creek's children develop strong basic skills. Sixty percent of the students who advanced into sixth grade in 1991–92 were ready for math typically reserved for seventh graders. Principal Hays recalls how one student named Justin saw himself at the bottom of the heap in a traditional class, where he ended up on the wrong end of the bell curve. But at Boeckman Creek, he became a third grader in class with second graders who turned to him for help.

"He said, 'Mom, I'm not the lowest kid in the class anymore,' " said Hays. "We saw him become a competent learner."

In an interview, Justin said he didn't used to like going to school. Now, he said, "I love it."

What a difference a little success can make.

Silver Ridge

In September of 1990, the same month Boeckman Creek opened, another pioneering elementary school opened on the Olympic Peninsula of Washington State in the small town of Silverdale at the foot of the Olympic Mountains. As in Boeckman Creek, the children in Silver Ridge are taking control of their own learning. What's striking at Silver Ridge is the web of technology students can tap to aid them on their educational journeys.

On one May morning in 1993, Cindy Parker and Josh Webb showed a school visitor how they build computer-based multimedia presentations. Visitors have become so common at this innovative school that a team of students trains to give tours. Josh, a lanky, freckle-faced fourth grader, was learning the ropes from Cindy, a perky sixth grader. Cindy flipped on an Apple computer, and there glowed a black-and-white picture of her smiling face along with the advisor and two classmates who helped her design this program on immigrants. She showed the visitor the zap shot digital camera her team used to shoot this picture and transfer it to the computer disk. She clicked a command with her computer mouse and a student's voice explained what an immigrant is. That, she explained, was done with hypersound, a digital recorder used to transmit and store sound on the immigrant computer program disk. She clicked the mouse again. The monitor began showing moving pictures of early immigrants as an audio narrative described them. The students programmed their computer to play a specific range of frames from the 25,000 recorded on the laser disk. With another click of the mouse, a still photo of an immigrant family popped up on the computer screen. The students used a computer scanner to take this picture from a textbook and load it into their program. After Cindy's team was graded on their multimedia presentation on immigrants, their disk was put on the shelf along with dozens of others in the multimedia library. These are available for younger students to watch. So the next third grader looking for more information on immigrants can get a good start by tapping Cindy's multimedia presentation.

Like Boeckman Creek, Silver Ridge is a school in transition. It still holds onto remnants of bell-curve practices such as age-based grouping, group instruction, and grades. But at the same time, it is departing from these conventions to give students more control over their own learning, primarily through the power of computer technology.

"The restructuring here is real," said Penny Beers, enrichment specialist for the school. "We empower children here. We give kids a lot of responsibility in this school."

Each week, for example, a team of fourth, fifth, and sixth graders produce a short television show with news and features about their school called "Good Morning, Silver Ridge." They show their work to the school every Friday morning through a network linking television sets in every classroom. The students use a computer program called VCR Companion to add interesting graphics and introductions to their productions.

"Mostly students work with this program," said Chelsie Webb, Josh's older sister, as she demonstrated how VCR Companion works. "I don't think adults do."

"They don't know how," added Amby Iles, a fourth grader on the production crew.

In addition to giving tours, students handle other jobs in the school. One team sells espresso café lattes to teachers and other adults in the school each morning. They keep track of supplies, money, everything that goes into the business. The coffee kids earned $1,200 in one school year and were looking to expand to the junior high next door. Other kids wear a set of tools strapped to their belts and do routine computer maintenance. Children also run a store, help care for two-year-olds in the school day-care center, and run an in-school postal system. In all, more than 100 of the school's 730 students have jobs.

Students say they spend part of nearly every day working on individualized reading and mathematics programs on the computers. The programs allow them to advance at their own pace.

"You get with the level you are on, and it is easier for you," said Kathy Lush, a sixth grader.

"I've been on computers since kindergarten," said fourth-grader Joel Cowgill.

Teachers are doing more pretesting so they can determine what students already know. Students skip lessons they've already learned and move on. Many students have surged ahead at least a grade level. As the school finds more ways to allow students to take individual learning paths, it is also permitting more students to break away from the pack and mix with students of different ages. Some students leave the school for part of the day to take more advanced courses at the junior high. One ten-year-old boy has been allowed to skip two grades to sixth grade and is already studying algebra. Because the school is so fluid, it can accommodate a great diversity of students. Severely mentally and physically handicapped children and extraordinarily gifted students all mix with the mainstream. An autistic girl who was chewing her clothes and pinching herself a year ago now sits quietly on a carpet with a group of her peers and listens to her teacher tell a story. Everyone fits in at Silver Ridge.

On Thursday mornings, the school completely removes age barriers and mixes all grades in teams of students for special projects. Every adult in the school, including the principal and custodian, help lead a team on a project. The school picks a theme, such as community service, and each adult chooses a project that suits him or her. The school counselor, for example, might choose to help a team learn cardiopulmonary resuscitation, while another teacher offers to lead a group in preparing local residents for an earthquake. Students choose which project they want to work on. Each team requires children from grades 1 through 6 to work together.

"We believe it is real artificial for kids just to be with kids the same age," said Principal B. J. Wise. "Only in public schools are we only with people the same age."

Teachers are using these weekly projects to experiment with new ways of teaching, said Wise. They try to avoid traditional direct, group-oriented instruction and let the teams of students take charge of their own learning. One student panel critiqued the projects and basically told teachers, "Quit talking so much; we know what to do." In some ways teachers dread the projects because trying to change is so hard. "It is a terrible stretch," she said.

But teachers have learned that they must keep stretching if they are going to keep up at this rapidly evolving school. Unlike in traditional schools, teachers here cannot retreat into the privacy of their classrooms. There is no privacy. The whole school is open. Classrooms are organized into one of four pods, named for the classical four elements: earth, fire, water, and air. Each pod has six classrooms representing at least three grade levels. One, for example, includes two fourth grades, two fifth grades, a third grade, and a kindergarten. Students stay with their teachers for two years. Each classroom has one wall missing where it opens onto a commons area filled with a bank of thirty computers. The remaining three walls of the classrooms form trapezoids. That shape—along with carpeting, sound-absorbing walls, and a speaker system producing white noise that nullifies classroom noise—keeps the open school remarkably quiet.

The open pods foster collaboration among teachers across grade levels. First-grade teachers Barbara Johnson and Jeanne Beckon like the openness so well they removed the wall separating their classes so they can share students and team-teach.

"The children get the best of both worlds," said Beckon. "[Johnson] is more creative; I'm more organized."

On Thursday afternoons, school closes at 1 P.M. so teachers can share ideas and launch joint projects. While the teachers are meeting, students can either go home or stay to participate in a variety of sports, music, and art activities.

Teachers also keep in touch through an electronic mail system on their classroom computers. Kindergarten teacher Marilyn Boyton may go days without seeing another kindergarten teacher in another pod, but they exchange messages every day through E-mail. Though Silver Ridge keeps them stretching, and perhaps because it does, teachers say they want to press deeper into the new territory they are exploring.

"I can't think of anyone at this school who would prefer to go back to traditional schools," said Boyton.

After three years, the school is beginning to see the fruits of its innovations, said Wise, who was named Washington State's Principal of the Year in 1992. About 95 percent of its students are fluent readers by the time they complete second grade. The school is so full of readers that the library shelves look half empty. Children note they can check out up to six books a week. By the time they reach sixth grade, Silver Ridge students can work beautifully in groups, use technology transparently, and skillfully take charge of their own learning, Wise said.

"This business of changing schools is an absolute journey, and it needs to happen," she said. "I think we're heading toward a place where kids will be making more decisions, not so much about what they are going to learn, but how they are going to learn it."

The bell curve is far from dead at Boeckman Creek and Silver Ridge schools. Teachers still cling to old ways even as they search for new ones. They still generally group students by age, and much of their instruction continues to be group-oriented. Silver Ridge still uses letter grades, though the whole Central Kitsap School District that it belongs to will soon be dropping Cs, Ds, and Fs. Implicit in that move is the notion all students should earn an A or B on a lesson, which is to say master it, before they advance to a higher level. Children, however, will continue to be looking at how they stack up against their peers as long as they are grouped by age. Boeckman Creek and Silver Ridge also lack the clear outcomes that can become powerful draws for students moving at their own pace. Teachers steer students through a traditional curriculum without spelling out precisely what students need to know and be able to do, say to advance to junior high school. Students master one lesson and simply move on to the next, with only a vague sense of where they are headed.

In their tentative departures from traditional practices, though, teachers in these schools are seeing how powerfully education can grip students when the bell curve is pushed aside. The instructional focus quickly shifts from group norms and standardized textbooks and lessons to individual needs and ways to meet them. Just giving children a portion of their day to read books they choose, to study at their own level and pace on a computer, or to work on a team with children of other ages is making these students more engaged in school. Many, if not most, of them are rapidly becoming competent independent learners. Even with their modest loosening of structure, these schools are able to accommodate a broader diversity of children. One can only imagine what students would be capable of in a school fully liberated from the bell curve and focused on clear standards.

Alternative Schools

Alternative schools, forced to be more flexible and responsive to children who do not fare well in traditional schools, in some ways have gone farther than most schools in breaking their ties with the bell curve. Vocational Village and Oregon Outreach are alternative schools in Portland, Oregon, that have discovered they must sever ties with the bell curve if they are going to connect with alienated students.

A stroll through Vocational Village, home for about 240 students, revealed one of the quietest, most orderly schools in the city. Three students sat at separate tables in the library, silently reading; another three were busy at a table in the student-run delicatessen, doing paperwork for their business; the business room clattered with students at work on computer keyboards; Russian immigrant students practiced their new language in an English class; and a team of students at a table were immersed in a group project in health occupations. The atmosphere was relaxed and purposeful.

There was not a scrap of litter on the polished tile floors, not a smudge of graffiti on the yellow-brick walls and this was near the end of the 1992–93 school year. The school is as tidy as a fire engine. Many outside teachers who visit are shocked. They've assumed this school must be a zoo because they've sent their most troublesome students here.

Vocational Village serves students such as Charles Santos, a short, burly eighteen-year-old who coasted through two years at Roosevelt High School in Portland and then began growing bored, getting in trouble, and slipping behind during his junior and senior years. Charles's biggest problem in public schools was the slow group pace he was forced to endure. He could recall fighting boredom as early as third grade, when he'd finish his work before most other students and begin tossing erasers. That's when he began making trips to the principal's office and spending punishment time isolated in a study hall. His problems grew worse at Roosevelt High where classes, such as a science class on Antarctica, seemed irrelevant.

"I didn't care about the South Pole," Charles said. "I'm not going to go there."

Teachers seemed cold and distant in even a moderate-size high school of 1,000 students. "Teachers would tell you 'You can do the work or not; I'm already getting paid; I'm already out of school,' " he recalled.

Charles figured he would keep slipping farther behind at Roosevelt. So, at his mother's urging, he transferred to Vocational Village. There he discovered he could build a learning schedule that fit his needs. Classes were all individualized and based on learning goals. Once students met the standards in a required course such as English or science, they would get a credit. The school has a ten-period day stretching from 8:30 A.M. to 5:30 P.M., allowing students to carve out that portion of the day that fits their needs. At Vocational Village, Charles was never frustrated, never bored, never sent to the principal's office. There he found his way.

"At this school, instead of being a number you are actually a name and a person," he said. "It is more versatile than a regular school. . . . Here I can learn about things I want to know about."

After a year at Vocational Village, Charles planned to earn his diploma and enroll in an emergency medical technician and fire-fighter program at a community college.

Vocational Village parted company with the bell curve when it opened as an alternative school twenty-five years ago. It had to. It was serving students who fell outside the mainstream, students whose academic pace was faster than, slower than, or different from that prescribed by the bell curve. They were misfits. Vocational Village needed to become more flexible, practical, and individualized to meet the needs of this diverse group of students.

"We are here to meet the needs of the individual whereas in the traditional schools you are there to meet the needs of the program," said Lynda Darling, who has been teaching reading at Vocational Village for more than two decades. "The kids we get from the traditional school are so locked into failure they are afraid to try. They know in their hearts they are going to flunk another test."

So the teachers at Vocational Village eliminate grades, grading, and any possibility for a student to fail.

"The longer I'm here, the more I understand grades are very tyrannical," said Principal Paul Erickson. "There are some wonderful C students who don't feel good about themselves."

Students entering Vocational Village are required to study an occupational area, such as metals, health, or business, along with their academic studies. Once students set a career goal, they become more willing to meet academic requirements to pursue it. To help them chart and stay on their individual learning paths, the school's academic and vocational teachers form pairs of advocates for small groups of students. Darling and a business teacher, for example, serve as advocates for about thirty students. The advocates check with their charges twice a day to make sure the students are on course.

Many of the students have family problems that sometimes force them to leave school for a time. But until they are twenty-one they can come back and pick up where they left off. Consequently, to sustain a daily attendance of about 240 students, the school must enroll twice that many, said Erickson. Each year about 40 to 50 graduate.

"We don't know what a dropout is," he said.

When they arrive at Vocational Village, most students have been jaded by bell-curve comparisons that repeatedly relegated them among the ranks of losers. They are placed slightly below their performance levels in every subject so they can succeed easily and advance. Once they rediscover their competence, many students become intoxicated with learning and rush ahead at breakneck speeds. One girl, an orphan living on her own, earned eighteen of the twenty-two credits she needed to graduate in the single 1991–92 school year, Erickson said. She attended school thirteen periods a day. (Budget cuts forced the school later to cut its day to ten periods.) In Darling's reading class, students typically make reading gains in seven to nine weeks equivalent to what they would be expected to make in one to two years in traditional schools.

"Once a student sees some gains in his reading ability, he starts to believe us when we tell him he can do it," Darling writes in a reading manual she coauthored about her program. "When he arrives at this point and begins to believe in himself, there is nothing to hold him back."

That was the case for Shannon Montgomery, a smart, shy, soft-spoken seventeen-year-old with long brown hair. Shannon enjoyed most of her school years on the winning side of the bell curve, earning As and Bs in elementary and middle school. But when she entered high school, she got lost. Like Charles, she found the size of the school daunting and the teachers distant. She was put in classes she found too hard and was chided when she asked to be moved lower.

"It made you feel dumb," she said, "when you go and tell your counselor your classes are too hard and you want them lowered, and he just says, 'You want the easy way out; you tested this high, and we're not going to move you down.'"

She began slipping behind. By the end of her sophomore year, she could see she was in trouble and in danger of quitting. A friend told her about Vocational Village and she transferred.

Instead of losing ground, Shannon surged ahead at Vocational Village. By June she was making plans to graduate early in December of her senior year. She became interested in graphics and desktop publishing and got chances to go beyond the classroom for knowledge. For her U.S. history credit, for example, she read some books, visited Portland historical museums, and was planning a tour of missions and historical sites in California during the summer, after which she would write papers on what she learned.

"You learn more going out doing things than just sitting in a classroom," she said. "It is a lot easier because you are working at your level and at your own pace instead of working in a class where some students are behind and some students are way ahead. You can work on stuff that you want to work on instead of being forced to work in books you have no interest in."

Shannon entered the business program and helped run the delicatessen. The young woman who had only months earlier been thinking about quitting high school had now set her sights on going to college for a four-year degree in business. A misfit in a group-oriented system found a place in a school geared to individuals.

Like Shannon, Antwan Ross, seventeen, did well in elementary and middle school, but fell out of step with the mediocre pace of the mainstream when he reached high school. He grew bored and began skipping school with friends.

"It was like I was repeating what I learned," he said. "We would hang out at the gym and play basketball all day until the teachers would kick us out. Or we would just leave school and go to the mall."

Antwan fell behind and lost interest in even trying to catch up. He had begun to think about quitting and trying to get a general education development certificate. But then he heard about Vocational Village and decided to give it a try.

He quickly fit into the smaller school. There he began to study marketing, went to work for the deli, and became vice president of DECA, a school business club. Antwan liked the self-paced learning options the school offered. In personal finance, he branched off into his own independent study of money management and learned how to keep checking accounts, fill out tax forms, and figure car loans. In global studies, he got a chance to study problems in the Middle East, which became of interest to him after his brother-in-law went to Saudi Arabia during the Gulf War.

"You can explore it as far as you want to go or you can just do so much and stop if you want to," he said. "But once I start learning something, I don't like to stop."

Antwan said he has broad interests and has not yet settled on a career, but he does know he wants to go to college.

Teachers and students interviewed at Vocational Village said they believed the more individualized, goal-based approach they used ought to be used in traditional schools. If it works for students who struggle in traditional schools, they say, think how well it would work for those who don't. "It would enable them to fly higher than they are able to now," said Erickson, the principal.

Oregon Outreach, a small, private, nonprofit organization is even more flexible, unstructured, and strapped for money than Vocational Village. It serves about fifty students who have been rejected repeatedly from other public and alternative schools. Some have been out of school for years. Some belong to street gangs. Some have been in trouble with the law and forced to attend the school by their parole officers. Some have not even begun middle school while others are only a few credits away from graduating. And some, who have failed at every school they've attended, give up at Oregon Outreach too. But others succeed there where they could not anywhere else because the school is so flexible.

"Most of them have a lot of attention problems," said Valerie Anderson, a teacher at one of the school's two centers (which have merged since this interview) in the basement of Vernon Presbyterian Church in northeast Portland. "A lot of times they come only when they can."

Entering students take tests that allow Anderson to determine what they know and can do and what they still need to learn. Students then work with Anderson to set goals and develop a personal learning plan or contract. Most choose to work on credits toward their high school graduation. As at Vocational Village, they can earn these credits by demonstrating that they have learned what the course demands, whether it takes them a semester or eighteen months. A student, for example, might zoom through a U.S. history course in nine weeks, in which case he or she would get a year's credit.

"Credits are based on outcomes, not seat time," said Anderson.

If students miss a day or a week, or even several weeks, they can return and pick up where they left off without having to repeat the course.

The school runs on a shoestring budget and is open only noon to 3 P.M. four days a week, which forces students to do much of their work on their own at home. Anderson was the only certified teacher at the Vernon center, but she had many other adult assistants and volunteers helping her tutor students. The students must take charge of their own learning, both in school and out, if they are to make progress. The school can afford only the most basic of learning materials: paperback workbooks, trade books, and a single computer. At Vernon, students met in a basement furnished like a coffeeshop with round tables. Anderson observed that while the school offers students the flexibility these students need, it also must find ways to offer a richer learning environment, more structure, and higher expectations. Too many students lack the drive to overcome so many years of failure, and their progress is "painfully slow," she said.

Still, for all its shortcomings, several students said they prefer Oregon Outreach, where they can chart their personal learning path, to a public school regimen they found either too irrelevant and dull or too difficult, frustrating, and demeaning. Even with the barest of resources and time, this school sometimes succeeds where others fail because it has rejected the bell curve.

Mike Whiteley, a husky, blond fifteen-year-old, loves baseball and football but became so bored with high school his sophomore year that he just stopped going. He missed so many days, the school barred him from coming back. So he turned to Oregon Outreach with hopes of salvaging his school year and a place in sports. He discovered he could make headway if he pushed himself.

"Before I was irresponsible," he said. "I feel a little more confident in doing my work now because I'm more mature."

He discovered he was more competent than he had believed in math as he whisked through algebra. "I'm starting to become a nerd now," he said with a grin. Mike expected to earn the credits he would need to allow him to return to high school with full junior standing by the following fall.

Tina-Marie Simmons showed up at Oregon Outreach three years after she gave up at a Portland high school early in her freshman year. She started at Vernon without a single credit toward her diploma. She had once liked going to school, but she fell behind and school became more and more of a nightmare as she advanced from grade to grade.

"All through my school years, they have passed me through with straight Fs because of my height," she said. "I was too big to stay behind."

At least part of her inability to keep up stemmed from dyslexia. She could write an entire essay backward, so it could be read in a mirror, without realizing she was doing it. By the time she reached her freshman year, school had become incomprehensible and too humiliating to endure.

"I just didn't understand anything," she said. "I wanted to learn, but the teachers just didn't have any time because there were too many kids in the class. I felt like I was getting stupider, not smarter."

So Tina-Marie quit and mowed lawns, baby-sat, and did other odd jobs for three years until one job brought her to Vernon Presbyterian Church to do some painting. That's when she learned about Oregon Outreach and decided to give it a try. She hopes that by working hard, she can earn her high school diploma within two years.

"Before I felt stupid in front of my classmates and I got yelled at by my teachers," she said after finishing a spelling assignment in the Vernon learning center. "Since I came to this school here, they let you work at your own pace, and they don't get mad at you. They just teach you. . . . I have to work twice as hard, but it will be worth it when I'm done."

Jennifer, a slim, articulate girl with dark eyes and a soft, friendly smile, had about given up on school after she became pregnant at age twelve and was forced to skip seventh grade. Her life had tumbled out of control more than a year earlier after she told an elementary schoolteacher that her stepfather was sexually molesting her. The Children's Services Division stepped in and Jennifer was placed in a foster home. She became incorrigible and was shuffled from one foster home to the next. She rebelled at school, goofed off, got in trouble, in part, she recalled later, to mask her fear of being unable to handle the school work. Her son was born premature, weighing only two pounds, and was placed in private foster care, where Jennifer was allowed to visit him once a week. Meanwhile, Jennifer stayed in a foster group home with fourteen other girls. She rode city buses for an hour each way to Oregon Outreach because the school was working for her. Like other students, she had discovered she was smarter than she thought. She failed math in traditional schools, for example, but at the Vernon center she discovered that with a little help, she could make respectable academic progress.

"I can work at my own pace and my own level so it is good," she said. "I get a lot done. It is easier. I think if I were in a regular school, I still would be way behind. I would probably still be goofing off. But here I'm learning a lot more and learning faster than I would in a regular school."

The bell curve took its toll on these students in traditional schools. But in a bare basement at Oregon Outreach, they've been able to escape the curve's clutches and discover that knowledge is still within their reach. The tragedy is that for so many this opportunity has come so late, after years of pain and failure.

Because Vocational Village and Oregon Outreach get students so late in their school careers, they cannot realistically set academic standards as high as they should for students entering the modern world. If these teenagers had had the opportunity to attend individualized schools earlier, however, then they all could be expected to meet high standards. That's why all schools, from the primary grades on up, need to become more like these alternative schools.

Accelerating Change

Across the country, schools that are embracing change are becoming easier to find. Many districts are in some stage of developing school-based councils to give parents and teachers more say in school improvement. More encouraging is that where schools are making changes, they are consistently moving away from at least some instructional practices tied to the bell curve. Scores of schools across the country are giving children more control over their learning, expanding the classroom beyond four walls into computer and science laboratories and the broader community, and moving, like Boeckman Creek, toward mixed-age grouping in their primary grades. Kentucky requires some of these practices, and other states such as Oregon encourage them.

The century-old Laboratory School on the University of Northern Colorado campus began mixing grades for its 570 students in 1987. The school takes preschool children and will keep them, if necessary, until they are age twenty. Elementary children are grouped in two-grade blocks, but grades are mixed in middle school and in high school. A sixth grader, for example, may be taking eighth-grade-level math and an eighth grader may be in a sixth-grade English class. Students do not get grades on their work until they reach high school. All students have an adult advocate, usually a teacher, who meets with them every day to make sure school is meeting their needs. The advocate stays with the children at least two years, sometimes longer. The school also strives to give all students time each day to study one of their passions in depth, said Gary Galluzzo, director of the school and associate dean of the university's college of education. One of the school's chief objectives is to teach every child to be a self-directed learner.

"We are of the mind that in the information explosion it is not just what you know but how you know that's important because there is just so much to know," said Galluzzo. "The first time I got time to be responsible for my own education was in my doctoral studies. Typically, we learn other people's subject matter in courses they run."

Children at the laboratory school begin taking charge of their learning early. Kindergartners are put in an empty room at the beginning of the year and allowed to fill it as they see fit. By spring, they have filled one corner with books, another with computers, and the room's support poles have become trees, sprouting exotic, kid-made branches. As the school becomes more fluid, individual subjects are falling by the wayside. Teachers are working in teams to integrate their lessons and make more meaningful connections between what students learn and the world they live in. The high school physics, art, and math teachers team up to offer a course on flight and aerodynamics. The English, social studies, and earth science teachers join forces to provide a course on Southwest Native Americans. Students will read Native American literature, visit clifftop pueblos, and study the region's geology. The school's move away from traditional group-oriented, lockstep practices is paying off. Ninety-two percent of its graduates go on to college, and each year their college entrance exam scores keep climbing. The school is not elitist; it takes whatever students choose to come. About 25 percent of them are minority and 13 percent come from low-income families.

As in the laboratory school, classroom walls are toppling in schools across the nation as students or teams of students leave the classroom to scout libraries, computer networks, and their communities for new knowledge and skills. All of Cambridge, Massachusetts, has become a classroom for high school students at the Rindge School of Technical Arts. One group of teenagers set out to design a plan for a new restaurant in a building they chose for renovation. They met with city zoning officials, studied nutrition to design a menu, and visited a graphic-arts studio to design business cards.[1] Other schools are re-creating communities within their own buildings. Two elementary schools in Massachusetts and three in New York have established Microsociety programs created by George Richmond, a painter and teacher raised in Manhattan's Lower East Side. Students in these schools learn math by running banks and businesses and paying taxes. They learn government by drafting their own constitution, arguing cases in courts, and running a city council. The schools have "demonstrated the potential to accelerate learning, provide ladders of economic opportunity and give children a sense of how their society works," writes *Time* magazine.[2]

In another pattern of change, schools are setting high expectations for all students, rather than tracking children and expecting more of some than of others. Public School 67 in New York's South Bronx and Three Oaks Elementary School in Ft. Myers, Florida, adopted a rigorous curriculum designed by educators working with E. D. Hirsch, Jr., author of *Cultural Literacy*. Elementary students in these schools are expected to learn a body of knowledge that includes classical literature, history, and art—and they do, gladly. This Core Knowledge program has been so successful that it has spread to fifty more schools and given rise to a network of 4,500 principals, teachers, and parents.

A public school in Watts, California, where 87 percent of the children score below average on standardized tests, also decided to demand more of its students. Fifth graders print a newspaper and sixth graders study tenth-grade biology and perform the Rossini opera *Barber of Seville*. This is one of a network of "accelerated schools" pioneered in 1986 by Henry Levin, a Stanford University education and economics professor, that since has spread to more than three hundred schools across the nation. Instead of expecting less of students by putting them through watered-down remedial courses, the accelerated schools give them a rich and challenging diet of literature, science, and problem solving. The result has been significant jumps in student achievement.[3]

Another approach to raising expectations for all students is to set high performance goals for them. As noted in Chapter 8, this out-comes-based approach to education rapidly gained appeal across the nation in the early 1990s. A growing number of school reform leaders concluded that setting learning goals would be one way to counter the tendency of norm-referenced tests to water down in-struction. They would focus on high academic standards rather than on the average or lowest common denominator. This practice quickly spread from state-level policy to school-level improvement plans. In a nationwide survey, 26 percent of public and private high schools in 1993 reported they had established specific learning goals or standards for graduation. Sophomores in the University of Northern Colorado's Laboratory School, for example, will be re-quired to demonstrate for their graduation in 1995 a mastery of standards in six areas: communications, arts, global awareness, problem solving, ethics, and wellness.

What's encouraging about this move to high standards is that it creates an incentive for districts to abandon age-based grouping, monolithic group instruction, comparative grading, and other practices rooted in the bell curve. To do otherwise restricts success. Many of the new statewide goal-based education plans emerging across the country encourage schools to part with their bell-curve ways. Educators are recognizing that simply setting high standards without making changes in the way schools organize learning will mean large numbers of students will fail to meet the standards.

So the nation is beginning to see promising patterns of change converge. Some broad state education improvement plans combine a shift to more individualized instruction with a move toward high standards, much like the structure Vance County School System built. This is exactly what needs to happen. This convergence can be seen in Oregon's school improvement plan, one of the most ambitious in the nation.

The Oregon Plan

On a cool but sunny day in late August 1992, some of Oregon's top educators gathered in a small meeting hall in Silver Falls State Park twenty miles east of Salem. Members of the state Board of Education, the state Department of Education, and a handful of superintendents, local board members, and parents from around the state were there. They dressed casually. State Superintendent Norma Paulus wore white shorts and a white sweatshirt, as if ready to take a day hike. The small hall was warm and cozy with its pine-planked ceilings, paneled wall, and pot of coffee steaming next to a stack of rolls on a table at one end. The task at hand was anything but casual, however. The educators assembled for three days to escape distractions, clear their heads, and focus on how they were going to carry out Oregon's school reform plan.

There was some irony in the setting, for the park was filled with remnants of the big, towering Douglas fir trees that formed the backbone of the state's economy for most of the century. These big trees, however, were disappearing, and many of those that remain were being protected as home for the endangered spotted owl. Consequently, Oregon's timber industry was depressed. Mill closures had left whole towns jobless. There in the shade of a once-great resource, educators were laying plans to prepare the state's youth for a future without trees.

That mission was at the heart of the Oregon Educational Act for the twenty-first century, or House Bill 3565, passed in 1991. It is commonly called the Katz bill after its chief sponsor, Representative Vera Katz (D-Portland), who two years later became Portland's mayor. Patterned after European education systems such as Germany's, the plan calls for ending traditional high school at grade 10 and allowing students to begin preparing either for work or college during their final two years. It envisions a massive expansion of youth apprenticeship training, probably through a combination of community college and business partnerships with high schools. The Katz plan drew heavily on recommendations of a report by the Commission on the Skills of the American Workforce, created by the National Center on Education and the Economy. Those recommendations were also at the base of President Clinton's push to expand work training for youth. Both Katz and Hillary Rodham Clinton served on the center's board.

The Oregon plan eliminates the traditional high school diploma in 1999 and replaces it with two certificates of mastery. (See Figure 9.1.) Students will be expected to earn the initial certificate of mastery around age sixteen or the end of tenth grade. To do so, they must meet a set of learning goals or outcomes. During its retreat in Silver Falls, the state board settled on eleven learning goals recommended by a task force. In summary, the goals require students to show they can: think; take charge of their own learning; use technology; work together; deliberate on public issues; understand diversity and speak in a second language; interpret human experience through art and literature; understand positive health habits; understand mathematical concepts; understand how science and math affect our world; and read, write, and speak well.

Teachers will use a variety of measures, most of them performance-based, to judge whether students meet the goals. To gauge whether students can apply math and science, for example, teachers might require them to use a computer and principles of statistics to study cancer incidence among people living near the Hanford nuclear site in Washington. The students could be required to construct the study, carry it out, and draw conclusions based on findings in a final report.

Academic performances such as this will be scored on consistent, clearly defined scales used by all teachers across the state. Once state educators develop these scales, they then will decide how high students must climb on each to meet learning goals for the certificates of mastery. Teachers could, for example, judge a student's ability to apply math and science on a six-point scale. The state then might adopt a level 4 performance as its standard for meeting the goal.

Students will keep samples of their best work—such as essays,

The Oregonian

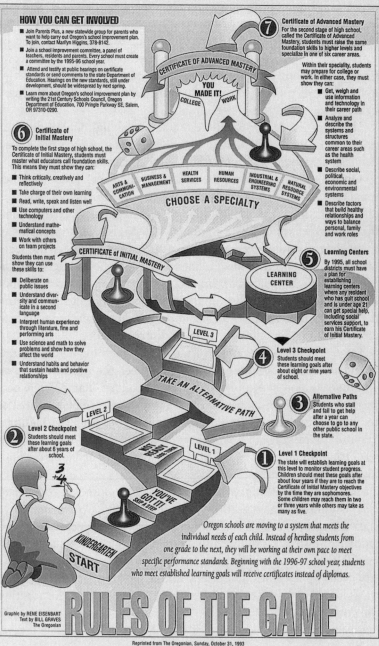

HOW YOU CAN GET INVOLVED

- Join Parents Plus, a new statewide group for parents who want to help carry out Oregon's school improvement plan. To join, contact Marilyn Higgins, 378-8142.

- Join a school improvement committee, a panel of teachers, residents and parents. Every school must create a committee by the 1995-96 school year.

- Attend and testify at public hearings on certificate standards or send comments to the state Department of Education. Hearings on the new standards, still under development, should be widespread by next spring.

- Learn more about Oregon's school improvement plan by writing the 21st Century Schools Council, Oregon Department of Education, 700 Pringle Parkway SE, Salem, OR 97310-0290.

(7) CERTIFICATE OF ADVANCED MASTERY

YOU MADE IT!
COLLEGE   WORK

Certificate of Advanced Mastery

For the second stage of high school, called the Certificate of Advanced Mastery, students must raise the same foundation skills to higher levels and specialize in one of six career areas.

Within their speciality, students may prepare for college or work. In either case, they must show they can:

- Get, weigh and use information and technology in their career path

- Analyze and describe the systems and structures common to their career areas such as the health system

- Describe social, political, economic and environmental systems

- Describe factors that build healthy relationships and ways to balance personal, family and work roles

(6) Certificate of Initial Mastery

To complete the first stage of high school, the Certificate of Initial Mastery, students must master what educators call foundation skills. This means they must show they can:

- Think critically, creatively and reflectively
- Take charge of their own learning
- Read, write, speak and listen well
- Use computers and other technology
- Understand mathematical concepts
- Work with others on team projects

Students then must show they can use these skills to:

- Deliberate on public issues
- Understand diversity and communicate in a second language
- Interpret human experience through literature, fine and performing arts
- Use science and math to solve problems and show how they affect the world
- Understand habits and behavior that sustain health and positive relationships

CHOOSE A SPECIALTY

ARTS & COMMUNICATION | BUSINESS & MANAGEMENT | HEALTH SERVICES | HUMAN RESOURCES | INDUSTRIAL & ENGINEERING SYSTEMS | NATURAL RESOURCE SYSTEMS

CERTIFICATE of INITIAL MASTERY

LEARNING CENTER

(5) Learning Centers

By 1995, all school districts must have a plan for establishing learning centers where any resident who has quit school and is under age 21 can get special help, including social services support, to earn his Certificate of Initial Mastery.

LEVEL 3

(4) Level 3 Checkpoint

Students should meet these learning goals after about eight or nine years of school.

TAKE AN ALTERNATIVE PATH

(3) Alternative Paths

Students who stall and fail to get help after a year can choose to go to any other public school in the state.

LEVEL 2

LEVEL 1

(2) Level 2 Checkpoint

Students should meet these learning goals after about 6 years of school.

3
+4

(1) Level 1 Checkpoint

The state will establish learning goals at this level to monitor student progress. Children should meet these goals after about four years if they are to reach the Certificate of Initial Mastery objectives by the time they are sophomores. Some children may reach them in two or three years while others may take as many as five.

YOU'VE GOT IT! SKIP A STEP

KINDERGARTEN START

Oregon schools are moving to a system that meets the individual needs of each child. Instead of herding students from one grade to the next, they will be working at their own pace to meet specific performance standards. Beginning with the 1996-97 school year, students who meet established learning goals will receive certificates instead of diplomas.

RULES OF THE GAME

Graphic by RENE EISENBART
Text by BILL GRAVES
The Oregonian

Reprinted from The Oregonian, Sunday, October 31, 1993

reports, and math problems—and their performance scores in a master portfolio. When students accumulate enough evidence to prove they have mastered a given goal, they can take the portfolio before a review board. The board will look at the work and decide whether the students have met the goal.

Beginning in the 1996–97 school year, students will be allowed to get a certificate of initial mastery whenever they can show they meet the 11 goals. Course credits will be as irrelevant for a certificate of mastery as they are for a driver's license. No longer will age and the time students have spent in class determine their advancement in school.

Once students have the initial certificate, they will spend their final two years or so of high school meeting ten more learning goals to get their certificate of advanced mastery. During this period, they also must explore one of six career pathways: arts and communications, business and management, health services, human resources, industrial and engineering systems, and natural resource systems. These areas of study will be similar to majors in college. The students will be free to follow their career path to college or into a technical or professional studies program. All students will be expected to study beyond high school, because doing so is necessary today to prepare for high-wage work.

In response to this plan, by fall of 1999 the Oregon State System of Higher Education will change its admission criteria from course credits and grade point averages to performance-based standards. It aims to align its admissions standards as much as possible with the public school certificate standards, creating a seamless transition from high school to college.

The certificates of mastery shift the focus of Oregon public education from the resources going into schools to learning goals defining what students must be able to know and do to get out. Standards for the certificates of mastery are to equal the highest academic standards in the nation by the year 2000 and in the world by 2010. Oregon educators realize that to meet this goal, schools are going to have to change.

"The certificate of initial mastery redefines everything that comes before it," said Jeana Woolley, chair of the state Board of Education.

Indeed, the Oregon plan encourages schools to eliminate primary grades and to use more individualized practices. It recommends that schools establish more fluid systems with academic performance benchmarks that will guide students on their way to the certificate-of-mastery standards. The plan advocates giving students more freedom to advance at their own pace, choose their own schools, and spend more time in independent studies, projects, and community services. In short, it implicitly recommends that schools reject the bell-curve practices of mass education.

In 1993, the legislature in neighboring Washington State passed a similar plan that also will trade high school diplomas for certificates of mastery. Wisconsin, Kansas, Colorado, Florida, Pennsylvania, and at least twenty-four other states are also moving to learning goal-based systems. While these all represent little more than plans right now, they are inspiring hundreds of schools to change in ways that generally appear to be moving away from standardized instruction, rigid age-based grouping, tracking, and other practices based on the bell curve.

In Oregon alone, scores of schools have begun mixed-age grouping, as Boeckman Creek is doing. Similarly, middle schools are beginning to divide students into teams, integrate their subjects, and sometimes keep them with the same teachers year after year. Many high schools in the state, such as Crater High in Central Point and Ashland High and Lake Oswego High School south of Portland, have moved from eight to four periods a day so teachers can integrate subjects and students can study them in more depth. Cottage Grove High School near Eugene issued the state's and nation's first certificate of initial mastery to 107 sophomores in the spring of 1994. Roosevelt High School in North Portland overhauled its curriculum to tie courses to the practical requirements of the six broad career areas required for the certificate of advanced mastery. The school has established partnerships with more than fifty area businesses willing to accommodate students for worksite visits and internships. After its first year, the venture cut the freshman dropout rate in half. Marshall High School in southeastern Portland embarked on a three-year journey to make a clean break with uses of the bell curve.

The Marshall Plan

At Marshall High School, Principal Colin Karr-Morse slipped a magnetic card capable of storing 4 megabytes of digitized information into a computer. Up on the computer monitor appeared a portrait of Mona Lisa and the student name Lisa Monahan. Karr-Morse punched a few keys and Lisa's academic profile was summed up with a color bar chart across the screen. Each bar represented Lisa's progress toward one of the performance goals required by Oregon's certificates of initial and advanced mastery. The graph showed that Lisa already had met communication goals for both certificates, had mastered standards for the social studies goal for the initial certificate, and still fell short of both certificate goals in math and science.

The optical memory card produced by LaserCard Systems Corporation in Mountain View, California, also stored records of the schools Lisa had attended, any discipline problems she'd had, her student records, and a profile of her academic and skill levels. The card was capable of storing up to 1,200 pages of information. It might show that Lisa understood probability, statistics, and linear equations, but was still weak in geometry. It might show that she could type at 42 words per minute, use a spreadsheet on an IBM computer, and recite the Gettysburg Address from memory. In short, the card could store a detailed summary of what Lisa knew and could do and what she still needed to learn. Based on the latter, the computer could design Lisa's learning schedule or individualized learning path.

Karr-Morse issued these profile cards to a trial group of 180 students in the spring of 1994 to demonstrate how they could be used to individualize education. He gave them to the whole freshman class in the fall. In recent years, Karr-Morse had, largely through grants, filled his 1,450-student school with about 350 computers that have a complex variety of capabilities. He had computers linked to video-image compressors, compact disks, laser disks, CD-ROM encyclopedias, and information databases. But so far this high-tech network had had little effect on his otherwise traditional high school.

"I don't think technology is going to solve the problems of education," said Karr-Morse, "but it is an absolutely essential part of the solution."

He believes the profile card and other technology will allow him to dramatically restructure his school into one that sets high standards for all students and has the flexibility to let each student meet those standards at his or her own pace in his or her own way. To help individualize instruction, Karr-Morse has a plan to eliminate grade levels, grading, and compulsory attendance. In other words, he plans to blast the Bell-Curve Syndrome out of his high school.

As in most traditional American high schools, the bell curve takes a heavy toll at Marshall, which lies in southeast Portland, a working class area not far from Creston Elementary School where Fran Lee teaches. About 25 percent of Marshall's students drop out. Another 25 percent stagger through with Ds and Fs and graduate unprepared for work or college. Even the half who fall on the sunny side of the bell curve are getting only a mediocre education, Karr-Morse says.

"The school doesn't work too badly for middle-class and upper-class people; it doesn't work very well in lower socioeconomic communities," he said. "We have a class system and our schools perpetuate the class system.

"Because schools are so deeply embedded in a historic period that no longer relates to our culture, we tend to become sort of a dysfunctional school. It is because we are stuck in patterns that don't work worth a damn.

"We try to deal with students as groups rather than individuals. We historically have not had the capability to individualize instruction because we just don't have the time and resources to do that."

Teaching students in groups is becoming increasingly difficult because students today are so diverse, Karr-Morse said. Marshall enrolls students with more than a dozen other languages as their first language. Some students have multiple handicaps; others have exceptional academic gifts. Students come into class with widely varying motivations, knowledge, skills, and expectations. Karr-Morse explained:

"The teacher says 'I can't deal with that. My job is not to deal with it. I'm going to teach algebra. I'm going to teach history.' So we become subject teachers instead of people teachers.

"What we know happens is generally teachers try to sort of teach to the middle. They can't teach to the high end, because then the rest of the kids will drop out. They can't teach to the low end for the same reason. So they say 'What can I do that sort of teaches to the middle?' It unquestionably slows down the bright ones, and it leaves the slower ones behind, and it catches some of the ones in the middle. School can become incredibly boring for some."

Karr-Morse, however, believes technology will allow teachers to individualize instruction and convert schools into models that reject factory practices for standards of the modern workplace.

"In a community that is very diverse, what we ought to be trying to move toward is what I call a designer curriculum," he said. "Instead of making the kid fit this archaic assembly-line school structure, let's see if we can't, by using technology and some other things, make the system fit the student."

Karr-Morse and his school committee of teachers and parents plan to convert Marshall into an individualized school with high standards for all students by 1997. Karr-Morse hopes to establish performance exams and standards and eliminate grades and grade levels by the 1995–96 school year. The staff voted seventy-two to five in support of the plan, though it is so ambitious that many teachers are skeptical about it ever becoming a reality. Many, however, hope it will.

"The staff is ready for change," said John Coady, a computer teacher. "They realize what we are doing is flat out not succeeding."

In the 1993–94 year, Marshall put eleven teams of teachers to work designing performance exams and standards to judge students for certificates-of-mastery learning goals. They also will define precisely how students will be expected to show they know and can do what the standards require.

"If we wait for the state, we will be here for one hundred years," Karr-Morse said. "So we are going to push the state."

To meet the standard showing they understand math and science, for example, students will be told precisely what principles and vocabulary they will be expected to understand, the kind of problems they will be expected to solve, the projects they must produce, and what they must include in their portfolios. They also will know the scoring scales that will be used to judge their work and the proficiency level, or standard, on those scales they must meet to satisfy the learning goal. All of this information will be at every student's fingertips in the school's computer system. Like Boy Scouts seeking a higher rank or merit badge, Marshall students will know precisely what they need to do in every subject and career path to get their initial and advanced certificates.

Teaching will be separated from assessment. Students who want to show they've mastered a learning objective will go to an assessment center, just as they now go to the Division of Motor Vehicles after completing their driving education courses to be tested for a license. Science teacher Jill Semlick saw the benefit of this split when she taught driver's education and helped students prepare for their license exams. Rather than an adversary, she said, "I was their ally."

The school will be reorganized to allow students to meet standards following paths that fit their learning needs, styles, and paces. For starters, Karr-Morse and his team hope to get a waiver from the state that will make attendance noncompulsory. Students will come only if they want to. If they come, however, they will be guaranteed a state scholarship of about $20,000, enough to pay for the up to four years of education they may need to get their certificates. They must in turn agree to attend regularly and make an earnest effort to learn and obey school rules. Students who are disruptive will be rejected, in effect fired. They will be allowed to return when they are ready. If students work hard and earn their certificates early, they can use whatever remains of their portion of state money to help pay for their next stage of education, whether it is college or a technical school. A student who zooms through the program in two years instead of four, for example, could apply $10,000 in state money toward college.

Course credits will be dropped. Students will study whatever they need to learn to earn their certificates. An entering freshman, for example, might already have the knowledge and skills to go right into the assessment center and meet the communication standards for both English and Spanish. That student then would not be required to take more English in high school. Instead he or she could concentrate on other subjects.

The school's use of time also will be more flexible to accommodate students with jobs and other practical demands. It will be open twelve hours a day year-round, not by adding more teachers, but by staggering their shifts and yearly calendars to match the demands of students. The teenagers also will have the option to take time out, say leave for a year to work, and come back to complete work on their certificates. They can attend the school through age twenty.

Courses will be organized in nine-week blocks and created to meet student demands. At the end of each quarter, a central computer will read every student's academic profile and create courses for the next quarter according to what they all still need to learn.

The school will eliminate traditional classrooms and replace them with large-group lecture halls and small seminar rooms designed to fit student learning profiles. Groups of twenty-five to thirty students are too big to be personal or allow meaningful discussions, said Karr-Morse, and too small to make efficient use of one-way presentations, whether films, lectures, or presentations.

"It is the very worst of all models for teaching," he said. "If you had to invent the very worst way to teach, you would take thirty-to-one."

When teachers need to lecture, which sometimes make sense, they might as well do so to a class of 400 instead of 25. So that's what they will do at Marshall. By dealing with large groups in lectures, the school can regroup students into seminars of about nine students for more meaningful and in-depth discussion. For example, Marshall has five teachers who collectively teach seventeen courses in physical science. When they give their annual presentation on volcanos, they do so seventeen times. And they'll do so next year and the year after, each time wasting sixteen human hours, Karr-Morse said. Why not put all of those students in one class of about 450 and have the most dynamic of the five teachers give a single presentation? Better yet, why not embellish the teacher's presentation with a riveting computer-based multimedia presentation? Once built and stored on a computer disk, that presentation could be used repeatedly and easily updated as needed year after year. Marshall now has the equipment to design multimedia presentations and is beginning to develop some prototypes.

The savings in efficiency through large-group presentations will allow the school to reduce class sizes to about nine students per teacher. By having one teacher take 450 students for an hour, it frees up sixteen other teachers to meet with smaller groups of students in seminars, laboratories, and independent and small-group projects. Universities have used this strategy at some levels for decades. Many, for example, offer introductory zoology in a large lecture hall and put students in smaller groups for laboratory studies. So instead of having an egg-carton school of classrooms, Karr-Morse wants to reshape Marshall into a school with four large-group lecture and multimedia presentation halls and scores of small seminar rooms, science and computer laboratories, and a well-equipped library.

The large lecture presentations will bring together students at various levels of their educational journeys for broad common lessons that can benefit them all. A biology teacher, for example, might give a lecture on cell structure that all students will need to understand. But those same students will break up into seminars, specialized classes geared to the specific needs of small groups. A more advanced group, for example, might gather for a seminar on DNA and genetics whereas another studies amebae, euglena, paramecia, and other protozoans. The computer will identify and group students with similar needs in seminars. So a fifteen-year-old and nineteen-year-old might end up in the same English seminar because both need to work on grammar. Seminars will be created every nine weeks according to student needs. They will offer students a place to get in-depth, personal attention.

"That should be our standard class size so there is a lot of interactive time," Karr-Morse said. "There is time to ask questions. There is time for a teacher to ask his nine kids what's going on at home."

The Marshall staff also wants to separate academics from social and cultural activities. After spending part of their day in rigorous academic work, students will be able to go to another side of the school to indulge in sports, art, music, photography, and other activities that interest them. Students will be expected to meet performance standards in the cultural activities they choose.

Karr-Morse also envisions new roles for teachers. Instead of organizing in subject departments, such as English or math, they will organize into six broad career paths that students will be able to choose from as they work for their certificates of advanced mastery. So a team of teachers with expertise in art, architecture, writing, film and cinema studies, fine arts, graphic design, journalism, foreign languages, and advertising will form the arts and communications department.

Teachers will not all do the same thing. They will have different roles based on their strengths. The most interesting and dynamic lecturers will run the large classrooms; others will specialize in the laboratory work, or curriculum design, and most will spend at least part of their time in seminars. Teachers will put in a forty-hour work week, but they will spend only half of that, about four hours a day, with students. They will divide the rest of their time studying to keep up in their fields, meeting with other teachers and parents, and working in the assessment center.

Karr-Morse's plan is a powerful one because it combines the state's new high standards with a reorganization that abandons all uses of the bell curve. He doesn't expect it to cost more, except initially in planning and training costs, because he will be using the same people and resources in new ways. His plan would surely wipe out the Bell-Curve Syndrome at Marshall High School. It is hard to imagine how anyone could settle for the status quo after looking at the possibilities that Karr-Morse envisions.

Yet the principal faces stiff obstacles. Some teachers are skeptical of his plan. A year after he had worked out most of these details, he was still waiting for the school board and central office administrators to take a look at it. Karr-Morse figures he and his school committee will be forced to carry out this plan on their own or it will never happen. It is a small flame that cannot penetrate the darkness of a system so deeply tied to the bell curve. Karr-Morse is fighting deep-seated inertia. Why else would school officials do anything but give him all the resources and support he needed to carry out such a promising plan? Karr-Morse has no doubts about how well his restructured school will work.

"It would work great," he said. "The kids would love it, and I think the parents would love it, and I think the teachers would love it. We need drastic change. The system is out of touch with the culture."

Bottom Up Meets Top Down

A growing number of education pioneers like Karr-Morse are discovering the promise of a flexible, individualized structure geared to high standards. While these patterns of change emerge from the grass roots, they also are beginning to bud at the top, as described in Chapter 8. The bottom-up efforts of individual schools are mirrored in the top-down strategies across the country. National and state leaders are trying to create performance standards for teachers and students. These shift the focus of schools from a standardized educational journey to a standardized destination.

After a decade of foundering in search for passages to improvement, American education is finding its way. State and national leaders are building a framework much like Betty Wallace built in Vance County. And the nation's schools are beginning to respond in individual and diverse ways within that framework just as they did in Vance County. So as government refines standards, relaxes regulations, and fosters more diversity in schools, a growing number of Marshall plans and school pioneers such as Boeckman Creek and Silver Ridge are blooming across the country like desert flowers after a rain. If these patterns of change can be brought into harmony, they will become a powerful force that will reshape American schools. But they are still young and fragile. The old system and all of the institutions that grew up around it—testing and textbook companies, schools of education, school boards, and teacher unions—will resist breaks from the bell curve. Change will prevail only if Americans demand it. The stormy transition from the old to the new is under way.

The nation's monolithic education system is beginning to crack and about to molt its bell-shaped shell. What waits to emerge is the most powerful education system on Earth.

EPILOGUE

▼

Betty Wallace resigned as superintendent of Vance County School System on August 31, 1993. Her relationship with the school board had become so strained and distracting that there was no hope of reconciliation. She could not battle the board and lead the district.

The board continued to protect Ronald Gregory, even after U.S. Equal Employment Opportunity Commission (EEOC) investigators concluded that the assistant superintendent had sexually harassed six women. The EEOC also determined that the board had mishandled the case and gave victims the option to press their grievances in federal court. One of them, Laura Joyner, the district's talented public information specialist, quit and took a job with a local hospital. She later sued both the board and Gregory.

By mid-August the board received word that the EEOC would be ruling in favor of Wallace in her case. She had filed a complaint documenting how the board retaliated after she launched an investigation of the sexual harassment charges against Gregory. The EEOC's finding gave her the option of taking the board to court and holding its members personally liable for damages.

The board offered Wallace $100,000 in "personal tort damages," which was in effect an out-of-court settlement to prevent her from pressing her suit. It also agreed to give her $150,000 in compensation for the nearly two years left on her contract. Wallace had hoped to stay longer in Vance County, but the rock-throwers had pushed her to the edge of a cliff. She could no longer stay out in front of them. So she settled.

"I am heartsick that I cannot be a part of bringing to fruition the potential that lies within this county," she told the *Henderson Daily Dispatch*, in her final appearance on its front page.[1]

The people of Vance County were hardly surprised that Betty Wallace was leaving. They had seen her battles with the board, and they had seen so many other superintendents go before her. Some people expressed anger with the board. One even may have tried to intimidate Margaret Ellis, who had taken over as board chairwoman, though it is impossible to know for sure. A week after Wallace resigned, the *Henderson Daily Dispatch* reported that someone set fire to a 1962 Plymouth Reliant that belonged to Ellis and was parked on her property.

It is hard to imagine why the board did not draw more fury after so clearly revealing its priorities. Board members faced clear options. They could support Wallace, who had helped the district's 7,000 children begin improving their academic achievement after a decade of decline, or they could support Gregory, who, according to federal investigators, sexually harassed six school employees. The board members chose Gregory. In fact, five days after Wallace resigned, they put him in charge of district contracts and finances and made him board liaison. His lack of a superintendent's certificate may be the only reason they didn't put him in charge of the district.

A few weeks later the board hired A. Craig Phillips to replace Wallace as superintendent. Phillips had been North Carolina superintendent of public instruction for twenty years before he retired under a cloud in 1988. Several unfavorable articles about him appeared in *The News & Observer* during his final years in office. One report showed that he collected state reimbursement money for his stay in hotel rooms that were given to him for free. Another described how he spent a good part of his final year as superintendent traveling to Australia, England, Hawaii, and cities across the United States. A third showed he was collecting honoraria from textbook companies for speaking to them about issues in education.[2]

After Wallace left Vance County, conventions of the bell curve began to reappear in its schools like weeds. Grades were restored and fewer students were allowed to advance early to middle school. Grade levels began to reestablish their boundaries in some schools. Phillips began to centralize the district much as he had centralized the state education system during his tenure as state superintendent. Tim Simmons wrote a long account of Wallace's work in Vance County for *The News & Observer*. Phillips told him morale was good.[3] Simmons reported it was otherwise:

> But the teachers and principals clearly aren't comfortable talking about the latest round of changes in the schools.
>
> Those who supported Wallace won't talk publicly. Some won't even come to the phone. Teachers and staff were obviously happy to see Wallace when she recently returned to Pinkston Street Elementary for a short visit, but none would get close to a photographer's camera.
>
> "I checked around before I called you back, and the other principals say it's probably best just not to say anything," one principal said when asked about Wallace.[4]

Vance County's fatalism had prevailed. People took defeat in stride, as if it was all they could expect. Even the *Henderson Daily Dispatch* conveyed resignation by responding to Wallace's departure with a bloodless editorial. The newspaper acknowledged that Wallace "brought the system to the brink of state accreditation" but declined to criticize the board for its treatment of her. There was no outrage. The newspaper even praised the board for hiring Phillips.[5]

Wallace returned to the mountains for a spell and spent some time with her father before he died in December 1993. She then began dividing her time between her mountain farm and consulting work in Raleigh and at the Center for Creative Leadership in Greensboro, North Carolina. And she went back to school, enrolling at Western Carolina University to take classes on racism and on the history of the Cherokee. She also began writing a novel about the Scotch-Irish immigrants who settled on Cherokee lands in the Southern Appalachians during the eighteenth century. Wallace continued to receive invitations to speak about education and change before various groups in North Carolina and elsewhere. *The Charlotte Observer* asked her to write about education for its New Year's Day edition.

In the meantime, Betty Wallace could see at least some measure of her work surviving in Vance County. Ginger Miller and Oddis Smith, the impassioned principals of Zeb Vance and Pinkston Street elementary schools, kept on with their school improvement plans.

"We're continuing with what we've been doing," said Miller in the spring of 1994. "We've been working to add more active learning and more portfolio assessment."

That spring Zeb Vance Elementary posted the highest test scores in the county, higher even than state averages. More than two-thirds of its students who were working at what the state deemed fifth-grade level had scored above the state average in math and reading. But the school no longer cared too much about averages or grade levels.

"My staff does not want to go back to the old way of doing things," Miller said. "We continue to adjust and change and refine what we are doing. No one wants to go back to self-contained, age-based classrooms."

Wallace hoped that the fresh, young voices of new leaders would begin to challenge the old from all corners of Vance County, as some were starting to do before she left. She hoped that leaders like Abdul Rasheed, the economic developer; Richard Moore, a newly elected state representative; W. A. West, tobacco farmer and fox hunter; Mike Faulkner, owner of the Kittrell store; and dozens more like them would become more emboldened. Betty Wallace had led Vance County deeper into change than most school districts in the nation have ventured. Now these new leaders had to pick up where she was forced to leave off. It would be up to them to stop adults stuck in tradition from standing in the way of educators concerned about children.

All Americans stand at a similar threshold. They too must decide whether to embrace change—flexibility and high standards for schools and all the work that involves—or to resign themselves to the status quo. There are several reasons to believe they will choose change. For one, American society cannot tolerate for much longer an annual crop of a million or so ill-prepared teenagers leaving its schools. That growing sea of restless young adults eventually will deluge the various social institutions trying to accommodate their needs for more education, affordable housing, financial aid, and medical help. These frustrated young people also are contributing to a crime wave that is clogging courtrooms and jails.

Second, a network of professional educators and researchers is rapidly developing national standards in all subjects for students and for teachers seeking national certification. Schools that have the courage to adopt these standards will quickly take the lead in school reform, especially if they also adopt flexible systems that reject bell-curve habits. Students in these schools will advance so far beyond those in conventional schools that the difference will be striking. Other educators might try to ignore them, but parents won't.

Even without such models, a growing number of American parents favor changing schools to fit the change that they see reshaping their economy, neighborhoods, and lifestyles. In a 1993 statewide survey by the Oregon Business Council, 65 percent of Oregon parents said they believe major change is needed in their neighborhood schools.

Other forces, however, are working against change. Local political leaders often resist reform because disruptions in the status quo typically threaten their positions and power. Teacher unions are opposing student performance standards for fear that the standards, like test scores, could be used to judge teachers. The Oregon Education Association tried to gut the state's school improvement act by introducing legislation in 1993 that would scrap learning goals and certificates of mastery. The attempt failed. The association argued that schools could not be expected to teach students to meet these standards without more money.

Educators' perpetual worries about money could blind them to the need for meaningful change. Wise ones will see diminishing resources as a compelling reason to change. The days of hefty annual boosts in school spending have ended, at least for a while. Governments cannot afford to spend more on schools, and in many cases they are cutting back. Oregon public schools opened in 1993–94 with $124 million less in the budget than they had the year before. During the 1980s most schools got a chance to show what money could do and failed to make significant improvements. They cannot expect to get much more money until they improve, and they won't improve unless they change.

No one can know how Americans will respond if education leaders cling to the status quo and schools fail to get better. Americans could become more supportive of proposals to use tax credits or government money for private or charter schools. New technology and the information highway may make knowledge so accessible that public schools will become less important. Nevertheless, it seems less and less likely that Americans will settle for schools as they are. The consequences of mediocre education are becoming too severe for their children.

If, on the other hand, American schools can part with the bell curve and set their sights on high standards for all students, they could produce the nation's first highly educated generation by early in the next century. Only one is needed. An educated people will convey their love of knowledge and learning to their children, which will perpetuate a learning culture. Education pioneers like Betty Wallace have marked the way. We would be wise to follow.

GLOSSARY

▼

Terms Commonly Used for Guided Learning in Vance County and Other School Reform Efforts

BELL CURVE: A statistical model representing the pattern of naturally occurring events. Carl Friedrich Gauss of Germany discovered the model in the nineteenth century. Gauss showed that weight of eighteen-year-old men, the height of mature corn, and other naturally occurring qualities will tend toward an arithmetic average. This average will gain statistical accuracy as the number of samples increase for a given quality, say the height of corn. Gauss charted statistics such as these on a graph with a vertical axis representing the number of occurrences and a horizontal axis representing the height of corn or some other dimension of a naturally occurring event. Plotting these numbers on a graph consistently produces a bell-shaped curve, with the peak of the curve representing the average. The line slopes away on each side as it moves away from average. While the curve is a useful description of chance events, it does not accurately describe qualities of human accomplishment, say the age at which men marry, because these are affected by intention or will. Yet schools assume student achievement should describe a bell curve. So they use grades, tracking, test scores, and other practices to sort students into bell-curve patterns, unfairly demanding more academically of students above average than of those below. In short, they use the bell curve to prescribe rather than describe student achievement.

BELL-CURVE SYNDROME: The complex of symptoms resulting from educational practices based on bell-curve assumptions about student achievement. These practices include age-based grouping, comparative grading, tracking, and the use of instruction and textbooks geared to the average. Such practices give rise to high dropout rates, widespread academic failure, dull textbooks, mediocre schools, and other symptoms of the syndrome.

COACHING: A method of teaching that puts more responsibility on the student to take charge of his or her learning. Rather than lecturing to a group of passive students, the teacher acts as a supervisor, helping each student find information and hone skills needed to meet learning objectives. The student is active rather than passive. The teacher as coach offers guidance and feedback and corrects performance as needed until the student achieves mastery.

CONTINUOUS PROGRESS: A practice allowing each student to advance through the curriculum at his or her own pace. Students are not promoted on the basis of age or grade level, but according to their demonstrated knowledge and application of skills and concepts.

COOPERATIVE LEARNING: An instructional method that groups two to six students for purposes of working on a common project, problem, or learning objective. Students are expected to learn how to work with others and contribute to the success of the group mission while at the same time meeting standards for individual performance.

DEMONSTRATIONS: Presentations or projects—such as a panel discussion, mock trial, painting, or essay—in which students show what they know and can do.

GUIDED LEARNING: The name of the school reform plan Betty Wallace used in Vance County. The plan replaced grades and grade levels with academic standards or outcomes at four levels: primary, intermediate, middle school, and high school. Students were allowed to move from one level to the next as soon as they met the standards. Guided Learning allowed students to march at their own pace up individualized learning paths to common, high levels of academic achievement.

INDEPENDENT STUDY: Learning activities selected and directed by the student.

MASTERY LEARNING: An instructional method in which the teacher identifies learning objectives for a unit of study, teaches the objectives, test students, and provides additional instruction for students who have not attained mastery (usually defined as meeting at least 80 percent of the achievement goals). Students who learn the objectives early spend time on enrichment studies while they wait for the others to reach mastery. Mastery learning is a group-oriented instructional method that conflicts with the individualized, continuous progress approach adopted in Vance County.

MENTORING: A practice in which an adult, often a teacher, takes a student under his or her wing and becomes that student's learning advocate. The mentor encourages, supports, and guides the student to ensure he or she meets academic achievement goals at a reasonable pace.

PAIDEIA: A program developed by philosopher Mortimer J. Adler, founder and director of the Institute for Philosophical Research in Chicago, geared to teaching students to think. The program reorganizes the curriculum around classic studies. The program emphasizes three modes of learning: (1) the acquisition of organized knowledge through traditional subjects; (2) the development of thinking; and (3) the enhancement of understanding of basic ideas and values. Adler also sees three modes of teaching: coaching, the Socratic method, and the didactic, or traditional, lecture and textbook approach.

PEER TUTORING: The use of students as teachers of other students. Teachers believe that students reinforce and deepen their understanding of knowledge by teaching it to others.

INDIVIDUALIZED INSTRUCTION: A teaching approach that focuses on the individual learning needs of each student rather than on general needs of a group or class. Teachers can use trade books, computers, projects, and other tools to let students follow individual learning paths even while they are involved in a group activity.

INTEGRATED INSTRUCTION: The practice of blending traditional subjects, such as English, science, and history, in lessons that show how these various fields are related. Many teachers believe this approach fosters deeper understanding and better retention of knowledge.

LEARNING CENTERS: Stations within a classroom where students can learn independently. By setting up a variety of centers in the classroom—say one for reading, another for writing, a third for art, and a fourth for math—the teacher can allow many students to work at a variety of tasks at the same time. This helps foster individualized instruction.

LECTURE METHOD: Traditional, group-oriented, teacher-centered instruction in which the teacher lectures and relies heavily on textbooks, work sheets, and tests.

OUTCOMES-BASED EDUCATION: A school structure that puts emphasis on academic achievement goals or outcomes—on what students ultimately learn—rather than on the number of teachers, textbooks, dollars, and other investments that go into the school. Students must meet the learning objectives to advance in or graduate from an outcomes-based system. For example, licensing programs for automobile drivers, pilots, lawyers, and doctors are based on outcomes. In each of these cases, people are judged and licensed on the basis of what they know and can do rather than on the amount of time they invested in school.

SITE-BASED MANAGEMENT: A decentralized administrative approach that extends decision-making power from the school district's central office to the school site. Typically, site-based committees of parents and teachers oversee the instructional programs in this management approach. Educators have increasingly moved to site-based management in recent years with hopes it will energize schools and foster innovations that will improve education.

SOCRATIC METHOD: An instructional method used by Socrates, a philosopher and teacher in ancient Greece. The Socratic teacher uses leading questions and dialogue to help students develop their own insights into the material. This teaching practice is used heavily in the Paideia program.

WHOLE GROUP INSTRUCTION: Teaching geared toward a group or class. The teacher determines what students do. All students work on the same task.

WHOLE LANGUAGE: A language arts instructional approach that integrates reading and writing and relies on trade books and literature rather than textbooks. Students learn vocabulary and conventions of grammar in the context of their reading and writing rather than in isolation.

CHRONOLOGY

▼

Spring 1991—North Carolina Department of Public Instruction names Vance County School System among the lowest performing in the state, targeting it for possible takeover by the state Board of Education.

June 14, 1991—Vance County school board hires Betty Wallace as superintendent to improve academic performance and avoid humiliation of state takeover.

July 16, 1991—Wallace announces massive change in schools, including elimination of age-based grade levels and letter grading. She immediately launches a three-month campaign of daily community and parent meetings to describe the changes.

Sept. 3, 1991—AdVance Strategic Planning Commission, a county economic development group, endorses the reform plan.

Sept. 5, 1991—Vance County school board adopts the reform plan, which Wallace calls Guided Learning. Member Deborah Brown is sole dissenter.

Jan. 1, 1992—*Henderson Daily Dispatch* declares Wallace's reform plan the year's top story for the three counties in which it circulates.

Jan. 29, 1992—Vance County School System test scores drop on 1990–91 state report card, and state names it one of three systems in danger of state takeover.

March 23, 1992—State Superintendent Bob Etheridge visits Vance County Schools and praises district for its cutting-edge reforms.

May 20, 1992—State Board of Education names Vance Schools one of four districts to pioneer outcomes-based education. Vance gets $1.65 million grant.

June 1, 1992—Vance County school board endorses policy to end "social promotions" and to hold back students who do not reach benchmark outcomes at primary, intermediate, and middle school levels.

June 15, 1992—State Representative James P. Green announces public forum to discuss concerns expressed by parents of students who are not allowed to advance to higher levels in the school system.

June 17, 1992—County Commissioners, led by Chairman Bill Fleming, cut school funding, noting Representative Green's constituents are unhappy with outcomes-based education.

June 22, 1992—School employees accuse Assistant Superintendent Ronald Gregory of sexual harassment. Wallace suspends him pending further investigation.

June 23, 1992—Green's self-appointed citizens' committee blasts outcomes-based education and Wallace's leadership.

June 24, 1992—Green attacks Wallace and outcomes-based education in news media while state Department of Public Instruction defends Wallace's plan.

July 1, 1992—Wallace meets with Green's committee and is frustrated by Green's political grandstanding.

July 6, 1992—First state test scores since Wallace's Guided Learning plan was initiated shows a reverse in a decade-long downward trend. Students show gains in six of nine categories.

July 30, 1992—Wallace becomes finalist for superintendent position in Brunswick County, North Carolina.

Aug. 12, 1992—After a month-long investigation and three-week-long hearing, the Vance County school board rejects Wallace's recommendation to fire Gregory. Vote is 4–3 along racial lines. Gregory is reinstated, and Wallace learns she will not get job in Brunswick County.

Aug. 14, 1992—Zeb Vance Elementary School opens in new building under Principal Ginger Miller. Wallace predicts the school will be the flagship school for Guided Learning.

Aug. 25, 1992—Laura Joyner, one of six women who accused Gregory with sexual harassment, files charges with the federal Equal Employment Opportunity Commission against the Vance County school board for its handling of the case.

Aug. 27, 1992—Vance High School's college entrance exam scores plunge forty-one points. Wallace reminds public her reforms have not yet been launched in the high schools.

Aug. 31, 1992—Deborah Brown, chairwoman of the Vance County school board, transfers her daughter to a neighboring county, charging that Vance County's Eaton-Johnson Middle School is immoral and academically unchallenging.

Sept. 14, 1992—Wallace shows Vance County school board her 10-point plan for the coming school year and asks that the board either support it or come up with a new plan it can support. Meantime, angry parents began circulating petition demanding Brown's resignation.

Oct. 14, 1992—Kittrell community invites Wallace for lunch and pledges its support for her reform efforts.

Nov. 2, 1992—Vance County school board endorses Wallace's 10-point plan by a 5–2 vote, with members Deborah Brown and Roosevelt Alston dissenting.

Nov. 15, 1992—State Department of Public Instruction announces Vance County's dropout rate has declined to lowest level in county's history.

Nov. 19, 1992—Rep. James P. Green sends letter to North Carolina Board of Education asking that Wallace be fired and $1.65 million outcomes-based education grant rescinded. State later defends project.

Dec. 17, 1992—Wallace files complaint with federal Equal Employment Opportunities Commission. She charges the Vance County school board retaliated and failed to respond after Chairwoman Deborah Brown threatened to "bring down" Wallace and Personnel Director Gloria Lunsford-Boone for investigating sexual harassment charges against Ronald Gregory.

Dec. 18, 1992—Vance County School System is removed from state takeover list because of dramatic improvements in student performance and drop-out rate.

Jan. 1, 1993—Vance County Schools' outcomes-based education plan ranked top story of the year by *Henderson Daily Dispatch*. Gregory's sexual harassment suit ranks fourth, and school system's removal from takeover list ranks ninth.

Jan. 6, 1993—State Report Card shows first year of Guided Learning produced major gains. Vance County meets 68 percent of state standards compared to only 40 percent the year before.

Jan. 16, 1993—Wallace hires Bernard Allen, former chief lobbyist for the North Carolina Association of Educators, as her assistant superintendent for human resources. Allen will help her ease racial, cultural, and economic conflicts in the district.

Feb. 1, 1993—Vance County school board hires one of the state's most prominent law firms to fight Wallace's EEOC complaint. Board is criticized for hiring firm in secret session, violating state's Open Meetings Law.

Feb. 4, 1993—State Board of Education removes Vance County School System from state takeover list.

March 31, 1993—U.S. Equal Employment Opportunity Commission determines school board ignored evidence showing Ronald Gregory sexually harassed Laura Joyner and other women. The commission also says the board mishandled the case by voting to reinstate Gregory. It rules the board violated Title VII of the Civil Rights Act of 1964 as amended.

April 13, 1993—Police report that Henderson's crime rate is double that of the state.

May 1, 1993—*Annual Children's Index* issued by North Carolina Child Advocacy Institute names Vance County among the ten worst counties in the state for children. Vance ranked ninety-fourth out of one hundred counties by such criteria as infant mortality, low birth weight, births to single teens, graduation rates, juvenile arrests, child abuse and neglect, welfare payments, and foster care.

May 6, 1993—Wallace presents her plan to State Board of Education and draws praise and a pledge of total support.

June 29, 1993—Laura Joyner leaves Vance County Schools to work with local hospital.

June 30, 1993—Vance County school board member E. J. Cash gets permission from board to transfer his child to a public school district in another county.

July 26, 1993—Vance students post scores near state average on state tests in reading and mathematics for first time in more than a decade.

Aug. 3, 1993—Vance County school board rejects invitation to describe Guided Learning reform plan at the 1994 National School Boards Association convention.

Aug. 16, 1993—Wallace gives convocation speech to teachers and administrators and encourages them to press forward. She decides against revealing that she is negotiating a settlement with the school board over her complaint with the EEOC, which found in her favor.

Aug. 23, 1993—Vance County school system has smoothest and most enthusiastic opening in years as teachers grow comfortable with change and reform. The district seems to be finding its stride.

Aug. 31, 1993—Wallace resigns. Board pays her $250,000—$150,000 in taxable unearned compensation and $100,000 for tax-free personal tort damages. Wallace drops EEOC complaint and promises not to sue the board over other actions.

Sept. 2, 1993—Vance County school board names Ronald Gregory liaison to the board and puts him in charge of district finance.

Sept. 13, 1993—The Bell-Curve Syndrome begins to reestablish itself in the district. School board votes to restore letter grades on report cards.

Sept. 14, 1993—Vance County school board hires A. Craig Phillips, former state superintendent of public instruction for twenty years. Phillips begins dismantling Wallace's reform structure and re-establishes a traditional, centralized organization.

Oct. 1, 1993—Wallace leaves Vance County and does consulting in educational reform and technology. She also works on adjunct faculty at the Center for Creative Leadership in Greensboro, North Carolina.

Oct. 7, 1993—Laura Joyner files federal lawsuit against Vance County school board and against four board members who voted to reinstate Ronald Gregory.

Dec. 3, 1993—Ronald Gregory files countersuit against Joyner and adds Wallace as third-party defendant.

March 3, 1994—Gregory drops lawsuit against Wallace.

Aug. 15, 1994—Wallace enrolls at Western Carolina University to study Cherokee history and racism. She divides her time between consulting in Raleigh and living on her mountain farm in Franklin, where she begins writing a novel about Scotch-Irish settlers on Cherokee lands in Western North Carolina during the eighteenth century.

Aug. 24, 1994—Vance County high school senior SAT scores jump 35 points. Craig Phillips credits recent reform efforts for the increase.

NOTES

Chapter 1

1. The following account is based on observations made in Fran Lee's classroom at Creston Elementary School in Portland, Oregon, on December 1 and December 4, 1992.
2. David T. Conley, *Roadmap to Restructuring: Policies, Practices and the Emerging Visions of Schooling* (Eugene, OR: University of Oregon, ERIC Clearinghouse on Educational Management, 1993), p. 44.
3. Tord Hall, *Carl Friedrich Gauss* (Cambridge, MA: The MIT Press, 1970), p. 82.
4. Elaine Mensch and Harry Mensch, *The IQ Mythology: Class, Race, Gender and Inequality* (Carbondale: Southern Illinois University Press, 1991), pp. 75–76.
5. The Commission on the Skills of the American Workplace, *America's Choice: High Skills or Low Wages!* (Rochester, NY: National Center on Education and the Economy, 1990), p. 20.

Chapter 2

1. U.S. Department of Education, *Digest of Education Statistics 1992* (Washington, D.C.: National Center for Education Statistics, 1992), pp. 154–155.
2. John Jacob Cannell, a West Virginia physician, documents widespread cheating on standardized tests in his book, *How Public Educators Cheat on Standardized Achievement Tests* (Albuquerque, NM: Friends for Education, 1989). One investigation, for example, found cheating in nineteen Chicago schools (pp. 4, 5, 14, 15).
3. William Ruberry, "Study Blasts Standardized Tests," *Richmond Times-Dispatch,* Oct. 16, 1992, p. B7.

4. Mary Ann Roser, "Teaching of Science Low on School's Priority List, U.S. Report Says," *The Oregonian,* Mar. 27, 1992, p. A17.

5. Chester E. Finn Jr. and Monty Neill, "To Test or Not to Test, That Is the Question," *The Washington Post,* Apr. 5, 1992, PER 1.

6. Kim I. Mills, Associated Press, "Math Students Do Sum Better," *The Oregonian,* Apr. 9, 1993, p. A10.

7. U.S. Department of Education, *Digest of Education Statistics 1992,* pp. 114, 118.

8. Ibid., pp. 112–124.

9. U.S. Department of Education, *Digest of Education Statistics 1992,* pp. 107, 114, and 122, and U.S. Department of Education *Digest of Education Statistics 1991* (Washington, D.C.: National Center for Educational Statistics, 1991) pp. 114 and 120.

10. Diego Ribadeneira, "Even the top students lag, colleges say" *The Boston Globe,* Dec. 20, 1992, Metro/Region section, p. 1.

11. Thomas Toch, "The Crisis in Education Is Not Confined to Inner City Schools" *The Baltimore Sun,* Jan. 19, 1992, p. 5J.

12. Diego Ribadeneira, "Even the top students lag, colleges say," *The Boston Globe,* p. 1.

13. Ray Marshall and Marc Tucker, *Thinking for a Living* (New York: Basic Books, 1992), p. 67.

14. Peter Callaghan, wire dispatch from Tacoma, Washington, by McClatchy News Service, Aug. 5, 1992.

15. Marshall and Tucker, *Thinking for a Living,* p. 66.

16. U.S. Department of Education, *Digest of Educational Statistics 1992,* p. 402, *Digest of Educational Statistics 1991,* pp. 390, 399.

17. Howard Gardner, "Educating for Understanding," *American School Board Journal* (July 1993): 22.

18. Richard C. Anderson, Elfrieda H. Hiebert, Judith A. Scott, and Ian A. G. Wilkinson, *Becoming a Nation of Readers: The Report of the Commission on Reading* (Washington, D.C.: The National Institute of Education, 1984), p. 80.

19. Harriet Tyson-Bernstein, *A Conspiracy of Good Intentions: America's Textbook Fiasco* (Washington, D.C.: The Council for Basic Education, 1988), p. 26.

20. Harold W. Stevenson and James W. Stigler, *The Learning GAP: Why Our Schools Are Failing and What We Can Learn From Japanese and Chinese Education* (New York: Summit Books,

1992), (pp. 163–164). Stevenson and Stigler note, "When we informed the Chinese teachers that American elementary school teachers are responsible for their classes all day long, with only an hour or less outside the classroom each day, they looked incredulous. How could any teacher be expected to do a good job when there is not time outside of class to prepare and correct lessons, work with individual children, consult with other teachers, and attend to all the matters that arise in a typical day at school?"

21. Tyson-Bernstein, *A Conspiracy of Good Intentions,* pp. 20, 21.

22. George A. Plimpton, ed. *The Writer's Chapbook: A Compendium of Fact, Opinion, Wit and Advice from the 20th Century's Preeminent Writers* (New York: Viking, 1989) pp. 242–243.

23. James D. Charlet, William S. Powell, and Dixie Lee Spiegel, *North Carolina: Our People, Places and Past* (Durham, NC: Carolina Academic Press, 1987), pp. 204–205.

24. Coauthor Bill Graves spent many days in this teacher's classroom during the 1991–92 school year as part of a newspaper project on high school.

25. Ann Bradley, "Not Making the Grade," *Education Week,* Sept. 15, 1993, p. 1.

26. Richard Stiggins made these comments during an interview in Portland, Oregon, on Dec. 22, 1992. Stiggins was former director of the Center for Classroom Assessment at the Northwest Regional Educational Laboratory in Portland. He recently coauthored a book, *In Teacher's Hands: Investigating the Practices of Classroom Assessment* (New York: State University of New York Press, 1992).

27. Thomas Sowell, *Inside American Education: The Decline, the Deception, the Dogmas* (New York: The Free Press, 1993), p. 2.

28. William Cole, "By Rewarding Mediocrity We Discourage Excellence," *Chronicle of Higher Education,* Jan. 6, 1993, p. B1.

29. Executive Summary, *Reinventing Chapter 1: Final Report of the National Assessment of the Chapter 1 Program* (Washington, D.C.: U.S. Department of Education, Office of Policy and Planning, Feb. 1993), pp. 14–16.

30. Joseph Berger, "Guiding Students to Failure" *The New York Times,* Aug. 24, 1992, p. A18.

31. U.S. Department of Education, *Digest of Educational Statistics 1991*, p. 61.

32. John Taylor Gatto, "I May Be a Teacher but I'm Not an Educator," *The Wall Street Journal*, July 25, 1992, Op-Ed Page.

33. U.S. Department of Education, *Digest of Education Statistics 1991*, p. 130.

34. Laura Mansnerus, "Should tracking be derailed?" *The New York Times*, Nov. 1, 1992, p. ED14

35. Jeannie Oakes with Tor Ormseth, Robert Bell, and Patricia Camp, *Multiplying Inequalities: The Effects of Race, Social Class, and Tracking on Opportunities to Learn Mathematics and Science* (Santa Monica, CA: The RAND Corp., July 1990), p. 45.

36. Ibid., pp. 105, 106.

37. Nena Baker, "The Hidden Hand of Nike," *The Oregonian*, Aug. 9, 1992, p. 1.

38. Willard R. Daggett in a speech on Feb. 28, 1990, at Sprague High School in Salem, Ore.

39. Frank Swoboda, "Incomes of Workers Lose Ground in '80s," *The Oregonian*, Sept. 8, 1992, p. A14.

40. Linda Darling-Hammond, "Reframing the School Reform Agenda," *Phi Delta Kappan* (June 1993): 754.

41. U.S. Department of Education, *Digest of Education Statistics 1991*, pp. 105, 290.

42. Ibid., p. 128.

43. Jeannie Oakes with Tor Ormseth, Robert Bell, Patricia Camp, *Multiplying Inequalities: The Effects of Race, Social Class, and Tracking on Opportunities to Learn Mathematics and Science* (Santa Monica, Calif.: The RAND Corp., July 1990), pp. 24, 25.

44. Ibid., p. 104.

45. Gilbert T. Sewall, *Necessary Lessons: Decline and Renewal in American Schools* (New York: The Free Press, 1983), pp. 46–57.

46. Bill Graves, "Teachers find class distinction," *The Raleigh Times*, Oct. 3, 1988, p. A1.

47. *Chicago Tribune* reporters did an extensive investigation of Chicago public schools in 1987 and published a series of stories on what they called a case of "institutionalized child neglect." The se-

ries was reprinted in 1988 in a book called *Chicago Schools: "Worst in America"* (Chicago: The Chicago Tribune).

48. Philip Morrison, "The Bell Shaped Pitfall," Paul L. Houts, ed., in *The Myth of Measurability* (New York: Hart Publishing Co., 1977), pp. 88, 89.

49. Howard Gardner, *Frames of Mind: The Theory of Multiple Intelligences* (New York: Basic Books, 1983), p. 276.

50. Ibid., p. 356.

51. Adria Steinberg, ed. "When Bright Kids Get Bad Grades," *The Harvard Education Letter* (November/December 1992), pp. 1–3.

52. The twenty-eight-member Commission on Chapter 1, chaired by David W. Hornbeck, codirector for the National Alliance for Restructuring Education, issued its report after a two-year study. The report was called "Making Schools Work for Children in Poverty."

53. Bill Graves interviewed Poelman and other students, government officials, and educators during a two-week visit to Germany and Holland in November 1992. The trip was sponsored by the German Marshall Fund.

54. Stevenson and Stigler, *The Learning Gap*, p. 95.

55. Stevenson and Stigler carefully document the superior math and reading performance of Japanese children in *The Learning Gap*.

56. Jay Matthews, *Escalante: The Best Teacher in America* (New York: Henry Holt and Company, 1988), pp. 249, 301.

57. Alfred Ntonga, a journalist from Malawi, was struck by this mismatch between American culture and its schools during his visit to Portland in the fall of 1992. Children must feel rebellious when they enjoy freedom of choice and independence outside of school yet are compelled to attend a particular school and a particular set of subjects with few choices at all, he observed.

Alexander Yegorov, a history teacher from Magnitogorsk, Russia, discovered that U.S. schools were much like Russia's, even before the Cold War ended. In the August 1993 issue of *The School Administrator*, Yegorov writes, "I began to see whatever the differences are, the United States and Russia probably have more similarities in education than in any other field."

Chapter 3

1. John Adams, "Liberty and Knowledge," in Diane Ravitch, ed., *The American Reader* (New York: HarperCollins, 1990), p. 12.

2. Samuel Thomas Peace, Sr., *Zeb's Black Baby, Vance County, North Carolina: A Short History* (Henderson, NC: Vance County Historical Society, 1955), pp. 84–90.

3. Joel Spring, *The American School: 1642–1990* (White Plains, NY: Longman, 1991), p. 30.

4. M. C. S. Noble, *A History of the Public Schools of North Carolina* (Chapel Hill: University of North Carolina Press, 1930), p. 56.

5. Jack Larkin, *The Reshaping of Everyday Life: 1790–1840* (New York: Harper & Row, 1988), pp. 34–37.

6. Spring, *The American School,* p. 53.

7. Ibid., p. 56.

8. Horace Mann, "The Case for Public Schools," in Ravitch, ed., *The American Reader,* p. 80.

9. U.S. Department of Education, *Digest of Education Statistics 1992* (Washington, D.C.: National Center for Education Statistics, 1992), p. 49.

10. Frederick Douglass, "Independence Day Speech at Rochester," in Ravitch, ed., *The American Reader,* p. 118.

11. Spring, *The American School,* p. 136.

12. Noble, *A History of the Public Schools of North Carolina,* pp. 400–401.

13. Theodore R. Sizer, *Secondary Schools at the Turn of the Century* (New Haven, CT: Yale University Press, 1964), p. 16.

14. Noble, *A History of the Public Schools of North Carolina,* p. 324.

15. Ray Marshall and Marc Tucker, *Thinking for a Living: Work, Skills, and the Future of the American Economy* (New York: Basic Books, 1992), p. 19.

16. Sizer, *Secondary Schools at the Turn of the Century,* p. xi.

17. Spring, *The American School,* p. 197.

18. Ibid., p. 232.

19. David B. Tyack, *The One Best System, A History of American Urban Education* (Cambridge, MA: Harvard University Press, 1974) p. 48.

20. Spring, *The American School,* p. 169.

21. Tyack, *The One Best System,* pp. 177, 178.

22. Ibid., p. 200.

23. Spring, *The American School,* p. 174.

24. Harold W. Stevenson and James W. Stigler, *The Learning Gap: Why Our Schools Are Failing and What We Can Learn from Japanese and Chinese Education* (New York: Summit Books, 1992), p. 111.

25. Gilbert T. Sewall, *Necessary Lessons: Decline and Renewal in American Schools* (New York: The Free Press, 1983), pp. 20–28.

26. Spring, *The American School,* pp. 237–242.

27. Ibid., p. 242.

28. Marc Tucker, "Measure Up," in Scholastic, Inc., *America's Agenda: Schools for the 21st Century* (Fall 1992): 21.

29. Robert Hampel, *The Last Little Citadel: American High Schools Since 1940* (Boston: Houghton Mifflin, 1986), pp. 46, 51.

30. Gordon L. Swanson, "The Hall of Shame," *Phi Delta Kappan* (June 1993): 797.

31. Hampel, *The Last Little Citadel,* pp. 60–65.

32. Kenneth A. Tye, "Restructuring Our Schools: Beyond the Rhetoric," *Phi Delta Kappan* (Sept. 1992): 10.

Chapter 4

1. *The Boy Scout Handbook* (Irving, TX: Boy Scouts of America, 1990), p. 17.

2. Theodore R. Sizer, *Horace's School: Redesigning the American High School* (Boston: Houghton Mifflin, 1992), p. 174.

3. *Curriculum and Evaluation Standards for School Mathematics* (Reston, VA: National Council of Teachers of Mathematics, 1989), pp. 212–221.

4. Bill Graves, "Vermont Blazes Educational Trail with Portfolios," *The Oregonian,* Nov. 25, 1991, p. A1.

5. Bill Graves, "The World of Waldorf," *The Sunday Oregonian,* Dec. 6, 1992, p. D1.

6. Bill Graves, "A Poor Harvest: N.C.'s Rural Schools," *The News and Observer,* Mar. 26, 1989, p. A1.

7. Adria Steinberg, ed., "Why Kids Give Up on School—And What

Teachers Can Do About It," *The Harvard Education Letter* (Sept./ Oct. 1990), pp. 1–4.

8. Peter M. Senge, *The Fifth Discipline: The Art and Practice of the Learning Organization* (New York: Doubleday/Currency, 1990), p. 4.

9. Much of the following account of Paint Branch Elementary School is drawn from a report the author did for *The Oregonian*. See Bill Graves, "School Breaks Mold and Shows Results," *The Oregonian*, Sept. 22, 1991, p. 1.

10. Bill Graves, "Teachers Find Class Distinction," *The Raleigh Times*, Oct. 3, 1988, p. 1A.

11. This account was described in a news release on July 13, 1993, by *Sassy* magazine, which named Fred Kiger the "most beloved teacher in America."

12. Bill Graves, "New York Teachers Use Genesee River Valley to Spark Learning," *The Oregonian*, Dec. 8, 1991, p. C4.

13. David E. Barbee described the applications of technology for individualized learning more than twenty years ago in his book, *A Systems Approach to Community College Education* (Princeton, NJ: AUERBACH Publishers, 1972).

14. "Ulysses and Beyond," a knowledge system prototype, described by James E. Dezell, Jr., vice president and general manager of IBM Educational Systems, during a keynote address at IBM Schools Executive Conference, "Restructuring Education Through Technology," on Feb. 2, 1990, in Palm Springs, CA.

15. James E. Connor, "Cutting Edge: Going Beyond Nintendo," *Journal of Developmental Education* (Winter 1992): 30.

16. Barbara Kantrowitz, "An Interactive Life," *Newsweek*, May 31, 1993, pp. 42–44.

17. Lewis J. Perelman, *School's Out: Hyperlearning, the New Technology and End of Education* (New York: William Morrow and Co., 1992), pp. 23, 130.

18. Sizer, *Horace's School*, p. 199.

19. Vance County's mission statement and goals for 1991–92 and 1992–93 are listed in the appendix.

20. U.S. Department of Education, *Digest of Education Statistics 1991* (Washington, D.C.: National Center for Education Statistics, 1991), p. 155.

Chapter 5

1. Some of these comments are drawn from an article by Tammy Stanford, "Wallace Addresses Concerns Over Schools' Upgrading Plan," *Henderson Daily Dispatch*, Aug. 20, 1991, pp. A1, A7.

2. Samuel Thomas Peace, Sr., *"Zeb's Black Baby" Vance County, North Carolina; A Short History* (Henderson, NC: Vance County Historical Society, 1955), introduction and p. 6.

3. Tammy Stanford, "AdVance Groups Back Education Reform Plan," *Henderson Daily Dispatch*, Sept. 3, 1991, pp. A1, A8.

4. Tammy Stanford, "Forum-Goers Wary Over Speed of Reform Plan," *Henderson Daily Dispatch*, Sept. 6, 1991, pp. A1, A7.

5. William Woltz, "National Leaders Praise Vance School Reform," *The Herald-Sun* (Durham, NC), Oct. 27, 1991.

6. Tammy Stanford, "OBE Experts: Vance Schools On Track," *Henderson Daily Dispatch*, Oct. 25, 1991, p. 1.

7. Tammy Stanford and Scott Ragland, "Vance, Granville Grades Fall on N.C. Report Card," *Henderson Daily Dispatch*, Jan. 28, 1992, p. A1

8. Tammy Stanford, "School Chief Praises Vance for OBE, Details Benefits of Education Spending," *Henderson Daily Dispatch*, Mar. 24, 1992.

Chapter 6

1. Reggie Ponder, "Vance Legislator Sets Educational Forum," *Henderson Daily Dispatch*, June 16, 1992, p. 1.

2. Reggie Ponder, "Vance Parents Form Committee on OBE," *Henderson Daily Dispatch*, June 18, 1992, p. A8.

3. Reggie Ponder, "Vance Budget Ax Takes Swing at School Funding," *Henderson Daily Dispatch*, June 17, 1992, p. 1

4. Tammy Stanford, "OBE, Wallace Caught in Crossfire," *Henderson Daily Dispatch*, June 25, 1992, p. A12.

5. Tammy Stanford, "Green Gives Wallace Failing Grade After Meeting with Self-Appointed Panel," *Henderson Daily Dispatch*, July 2, 1992, p. 1.

6. Scott Ragland, "Two OBE Panel Members Say Progress Made," *Henderson Daily Dispatch*, July 3, 1992, p. 1.

7. Wilbur Boyd, "Committee Member Has Different View," Letters to the Editor, *Henderson Daily Dispatch,* July 4, 1992.

8. James P. Green, Sr., "Dispatch Dividing the Community," Letters to the Editor, *Henderson Daily Dispatch,* July 15, 1992.

9. Tammy Stanford, "Vance Leaders: School Turmoil Hampers Growth," *Henderson Daily Dispatch,* Aug. 11, 1992, p. 1.

10. Marsha J. Drane, district director, in determination issued on March 31, 1993, by the U.S. Equal Employment Opportunity Commission, Raleigh Area Office.

11. Tammy Stanford, "Wallace Offers Teachers Pep Talk, Cites 'Golden Opportunity' in '92–'93," *Henderson Daily Dispatch,* Aug. 22, 1992, p. 1.

12. Tim Simmons, "Chairman Takes Child Out of Vance Schools," *The News and Observer,* Sept. 9, 1992, p. 1.

13. Ibid.

14. Ad in *The Henderson Daily Dispatch,* Sept. 24, 1992, p. 7A.

15. Sarah Wente, "Talk, Understanding Served Up in Kittrell," *Henderson Daily Dispatch,* Oct. 15, 1992, p. 1.

16. Sarah Wente, "Group Asks State Officials to Oust OBE, Superintendent," *Henderson Daily Dispatch,* Nov. 20, 1992, p. 1.

17. Sarah Wente, "Superintendent, Others Ousted from Education Group Meeting," *Henderson Daily Dispatch,* Nov. 30, 1992, p. 1.

18. "School's Christmas Surprise Encouraging." *Henderson Daily Dispatch,* Dec. 22, 1992, p. A4.

19. Editorial, "Report Card Progress Is Encouraging," *Henderson Daily Dispatch,* Jan. 8, 1992, p. 4.

20. Sarah Wente, "Vance Schools' Grades Up on N.C. Report Card," *Henderson Daily Dispatch,* Jan. 7, 1992, p. 1.

Chapter 8

1. Albert Shanker "Outrageous Outcomes," *New York Times,* Sept. 12, 1993, p. E7.

2. Robert Rothman, "Taking Account: State Moves from 'Inputs' to 'Outcomes' in Effort to Regulate Schools," *Education Week,* March 17, 1993, pp. 11, 12.

3. Meg Sommerfeld, "Christian Activists Seek to Torpedo NASDC Project," *Education Week,* March 10, 1993, pp. 1, 18, and 19.

4. Marc Tucker, "Building Toward Economic Competitiveness," paper delivered April 29, 1993, at the American Association of Community College's 73rd annual convention in Portland, OR.

5. Ernest L. Boyer, in a speech to the Education Writers Association, April 16, 1993, Boston, MA.

6. Elizabeth Shogren, "Senate OKs Education Measures," *The Oregonian*, Feb. 10, 1994, p. A7.

7. American Federation of Teachers, "AFT's Shanker Praises Passage of Goals 2000," News Release, March 28, 1994, in Washington, D.C.

8. Ray Marshall and Marc Tucker, *Thinking for a Living: Education and the Wealth of Nations* (New York: Basic Books, 1992), pp. 147–150.

9. Lauren B. Resnick, "Why We Need National Standards and Exams," reprinted in *Partnership Papers* (Los Angeles: Los Angeles Educational Partnership, Fall 1992).

10. David T. Conley with Robert Brownbridge, Andrew Dungan and Karin Hilgersom. "Proficiency-Based Admission Standards Study (PASS)." (Eugene, Ore.: Office of Academic Affairs, Oregon State System of Higher Education, Jan. 28, 1994), pp. 84–86.

11. Bill Graves, "School 'Reform' by University Mandate," *The School Administrator*, Nov. 1992, p. 8.

12. Tim Simmons, "Program to Improve State Schools Still on Launching Pad." *The News and Observer*, May 20, 1991, p. A1.

13. Ann Bradley and Lynn Olson, "The Balance of Power: Shifting the Lines of Authority in an Effort to Improve Schools," *Education Week*, Feb. 24, 1993, pp. 9–12.

14. Edward B. Fiske, *Smart Schools, Smart Kids: Why Do Some Schools Work?* (New York: Simon & Schuster, 1991), pp. 35–48.

15. Marvin Cetron and Margaret Gayle, *Educational Renaissance: Our Schools at the Turn of the Century* (New York: St. Martin's Press, 1991), pp. 36–37.

16. Bill Graves, "Germany's Student-team Learning Program Offers Model for Oregon," *The Oregonian*, Feb. 14, 1993, p. A20.

17. Fiske, *Smart Schools, Smart Kids*, pp. 168–178.

18. Ernest L. Boyer and The Carnegie Foundation for the Advancement of Teaching, *School Choice*, (Princeton, N.J.: The Carnegie Foundation for the Advancement of Teaching, 1992) p. 49.

19. Jonathan Kozol, *Savage Inequalities: Children in America's Schools* (New York: Crown, 1991) pp. 58, 63.

20. John E. Chubb and Terry M. Moe, *Politics, Markets, and America's Schools* (Washington, D.C.: The Brookings Institution, 1990), pp. 217–226.

21. On April 4, 1992, a task force on school governance funded by The Twentieth Century Fund and the Danforth Foundation cited a variety of problems with the nation's school boards, particularly those in urban districts. Instead of being part of the solution, "school boards have all too often been part of the problem," the report says. The report adds that school boards have become barriers to school-based management, tend to micromanage the systems they oversee, maintain poor relationships with their superintendents, have poor relations with other local government agencies such as health departments and juvenile services, and have become increasingly politicized. Fewer and fewer people voting in school board elections raises questions about the legitimacy of board members, the report says. "Facing the Challenge: Report of the Task Force on School Governance" (New York: Twentieth Century Fund Press, April 1992).

22. As Jonathan Kozol shows so vividly in his book *Savage Inequalities,* Americans continue to have a shamefully high tolerance for segregated schools such as those schools in East St. Louis, Chicago, and Washington, D.C., where more than 90 percent of the students, and in some cases all, are black. Atlanta is 57 percent black, but 92 percent of its public school students are black. A survey of public schools in the nation's forty-seven largest cities shows only one in four children are white.

23. Karen Mills, "Graduation Day at Model School," Associated Press wire service, June 1, 1993.

24. James A. Mecklenburger, "The Braking of the 'Break-the-Mold' Express," *Phi Delta Kappan* (Dec. 1992): 283.

25. Ibid., pp. 284–287.

26. Peter Passell, "Edison Project Aims to Reform Education," *The Oregonian,* January 21, 1994, p. A5.

27. Anne Lewis, *Restructuring America's Schools* (Arlington, VA: American Association of School Administrators, 1989), pp. 72, 73.

28. Albert Shanker, "AFT's Message to School Administrators," *The New York Times,* July 20, 1988.

29. Stanley M. Elam, Lowell C. Rose, and Alec M. Gallup, "The 26th Annual Gallup/Phi Delta Kappa Poll," *Phi Delta Kappan,* (Sept. 1994): 45.

Chapter 9

1. Lynn Olson, "The Future of School," *Education Week,* Feb. 10, 1993, p. 16.

2. Kevin Fedarko, "Can I Copy Your Homework—And Represent You in Court?" *Time,* Sept. 21, 1992, pp. 52, 53.

3. Hillary Stout, "Remedial Curriculum for Low Achievers Is Falling from Favor," *The Wall Street Journal,* July 30, 1992, pp. A1, A9.

Epilogue

1. Sarah Wente, "Vance School Board Gives Wallace $250,000 to Quit, Drop EEOC Complaint," *Henderson Daily Dispatch,* Sept. 1, 1993, p. 1.

2. Author Bill Graves wrote the latter two of these reports in *The News and Observer:* "State Superintendent Spends Much of Final Year on Road," Apr. 24, 1988; p. A1 and "Publishers Curry Favor with N.C. Education Officials," June 19, 1988, p. A1.

3. Bill Graves called Phillips on March 24, 1994, to ask him what had happened in Vance County schools since he took over as superintendent. Phillips declined to talk, however, other than to say he was "trying to clear up a mess" that Wallace had left behind.

4. Tim Simmons, "Advance & Retreat," *The News & Observer,* Oct. 24, 1993, p. E1.

5. "Superintendent Search Begins—Again," *Henderson Daily Dispatch,* Sept. 15, 1993, p. A4.

SELECTED BIBLIOGRAPHY

▼

Anderson, Richard C., Hiebert, Elfrieda H., Scott, Judith A., and Wilkinson, Ian A. G., *Becoming a Nation of Readers: The Report of the Commission on Reading* (Washington, D.C.: The National Institute of Education, 1984).

Bell, Terrel H., *The Thirteenth Man: A Reagan Cabinet Memoir* (New York: The Free Press, 1988).

The Boy Scout Handbook (Irving, TX: Boy Scouts of America, 1990).

Cetron, Marvin and Gayle, Margaret, *Educational Renaissance: Our Schools at the Turn of the 21st Century* (New York: St. Martin's Press, 1991).

Chubb, John E. and Moe, Terry M., *Politics, Markets and America's Schools* (Washington, D.C.: The Brookings Institution, 1990).

Commission on the Skills of the American Workplace, *America's Choice: High Skills or Low Wages!* (Rochester, NY: National Center on Education and the Economy, 1990).

Conant, James B., *The Comprehensive High School* (New York: McGraw-Hill Book Co., 1967).

Conley, David T., *Roadmap to Restructuring: Policies, Practices and the Emerging Visions of Schooling* (Eugene, OR: University of Oregon; ERIC Clearinghouse on Educational Management, 1993).

Fiske, Edward B., *Smart Schools, Smart Kids: Why Do Some Schools Work?* (New York: Simon & Schuster, 1991).

Gardner, Howard, *Frames of Mind: The Theory of Multiple Intelligences* (New York, Basic Books, 1983).

Gatto, John Taylor, *Dumbing Us Down: The Hidden Curriculum of Compulsory Schooling* (Philadelphia, PA: New Society Publishers, 1992).

Hampel, Robert L., *The Last Little Citadel: American High Schools Since 1940* (Boston: Houghton Mifflin Co., 1986).

Illich, Ivan, *Deschooling Society* (New York: Harper & Row, Publishers, 1970).

Kearns, David T. and Doyle, Denis P., *Winning the Brain Race: A Bold Plan to Make Our Schools Competitive* (San Francisco: Institute for Contemporary Studies, 1988).

Kidder, Tracy, *Among Schoolchildren* (Boston: Houghton Mifflin Co., 1989).

Kozol, Jonathan, *Savage Inequalities: Children in America's Schools* (New York: Crown Publishers, Inc., 1991).

Larkin, Jack, *The Reshaping of Everyday Life, 1790–1840* (New York: Harper & Row, Publishers, 1988).

Lewis, Anne, *Restructuring America's Schools* (Arlington, VA: American Association of School Administrators, 1989).

Marshall, Ray & Tucker, Marc, *Thinking for a Living: Work, Skills and the Future of the American Economy* (New York: Basic Books, 1992).

Matthews, Jay, *Escalante: The Best Teacher in America* (New York: Henry Holt and Co., 1988).

Perelman, Lewis J., *School's Out: Hyperlearning, the New Technology and the End of Education* (New York: William Morrow and Co., Inc., 1992).

Ravitch, Diane, ed., *The American Reader: Words That Moved a Nation* (New York: HarperCollins Publishers, 1990).

Senge, Peter M., *The Fifth Discipline: The Art and Practice of the Learning Organization* (New York: Doubleday/Currency, 1990).

Sewall, Gilbert T., *Necessary Lessons: Decline and Renewal in American Schools* (New York: The Free Press, 1983).

Sizer, Theodore R., *Places for Learning, Places for Joy: Speculation on American School Reform* (Cambridge, MA: Harvard University Press, 1973).

———, *Secondary Schools at the Turn of the Century* (New Haven: Yale University Press, 1964).

———, *Horace's School: Redesigning the American High School* (Boston: Houghton Mifflin Company, 1992).

Spring, Joel, *The American School: 1642–1990* (White Plains, NY: Longman, Inc., 1991).

Stevenson, Harold W. and Stigler, James W., *The Learning Gap: Why Our Schools Are Failing and What We Can Learn from Japanese and Chinese Education* (New York: Summit Books, 1992).

Toch, Thomas, *In the Name of Excellence: The Struggle to Reform the Nation's Schools, Why It's Failing, and What Should Be Done* (New York: Oxford University Press, 1991).

Tyack, David B., *The One Best System, A History of American Urban Education* (Cambridge, MA: Harvard University Press, 1974).

Tyson-Bernstein, Harriet, *A Conspiracy of Good Intentions: America's Textbook Fiasco* (Washington, D.C.: The Council for Basic Education, 1988).

INDEX

$$\equiv \blacktriangledown \equiv$$